D1555132

Organized and Corporate Crime in Europe

Organized and Corporate Crime in Europe

Offers that Can't Be Refused

Vincenzo Ruggiero
Middlesex University, London

Dartmouth
Aldershot • Brookfield USA • Singapore • Sydney

Published by
Dartmouth Publishing Company Limited
Gower House
Croft Road
Aldershot
Hants GU11 3HR
England

Dartmouth Publishing Company
Old Post Road
Brookfield
Vermont 05036
USA

British Library Cataloguing in Publication Data
Ruggiero, Vincenzo
Organized and Corporate Crime in Europe:
Offers That Can't be Refused. –
(Socio-legal Studies)
I. Title II. Series
364.106094

Library of Congress Cataloging-in-Publication Data
Ruggiero, Vincenzo,
Organized and corporate crime in Europe : offers that can't be refused / Vincenzo Ruggiero.
p. cm. – (Socio-legal studies series)
Includes bibliographical references and index.
ISBN 1-85521-522-5
1. Organized crime–Europe. 2. Commercial crimes–Europe.
3. Corporations–Corrupt practices–Europe. 4. White collar crimes--Europe. I. Title. II. Series: Socio-legal series.
HV6453.E9R84 1996
364.1'06'094—dc20 95-22887
CIP

ISBN 1 85521 522 5

Printed in Great Britain by the Ipswich Book Company, Suffolk

Contents

Foreword

The importance of organized crime to criminology has been met by a neglect which, outside Italy and the USA, until very recent times has been almost total. Even in the USA, the otherwise prolific 'Chicago School' of the 1920s and 30s produced only one truly focused study of the subject (Landesco 1969). In the postwar period, US Government Commissions, notably that chaired by Estes Kefauver (1951), set the framework for the debate about its character academically as well as journalistically for three decades, propounding the 'Mafia conspiracy' view, elaborated by Cressey as the *Theft of the Nation* (1969). Against this standard model, critics such as Albini (1971) and Ianni (1972) proposed a counter-model which emphasized local networks and family ties. But the focus on a relatively narrow range of organized criminal activities – 'protection', drugs, vice and gambling in particular – was perpetuated in the process. In short, the definition of the problem has, in this field, been unusually productive not of opening up debate and stimulating research but of theoretical closure and a dearth of original studies. The study of 'white-collar' and 'corporate crime' has also proceeded in a somewhat compartmentalized way. The fact that this intellectual division of labour has produced some outstanding research – such as Gambetta (1992) and Hobbs (1995) on organized crime, Levi (1981, 1987) on white-collar crime and Braithwaite (1984, 1993) on corporate crime – only serves to emphasize the segmentation of the field.

Whatever the virtues of this ordering of inquiry in the past, Vincenzo Ruggiero argues that it is inadequate to the task of analysis posed by the growing tendency of these formations of crime both to interpenetrate each other and the legal worlds of commerce, industry and government. He begins his essay in reordering the field by asking how such definitions arose in the first place. In the pioneering work of Edwin Sutherland on 'white-collar crime', he finds the source of the confusion. Sutherland at a stroke challenged the conventional wisdoms of orthodox criminology by the force of his argument that a spectrum of crime eluded it. Fraudulent advertising, phoney bankruptcies, violations of safety regulations, and the like, may be dealt with by administrative agencies but constitute crimes nonetheless. In the process, however, he analytically separated the study of 'white-collar crime' from 'organized crime'. By arguing instead that 'white-collar and corporate crime are variants of organized crime' (p. 2), Ruggiero proposes a new framework capable of releasing energies in fresh analytic directions. His approach transcends the fragmentation implicit in treating each form of crime as a basis for a separate field of inquiry. He proposes and applies the uses of economic, organizational and labour market theory to this end.

As a result, he opens up a terrain which is awesome in its scope. In two key chapters, *Crime As Work* and *Work As Crime*, he provides an inventory of organized crime based on concepts distilled from these fields. In the process, he mounts a withering critique of what he terms 'deficit' theories of crime and delinquency, the pronounced view in criminology that deviance flows primarily from a *lack* of money, goods, employment or status. On the contrary, he concludes, the most developed and major forms of organized crime flourish in the sites of wealth and power, which generate forms of stratification parallel to those in the conventional world. The world of organized crime rests on 'disorganized' criminal labour. While Ruggiero's depiction and wholesale repudiation of deficit theories, are destined to raise discussion, I find his scepticism about their limitations compelling.

What Ruggiero's analysis entails, to a more devastating extent than hitherto, is a recognition of the active complicity of governments and key institutions in the sustenance of organized crime. It should energize and stimulate further analysis and research into what can no longer be morally neutralized as a dark and recessive underworld but must be acknowledged as increasingly central to the 'overworld', the mainstream economies in which our pension funds, endowment trusts and investments are a main part of the frame. As Merton argued long ago, it is only by grasping the functionality of organized crime, what Daniel Bell called the beauty of the racket, that we can take the first step towards remaking the world along better lines. This book, the outcome of an original mind confronting issues of timeworn complexity, is such a step.

Professor David Downes
Department of Social Policy
London School of Economics

Preface

There are recurring difficulties in defining white-collar, corporate and organized crime. On the one hand, these difficulties are due to the extraordinary variety of forms that these types of crime display. On the other hand, difficulties are caused by the very academic discipline which is expected to shed light on such complex forms of offending. The segmentation of criminology into sub-disciplines, for example, makes it hard to utilize the analytical tools developed by students of corporate crime when one is faced with forms of organized crime, and vice versa. This book attempts to provide a joint analysis of these types of crime, and is focused on specific cases occurring in Europe.

Chapter 1 discusses Sutherland's contribution to the study of white-collar crime, and tries to analyse the extent to which his writings embryonically contain a distinction between corporate and organized crime. In this chapter the discussion is also focused on the way in which subsequent criminologists contributed to crystallizing this distinction. Chapter 2 performs a similar exercise with respect to conventional organized crime, and concludes that the two forms of offending should be analysed jointly. Some categories which allow for this joint analysis will be derived from the theory of organizations and the theory of the firm. Chapter 3 is devoted to the examination and selection of such categories and theories. In Chapter 4 a number of cases of white-collar and corporate crime occurring in European countries are discussed against the background of the theories and definitions provided in the previous chapter. A similar discussion is provided in Chapter 5, in which specific activities performed by organized crime are examined through the theories of organizations and the firm. Chapter 6 concludes the joint analysis of corporate and organized crime in Europe by describing cases in which these two types of offending occur simultaneously. Based on the tautology that corporate actors and organized criminals sometimes commit crime together, this chapter reiterates the case for a joint analysis of the two types of criminality and identifies encounters between licit and illicit economies.

It would have been very easy to focus this book on the European countries that I know best: Italy and Britain. The former is almost proverbial for displaying large-scale economic and organized crime, while the latter, in my view, is formidable in concealing both. However, the drive behind this book is the search for typologies, namely the study of qualitative rather than quantitative aspects. For this reason, the European countries mentioned in the following pages will be treated even-handedly, as they all offer interesting material for reflection. Consequently, the selection of cases discussed below is based on the attempt to identify qualitative similarities rather than to single out the most sensational episodes.

Apart from the available academic literature in a number of languages, sources for this study were provided by informants with whom either meetings were held or correspondence was exchanged. Informants included judges, prosecutors, defence lawyers, investigators and members of organizations whose activity aims to expose corporate and élite deviance. Some of these were contacted after news regarding specific offences had become public – hence, in this study, the use of journalistic material from a number of European countries. Following journalistic accounts of precise episodes, informants involved in one way or another in those episodes were contacted. In some cases these were investigators, public prosecutors, judges and members of the above-mentioned organizations, whereas in other cases they were counsels for the defendants who were investigated or victims of the alleged offence committed. Finally, in a number of cases informants recounted episodes which were unrelated to specific journalistic accounts but were part of the illegalities occurring in their country of residence.

Some believe that academic conferences are attended less for their actual content that for the opportunity they offer of exciting travelling and pleasurable social encounters. Although both things alone make conferences worth attending, at times other unexpected benefits may be obtained. For me, one such case was the 11th International Congress of Criminology held in Budapest in 1993. There I had the good fortune to chair a series of well-attended sessions on organized and corporate crime, and I met some of those who were either to become my respondents or to act as mediators for contacts with other informants.

A final terminological note. If, as this book would like to suggest, white-collar, corporate and organized crime can be analysed by recourse to identical concepts, why not coin one definition encompassing them all? I have resisted this temptation, and chosen to utilize the traditional definitions, both because they make these forms of offending more easily identifiable by readers and to avoid adding to the existing terminological confusion. I have only added the adjective 'conventional' when referring to what is commonly termed 'organized crime'.

Acknowledgements

I wish to thank all those who agreed to be interviewed or to correspond with me, sharing both their general knowledge of and insight into the issues dealt with in this book. In particular, I should like to mention Robert Colover QC, who not only explained to me in detail some of the cases of white-collar offending in which he had been involved as a barrister, but also introduced me to a number of his London colleagues whose help was equally invaluable. In the Netherlands I am particularly indebted to Gerd H. Hoffmann, whom I contacted after being fascinated by his book, the autobiography of a private investigator with a lengthy experience in cases of corporate crime. In the Netherlands I also received support and information from Petrus van Duyne (Ministry of Justice), Jurjen Boorsma (Criminal Intelligence Division) and J. Regterschot (Organized Crime Task Force).

Insights and contacts in France were provided by Ermanno Gallo, Laurent Joffrin of *Le Nouvel Observateur*, and members of the Syndicat de la Magistrature. I thank them all warmly. Ida Koch from Copenhagen drew my attention to some interesting unpublished material. I am also grateful to Andrzey Marek, whose work on organized and economic crime in Poland provided an important pointer for my own research, and to judges and defence lawyers based in Germany, Italy, Hungary, Spain and Switzerland who wish to remain anonymous. MEPs and members of a number of organizations were also extremely helpful. These organizations include Friends of the Earth, the World Development Movement, the German Association of Haemophiliac Patients, the Herald Families Association, Anti-Slavery International, Amnesty International, the Campaign against the Arms Trade and the National Peace Council. Finally, a mention is due to Frank Treble of Middlesex University, who suggested the title of this book, and Les Levidow for some ideas and the patient subediting of the English, which to me, alas, remains a foreign language.

1 'Bad' Economies

Encolpius and Eumolpus are two low-rank tricksters who travel Italy from north to south stealing and cheating. A fortunate circumstance brings them to Trimalcio's villa where, amid delicious and abundant foods, they meet high dignitaries and merchants of the declining Roman Empire. The debauchery, corruption and robberies of which these distinguished patricians boast make the two tricksters resemble law-abiding people. The adventures of the two are told in *Satyricon*, a book that, so goes the legend, was given to Nero by his enemies so that the emperor could see himself in it (Petronio, 1949).

Examples of crimes of the powerful are not rare in international literature, a phenomenon which testifies to its widespread presence in all societies and, at the same time, to the awareness of these types of offences by both observers and the general public. In the light of great scandals uncovered in Italy in the early 1990s, one may caustically remark that the legacy of corrupt Rome was never washed away. Chaucer seems to suggest that fraud lurks in all respectable cliques of all societies – see, for example, *The Pardoner's Tale*, a mock sermon against avarice deliberately designed to make gullible folk part with their money. The Prologue to the tale goes: 'My theme is alwey oon, and evere was *Radix malorum est Cupiditas*'. Incidentally, this sounds like what is still the most immediate and common explanation for white-collar and corporate crime: greed!

Sutherland and Criminology

Thanks to the previous paragraphs I have managed to avoid the customary tribute to Edwin Sutherland that a chapter on white-collar and corporate crime could otherwise hardly escape. Certainly, Sutherland deserves more than a customary or perfunctory tribute. His refutation of some of the classic assumptions in criminology constitutes a revolutionary shift that cannot go unacknowledged. This shift persuaded one of the founders of British criminology, Hermann Mannheim, that if a Nobel Prize for this discipline were in existence, without any doubt it ought to be conferred on Sutherland. Examples of classical texts criticized by the author are 'sacred' texts such as the Glueks' investigation of juvenile delinquents and the highly celebrated research on the ecological distribution of offenders conducted by sociologists of the Chicago school. In reading these studies, Sutherland concludes that general theories of crime frequently confine themselves to the use of official statistics and individual case histories. In this way they inevitably end up by focusing on cases which are concentrated in the lower sectors of the socio-economic structure (Sutherland, 1983). It comes as no surprise that theories of criminal behaviour place much emphasis on disadvantage and poverty:

> The assumption in these theories is that criminal behaviour can be explained only by pathological factors, either social or personal. The social pathologies which have been emphasized are poverty and, related to it, poor housing, lack of organized recreations, lack of education, and disruptions in family life. (ibid.: 5)

In contrast with these widespread assumptions, Sutherland argues that the causal factor of crime is not poverty, in the sense of sheer economic need, but rather the social and interpersonal relations which are associated sometimes with poverty and sometimes with wealth.

This breakthrough in criminological theory has frequently been underestimated or even ignored by subsequent scholars: personal circumstances of poverty and disadvantage still form prominent themes of most criminological analysis. For example, in Britain the espousal of the 'poverty' thesis is somehow a way for criminologists to air, if obliquely, their criticism of the Conservative governments. The growth of crime, therefore, is often exclusively attributed to the exacerbation of poverty produced by these governments. Many criminologists are 'forced' to support this thesis lest they lose their oppositional identity. If they were to claim, as Sutherland did, that crime is a consequence of both poverty and wealth, they might seem to condone socio-economic policies which indeed worsen poverty and relative deprivation. Is theoretical reductionism a cost to be paid for the 'politicization' of criminology?

However, the neglect of these aspects of Sutherland's thought may also be part of an overall caution with which his work is regarded. In *White-Collar Crime* as well as in other writings, the author attempts to formulate a general explanatory theory which, in his view, can be applied to all types of crime. His desire to provide a complete aetiology of criminal activity is met with suspicion. His hypotheses on crime causation are deemed mono-factorial, whereby poverty and wealth are the complementary sides of one explanatory factor: economic conditions. Conversely, it is prevalent among criminologists to search for a multiplicity of factors which account for crime, a multiplicity that Sutherland discarded as an arbitrary pot-pourri of elements vaguely connected with one another (Sutherland, 1939; Sutherland and Cressey, 1960). The objective of criminology, he emphasized, is the development of a body of general and verified principles regarding the processes of law, crime, and the treatment or prevention of crime. A scientific explanation of crime, therefore, consists of a description of the conditions which are always present when crime occurs, and which are never present when crime does not occur.

It is not easy to share this somewhat ambitious agenda. To describe what Sutherland terms a hodgepodge of unrelated factors that most criminologists associate with crime, the author uses the following example. Two boys are engaged in a minor theft. When they are discovered, they run: one boy has longer legs, escapes, and becomes a priest; the other has shorter legs, is caught, sent to prison, and becomes a gangster. Sutherland argues: 'But "length of legs" need not be considered in a criminological theory for, in general, no significant relationship has been found between criminality and length of legs, and certainly many persons with short legs are law-abiding and many persons with long legs are criminals' (Sutherland and Cressey, 1960: 76). Subsequent experiences and associations of the two boys should be included in the explanation of their respective careers. If criminology is to be scientific, Sutherland concludes, 'the heterogenous collection of "multiple factors" known to be associated with crime and criminality should be organized and integrated by means of an explanatory theory which has the same characteristics as the scientific explanations in other fields of study' (ibid.: 74).

This search for general principles for the building up of a scientific knowledge of crime is still met with scepticism, which perhaps leads to a selective acceptance of Sutherland's thought (Lilly et al., 1989; Ceretti, 1992). In other words, many criminologists accept his analysis of white-collar crime, as if this were unconnected to the author's general theory of crime. This selectivity may also account for a number of problems encountered by other authors when dealing with white-collar crime, problems which compound the ambiguity inherent in the very definition of this crime.

White-collar Crime: Definitions

While Sutherland's general criminological theory is often overlooked, his study of white-collar crime has spawned a phenomenal amount of empirical research and theoretical thinking. However, the very definition coined by Sutherland has undergone elaboration and successive specifications. The formulation, 'white-collar crimes are crimes committed by persons of respectability and high social status in the course of their occupation' may be regarded as too broad, because white-collar offences entail diverse combinations of 'respectability, social status and occupation'. Critics argue that the original definition encompasses too many diverse and often unrelated behaviours and should therefore be broken down into more precise categories. As alternatives to white-collar crime, definitions such as élite deviance, official deviance, and corporate deviance have been used (Simon and Eitzen, 1982; Ermann and Lundman, 1978, 1982; Douglas and Johnson, 1977). Other definitions aimed at narrowing the original conceptualization and identifying more specific behaviours are corporate crime, business crime, political crime and government crime (Clinard and Yeager, 1980; Roebuck and Weeber, 1978; Conklin, 1977).

These types of behaviour cannot be solely identified on the basis of a coded prohibition, because the law may fail to prohibit them clearly and strictly. For this reason some authors suggest different conceptualizations based on deviance rather than criminality. Quinney (1970), for instance, considers the correspondence between deviant and criminal behaviour as crucial in the study of white-collar crime. The question he poses is whether or not the behaviour defined as criminal is also a deviation from the normative structure of the occupation: 'If it can be established that the behaviours are regarded as deviant, as well as criminal, by the occupational members, the criminal violations can truly be studied as deviations from occupational norms' (ibid.: 33). This, according to Quinney, resolves the problem that the behaviour studied by criminologists may not be regarded as criminal by the groups being studied.

The debate also centres on the social status of offenders. As Croall (1992) explains, this controversial aspect may hamper research and analysis as offenders of diverse social status and respectability may commit white-collar offences. On the other hand, it is felt that the definition 'occupational crime', whose original formulation is due among others to Quinney (1964), may resolve the issue by including both white-collar and blue-collar crime.

Green (1990: 13) defines as occupational crime 'any act punishable by law which is committed through opportunity created in the course of an occupation that is legal'. He argues that the criterion of *legal* occupation is necessary because without it the term 'occupational crime' could conceivably include all crimes.

> Only persons who have a legal occupation can commit occupational crime, according to our definition. Thus, the term would exclude persons with occupations which are illegal to begin with, such as bank robbers, organized crime

> figures who make money through illegal channels, or professional 'confidence men'. (ibid.: 13)

The author identifies four categories of occupational crime: crimes for the benefit of an employing organization (organizational occupational crime), crimes by officials through the exercise of their state-based authority (state authority occupational crime), crimes by professionals in their capacity as professionals (professional occupational crime), and crimes by individuals as individuals (individual occupational crime).

It should be noted that Green's definition is in complete accordance with Sutherland's original formulation. Sutherland, in effect, stresses that white-collar crime excludes many crimes of the upper class such as most cases of murder, intoxication, or adultery, since these are not a part of the occupational procedures. 'Also, it excludes the confidence games of wealthy members of the underworld, since they are not persons of respectability and high social status' (Sutherland, 1983: 7).

This specification has been transmitted to current students of corporate crime in a somewhat uncritical fashion. Many authors currently subscribe to the principle that professional or organized criminals should be excluded from the umbrella definition of white-collar criminals. Paradoxically, this principle also seems to apply when members of organized crime commit typical white-collar offences, their exclusion being therefore based less on what they do than on who they are. It would perhaps be more fruitful to focus on the nature, characteristics and methods of these offences rather than on the profile of the offenders. This avenue will be explored throughout the book and clarified in the final part of this chapter.

A further elaboration of Sutherland's seminal work pertains to the nature and definition of corporate crime. According to a relatively accepted formulation, this consists of illegal acts performed within a legitimate organization, and in accordance with the organization goals, which victimize employees, customers or the general public (Schrager and Short, 1977). Related to this formulation is the distinction between crimes *for* corporations and crimes *against* corporations, the latter representing what is commonly associated with 'corporate crime' (Box, 1983). But, although useful, this distinction is said to implicitly overstate the homogeneity of 'crimes *against* business'. If such crimes include fraud, for example, 'Even if one excludes from consideration many forms of business "malpractice" that are either not criminal at all or whose criminality is ambiguous, to write about commercial fraud is to write about a number of very different sorts of activities' (Levi, 1987: xix).

According to another specification, *criminal corporations* are also identified which are 'deliberately set up, taken over, or controlled for the explicit and sole purpose of executing criminal activity' (Box, 1983: 22). Examples of criminal corporations are provided by Hopkins (1980), who describes how an oil company was established with the sole purpose of effecting a series of illegal financial deals, and by Levi (1981), who documents how companies are set up with the deliberate intention of obtaining goods on credit for which payment is never intended. However, it is a relatively widespread conviction that: 'Although the crimes of criminal corporations are clearly serious, they should be kept analytically separate from corporate crime' (Box, 1983: 22–3).

While the activities of 'criminal corporations' have not been studied extensively, the broad distinction guiding Box's work between crimes for and crimes against corporations is now commonly accepted. This distinction is based on the characteristics of the actors benefiting from the respective crimes: corporations in the former cases, and individuals in the latter.

If white-collar crime embraces illegal behaviour adopted within a legal occupation, the nature of this occupation and the degree of power that this carries vary significantly. Some types of white-collar crime may be committed by secretaries or truck drivers, as well as by high-ranking officials or presidents within the same organization (Geis and Jesilow, 1993). Levi (1987: xix) also argues that the social composition of white-collar criminals is not homogeneous, as it includes members endowed with varying degrees of power and respectability. 'Even upmarket-sounding crimes like insider dealing – where shares are bought or sold unlawfully on the basis of confidential inside information – may be committed by the company chairman or the company typist.'

This approach alludes to the crucial importance of the techniques used for these types of offending as opposed to the characteristics of offenders. Failure to examine these techniques, which indeed may be learned by secretaries as well as by presidents, may give rise to identical problems to those mentioned above, namely that offences presenting the same dynamics are treated differently on the grounds of who commits them.

Work by Green (1993) offers an opportunity to reiterate this point. The author, while discussing embezzlement in the USA, poses the question whether this type of behaviour can be included in Sutherland's definition of white-collar crime. Sutherland, he argues, refers principally to business managers and executives, and considers social status and respectability to be independent of economic wealth. Other authors who study trust violators, for example, do not apply Sutherland's definition to the actors studied because these lack the requirement of social prestige that the original definition implies (Cressey, 1953). A further example is provided by a study of female embezzlers, where the author is at odds with Sutherland's definition in that her subjects cannot be characterized as having high social status

(Zeitz, 1981). According to Green, the definitional problems inherent in the term 'white-collar crime' become most evident when a crucial statement of Sutherland is examined. The author of *White-Collar Crime* regards this offence as a form of organized crime. This applies to offences which are collusive in nature and require the participation of different actors playing a number of differentiated roles.

> Bribery, price fixing, bid rigging, industrial espionage, and physician-fee splitting are examples of formally organized illegalities.... White-collar criminals are also formally organized in that they select administrators, and control legislation ... they use their economic and political influence to deflect criminal definitions from their illegal behaviour. (Green, 1993: 99)

Embezzlement, therefore, which does not necessarily require collusion and is often performed without the support of a formal organization, should not be described as white-collar crime. In sum, Green's embezzlers are not white-collar criminals because of the absence of a criminal organization planning and supporting their acts. The author concludes that problems arise when trying to determine whether an offender is of high social status, and that

> it may be more prudent to study job-related trust violation as a form of occupational crime. This approach highlights the source of opportunity for trust violation, allows for its differential distribution, and is not muddled by the concept of white collar crime. (ibid.: 106)

Again, this distinction, which is inscribed in a useful definitional diatribe, leaves aside an important aspect. The techniques used for the commission of embezzlement may be more important than its definition. These techniques may initially be experimented with by isolated individuals, but may be transmitted to others who participate in formal organizations. Individuals, in other words, may act as 'inventors' or innovators, whose techniques are then refined and applied on a larger scale. In this they can be likened to their private-sector counterparts. Descriptions of how embezzlement is performed may indicate that a variety of actors can engage in this behaviour. Furthermore, examples of organized embezzlement are not rare. Individuals can sell their know-how to organizations, either licit or illicit, and often establish joint ventures with them.

Paradoxically, the best way to avoid definitional muddles may well be the adoption of the original phrase coined by Sutherland, provided the caveat is made that this is intended to incorporate a set of analogous behaviours. This route is taken by Croall (1992), who includes in the definition the areas of both occupational and organizational or corporate crime. White-collar crime, she adds, 'also avoids the difficulties of including the social status of offenders within the definition of the offences, but at the same time does not rule out their significance for analysis' (ibid.: 19). The description white-collar crime, moreover, can be retained because 'by and large criminologists, lawyers, students and the public identify with such a description' (ibid.: 19). I shall postpone the specification of my own terminological choice, which will perhaps only become clear at the end of this chapter.

White-collar Crime: Characteristics

The legacy of Sutherland is strongly felt when the characteristics of white-collar and corporate crime are examined. The difficulties encountered by investigators and prosecutors in the face of this type of offending is among the most prominent of these characteristics. Sutherland is adamant on this point. Persons of the upper socio-economic class, he argues, escape arrest and conviction because they are politically and financially powerful. They do so to a greater extent than persons who lack such power. Powerful people can appoint experienced and skilled defence lawyers, who in turn may be well connected in legal circles. In these circles, where judges are also found, the reputation and perceived integrity of these lawyers may benefit the powerful clients they represent. Furthermore, as Sutherland suggests, wealthy persons can influence the administration of justice in their own favour more effectively than can persons of the lower socio-economic class.

However, this bias, which is taken by Sutherland as indubitable, is not given great importance by the author from the theoretical point of view. He warns that this characteristic of white-collar crime should not be overstated, nor should it be confused with the explanation of this type of crime. In other words, the problems inherent in detecting and punishing white-collar and corporate crime cannot be included in the rubric regarding the causation of these crimes. Sutherland concedes that crime committed by the upper socio-economic class differs from the criminal behaviour of the lower socio-economic class principally in the administrative procedures which are used in dealing with the offenders. But he insists that variations in administrative procedures are not significant from the point of view of causation of crime. The causes of tuberculosis, he explains, were not different when it was treated by poultices and bloodletting than when treated by streptomycin.

Other characteristics of white-collar and corporate crime are part of what Nelken (1994a) identifies as the fundamental ambiguity of these offences. The fact, for example, that the perpetrator has justification for being present at the scene where the crime takes place distinguishes this type of offending from conventional predatory crime (Clarke, 1990). On the surface, the ambiguity of white-collar crime makes this behaviour very similar to ordinary legal behaviour: 'For example, for fraud to succeed, it must obviously succeed in mimicking the appearance of legitimate transactions, and it is not unusual for those guilty of this crime to remain undetected for years, even a lifetime' (Nelken, 1994a: 373). In sum, difficulties in classifying white-collar offenders are compounded by difficulties in discovering that a white-collar offence has been committed in the first place.

All of this suggests that *invisibility* is perhaps yet another characteristic of crimes of the powerful. In many cases, this invisibility describes the condition of both offenders and victims. The perpetrator is made invisible by the circumstance whereby the setting of the offence does not coincide with the setting where its effects will be felt. This is also the case because the time when the crime is performed and the time when the damage caused becomes apparent do not correspond. On the other hand, victims themselves can be described as invisible in that they are both absent from the scene of the crime and are frequently unaware of their own victimization.

Recent analysis hypothesizes that changes in the perception of corporate crime are modifying its characteristics. While invisibility may still be one of these, more awareness of victimization on the part of the public may be in the process of developing. Increasingly, powerful offenders are said to be seen as being as threatening as street criminals to the well-being of the bulk of 'respectable' society (Geis and Jesilow, 1993). Those who do not live up to traditional Calvinistic values of sacrifice, temperance and deferred gratification have always been regarded with hostility by certain sectors of the population. They are usually seen as lazing in comfortable luxury which they do not deserve. 'Now members of the upper class, including powerful politicians, are deemed equally irresponsible and are seen as taking advantage of their position to make life harder and more expensive and less responsive to middle-class demands' (ibid.: 8–9).

It is controversial whether white-collar and corporate crime are now regarded as being more socially damaging than in the past. It is true that customer pressure groups, environmentalists and other activists may have contributed to a significant shift in the way these crimes are perceived. On the other hand, the increasing attention paid to this or that specific corporate offence may be due to causes which are related to the very competitive world in which corporations operate. Sgubbi (1990) posits that lobbies influencing both administrative regulations and the penal law include powerless and powerful groups alike. Groups active in specific business sectors may exert pressure aimed at the penalization of other business sectors. Competition between powerful groups, in other words, may be reflected in the arena of the law, where some corporate activities are favoured and others are hampered. The author's definition of crime as 'a social risk' alludes to the fact that many businesses start an activity regardless of whether current or forthcoming regulations will be breached. The proliferation of rules guiding both administrative and corporate activity puts any enterprising (or simply efficient) individual at risk of committing an offence. This argument is by no means intended to endorse the customary lament of corporate actors addressed to governmental regulations, which allegedly hinder free enterprise. Rather, it describes an uncertain panorama where definitions of crime may constantly shift. This may result not only from the pressure exerted by powerless groups against powerful ones and vice versa, but also from the pressures of powerful groups against one another.

Is this an extension of labelling theory? It is ironic that this theory, which originally attempted to put the anti-social nature of powerless offenders in perspective, is now invoked for the description of what characterizes corporate and white-collar crime. Pressures on the political establishment may indeed result in the criminalization of one corporate behaviour and the acceptance of others. This is somehow an expansion of Quinney's concept of the political nature of crime. According to Quinney, much of the behaviour that is labelled as criminal is destined to change substantially in the future. Behaviours commonly viewed as pathological or deviant will become more political in nature. 'The actions of the criminally defined are not so much the result of inadequate socialization and personality problems as they are conscientious actions taken against something' (Quinney, 1970: 180). Optimistically, the author applies his analysis of the 'politicality of crime' to the emergent social movements of the 1960s. He sees in those years a vivid example of how law takes on an overtly political nature in response to the rising 'new political consciousness'. An increasing portion of crime, he predicts, will be a reflection of this political confrontation. It is ironic that these notions are now also applied to the aetiology of white-collar and corporate crime, to which I shall now turn.

White-collar Crime: Aetiology

'A person becomes delinquent because of an excess of definitions favourable to violation of law over definitions unfavourable to violation of law. This is the principle of differential association. It refers to both criminal and anti-criminal associations and has to do with counteracting forces' (Sutherland and Cressey, 1960: 78).

As we have seen, the definition and characteristics of white-collar crime have undergone a notable process of elaboration since they were originally formulated. A similar process can be observed when its aetiology is examined. According to Sutherland, poverty and wealth can both lead to criminal behaviour when this behaviour is *learned* through social interaction. This statement is part of the concept of *differential association*. Criminal behaviour is therefore learned in a communicative process in which specific techniques of committing crime are transmitted along with the attitudes, rationalizations and motives underlying it. 'Differential social association' is Sutherland's alternative to the term 'social disorganization', which is regarded by the author to be not entirely satisfactory. The postulate on which Sutherland's term and related theory are based is that crime is rooted in the social organization and is an expression of that social organization. 'Most communities are organized both for criminal and anti-criminal behaviour and in that sense the crime rate is an expression of the differential group organization' (ibid.: 80).

The validity of this causation has been empirically assessed in a number of studies. Geis (1992) examined the violations of antitrust laws committed by the General Electric and the Westinghouse Electric Corporations, the two largest companies in the heavy electrical equipment industry of the United States. The violations, which were given court hearing in 1961, consisted of a comprehensive division of the market by way of price fixing and pre-established bids to submit to contractors. 'Sometimes, depending upon the contract, the conspirators would draw lots to determine who would submit the lowest bid; at other times, the appropriate arrangement would be determined under a rotating system conspiratorially referred to as the "phase of the moon"' (Geis, 1992: 81). The defendants in this case sought the causes of their offending in the structure of the corporation by which they were employed. None attributed their behaviour to a general law-breaking attitude making them prone to offending outside their occupational role. This role, they implied, included practices established by others before they were given the job, and in a sense violations were part and parcel of their occupational role as if inscribed in their job description. Geis remarked that many of Sutherland's concepts concerning illegal behaviour of white-collar offenders received substantiation. The origin of these offences seemed to be located in learning processes and associational patterns.

A large-scale comprehensive investigation of corporate violations was conducted in the USA in the mid-1970s. The author rightly claimed that the only previous study of a somewhat similar nature was Edwin H. Sutherland's famed *White-Collar Crime* (Clinard, 1979). In this study, corporate crime is defined as being white-collar crime of a particular type. It is organizational crime that occurs in the context of extremely complex and varied sets of structured relationships between boards of directors, executives and managers on the one hand, and parent corporation, corporate divisions and subsidiaries on the other. Clinard provides evidence from opinion surveys that corporate executives believe unethical and illegal practices to be common. The socio-cultural environment in which corporations operate is deemed conducive to these practices. Lawbreaking may become a normative pattern within certain corporations, a remark that brings Clinard's analysis very close to Sutherland's 'learning approach'. His study focuses on the criminal activity of 582 of the largest corporations in the USA, while data are based on all criminal proceedings initiated against these companies by 24 federal agencies. Findings indicate that 60 per cent of the corporations examined have an average of 4.2 actions filed against them. Most of the offences are committed against workers, customers and the environment. In a list of defences offered by corporations to explain their crimes, the following are included among others:

(*a*) all measures proposed constitute government interference with the free enterprise system;
(*b*) the government is to blame because the additional costs of regulations and bureaucratic procedures cut heavily into profits;
(*c*) the government is to blame because most regulations are incomprehensible and too complicated;
(*d*) the government is to blame because the aspects being regulated are unimportant;
(*e*) there is little deliberate intent in corporate violations, most of them being errors of omission rather than commission, and many simply being mistakes;
(*f*) although the damage from corporate crime may be high, this is so diffused among many members of the public that individually there is little loss;
(*g*) violations are due to economic necessity.

It should be noted that, among these defences offered to explain corporate crime, some overlap with those which are the very definitions and characteristics of this type of crime. On the other hand, the defences could be regarded as techniques of neutralization which follow rather than precede the commission of an offence (Sykes and Matza, 1957). However, even among the critics of Clinard's study, many accept these items as part of the aetiology of corporate crime, although further specifications are felt to be needed. Young (1981), for example, criticizes Clinard for omitting a number of explanatory categories: these include the concepts of capitalism, class, class struggle, community, surplus value, alienation, separation of production and distribution, profit rate, competition, and accumulation. According to Young, the modern capitalist state constructs an environment where violation of the law by corporations is not only likely but necessary. Capitalism, in other words, must commit crime to survive.

This line of analysis implies the existence of a monopoly in the definition of crime, whereby the crime problem is associated with the offences committed by the lower classes and excludes crimes of the powerful. As we have seen above, this view overlooks how definitions of what is crime may not only benefit powerful groups in general, but also specific powerful groups among others (Sgubbi, 1990). What is important to note here is that the causation of corporate crime, in the above orthodox analysis, simply reformulates labelling theory with categories such as class and power relationships. Students of corporate crime who share this approach tend to view such behaviour as one among other strategies used by corporations to enhance their power and profits. In this way, attention is drawn to the overall social structure within which corporations operate. 'Thus, in analysing "crimes of corporations", we are ultimately led to ask fundamental questions about the nature of American and the world's free enterprise system' (Pearce, 1976: 105). Conversely, the usual focus on lower-class criminals is deemed functional in maintaining a class-structured system.

It is true that to focus on specific forms of crime may be instrumental in understanding larger social dynamics and that the exposure of 'crimes of the powerful' may result in the indictment of the overall system of power. However, this type of analysis often ends up with moralistic overtones, to which the pioneer of the study of this kind of crime never resorted. Sutherland's notion that both poverty and wealth may be the causes of crime constitutes a definitive rupture with the positivist tradition. On the contrary, among orthodox analysts some traits of this tradition are still retained in their somewhat apologetic explanation of crimes of the powerless, and their moralistic view of crimes of the powerful. The former type of offending is often regarded as the inevitable consequence of poverty or powerlessness, the latter as the monstrous outcome of greed. In both cases the idea is conveyed that crime constitutes an exceptional behaviour and a social pathology. It is instead the 'normality' of crime which forms Sutherland's focus of analysis, along with the strategies and values contributing to this normalization. In sum, one important aspect often neglected by orthodox analysis is the blurring of the boundaries between criminal and non-criminal activities in which many corporate offences, and for that matter many economic-motivated offences in general, take place.

Every attempt to investigate the causes of crime is exposed to generalizations, all the more so when the offences studied are those committed by socially advantaged people. As Nelken (1994a) notes, accounting for white-collar crime in terms of the desire to make a profit does little to distinguish this type of offence from others. All economic-motivated offences, in fact, could be tautologically explained by the economic advantages they bring. Sutherland goes further: not only does he find general economic motives insufficient for distinguishing between conventional and corporate crime, he also finds this motivation unsatisfactory for distinguishing crime in general from conformist behaviour.

> Thieves generally steal in order to secure money, but likewise honest labourers work in order to secure money. The attempts by many scholars to explain criminal behaviour by general drives and values, such as the happiness principle, striving for social status, the money motive, or frustration, have been and must continue to be futile since they explain lawful behaviour as completely as they explain criminal behaviour. They are similar to respiration, which is necessary for any behaviour but which does not differentiate criminal from non-criminal behaviour. (Sutherland, 1939: 79)

Another aspect of the causation of corporate crime pertains more specifically to the economic field. Whether and how crime rates in general follow a precise pattern related to the economy is still a matter of criminological debate. As for corporate crime, some authors seem to regard this type of offending as business routine, or as an inevitable corollary of capitalism, whereas others try to identify 'cycles of offending' which are somehow related to 'cycles of accumulation'. Advocates of the former interpretation seem to put forward arguments which echo the renowned Marxist notion of 'the tendential decline of the rate of profit'. As accumulation is hindered by its own inherent mechanisms, the recourse to crime becomes inevitable if these mechanisms are to be countered. Instead, advocates of the latter interpretation suggest that corporate crime is rife in difficult economic circumstances, which may be transitory or cyclical, when every effort is made to maintain profits (Box, 1983; Passas, 1990). Strain elements due to capitalist competition are included in this analysis, and the attractiveness of illicit opportunities is said to increase when profitability declines. Similarly, 'firms in depressed industries as well as relatively poorly performing firms in all industries tend to violate the law to a greater degree' (Clinard and Yeager, 1980: 129). Other authors, however, cast doubt on this assertion: that firms in financial difficulty are more likely to offend than profitable ones has not yet found empirical corroboration (Braithwaite, 1985).

In his study of the role of middle management, Clinard (1983) finds a variety of causes for the explanation of corporate unethical behaviour. The middle-management executives he interviews feel that the source of this behaviour lies primarily within the corporation itself, not in external factors. External factors such as competition, or indeed unfair competitive practices, are deemed as unimportant as the poor corporate financial situation in determining unethical behaviour. Rather, 'the general theme expressed by most middle-management executives was that top management, and in particular the chief executive officer (CEO), sets the corporate ethical tone' (ibid.: 132). Some 'financially oriented' top managers are more prone to securing quick prestige and profits and therefore are more likely to engage in illicit practices. This occurs to a lower degree among 'technical and professional type' top managers. Finally, a distinction is drawn between the ethics of top managers who are occupationally unstable and move from one corporation to another, and those who are more permanently established within one single corporation. The former are found to be more aggressive, 'interested in their own rapid corporate achievements and consequent publicity in financial journals; they have limited concern for the corporation's long-term reputation' (ibid.: 137).

According to other interpretations, the study of corporate crime should be coupled with the study of how 'trust' is distributed, maintained and abused within both the social structure and specific organizations (Shapiro, 1990). The nature of the social structure, but also the specific layout of an organization, may be conducive to abuses and malpractice. However, while the point can be accepted that structural factors create conditions where abuse of trust occurs, the precise mechanisms that lead to these conditions await further investigation. So do the mechanisms whereby, in the same conditions, some corporate actors do refrain from abuse. Are abuse and restraint related to the varying stringency of existing sanctions? (Pearce and Tombs, 1990; 1991). Authors who believe they are seem to imply that strong sanctions affect only crimes of the powerful, and that they lose their deterrent effect when addressed to conventional crime. These issues bring us back to Sutherland's observation that the causes of corporate crime cannot be found in the institutional responses to it, just as the causes of tuberculosis are not found in the type of therapy chosen.

The difficulties encountered in explaining corporate crime arise from the misgivings surrounding the precise identification of this kind of crime. On the other hand, they may also mirror uncertainties regarding the aetiology of all crimes. Nevertheless, attempts have been made to identify causations which would be potentially applicable to all sorts of lawbreaking. This avenue is taken by Gottfredson and Hirschi (1990), who resume where Sutherland left off, by attempting to explain criminal behaviour with an all-inclusive theory. The two authors discard the basic thesis of differential association, namely that crime is caused by culturally induced motives. They instead posit 'propensity event theory', which is centred on differences between people in terms of self-control. Individuals endowed with the lowest self-control are said to commit the majority of crimes, irrespective of the type of offence. White-collar offenders, street robbers, adolescent deviants and prostitutes, therefore, share a lack of self-control which manifests itself in a number of symptoms. Green (1993: 104) adopts this causation in his study of embezzlement and identifies these symptoms with the following:

> 'risk-taking', or a quest for exciting and dangerous behaviour; 'simplicity', or an avoidance of difficult tasks; 'low frustration tolerance'; 'physicality', or a desire for physical rather than mental activity; 'immediate gratification', or impulsivity; more concern with immediate than future pleasures; and 'self-centredness' – looking out for oneself first or tending to blame oneself last'.

Green also finds further indirect support for this theory as an explanation for embezzlement. Propensity event theory, he explains, assumes that offenders have low self-control and that this condition is relatively stable over time. Offenders, in other words, do not display their criminal behaviour in one episode only, but manifest their low self-control in a career on the one hand, and in a variety of offences on the other. Thus embezzlers turn out to have been involved in other crimes as well prior to the embezzlement, a claim that Green substantiates through reference to other studies.

Coleman (1987) relies on a theory of white-collar crime based on the hypothesis that criminal behaviour results from a coincidence of appropriate motivation and opportunity. Motivation is held to consist of 'a set of symbolic constructions defining certain kinds of goals and activities as appropriate and desirable and others as lacking those qualities' (ibid.: 409). An opportunity is defined by the author as a course of action which is part of a person's repertoire of potential behaviours. Furthermore, he argues, a potential course of action becomes an opportunity only when there is awareness of it. Coleman does not believe in the inadequacy of both the biological make-up or socialization of white-collar criminals, and considers the interactionist approach to be the best suited for the explanation of their offences. The meaning that individuals attribute to a particular situation and to social reality in general makes certain actions seem appropriate. Individual perceptions also include an anticipation of other people's responses to one's behaviour. Social behaviourists such as Mead (1934) provide a crucial framework for this type of analysis. In performing a certain act, Mead suggests, one has to predict the reaction of others, and in a sense take over into one's self all the attitudes of others, or the *generalized other*. The adoption of this hypothesis leads Coleman to identify rhetorical techniques of neutralization used by white-collar offenders, among which the 'denial of harm' is said to be the most common. 'When convicted white-collar offenders are asked to explain their behaviour, they frequently claim that their actions did not harm anyone, and they have therefore done nothing wrong' (Coleman, 1987: 411).

Coleman is aware that interactionist analysis, while offering a convincing account of the ways in which white-collar offenders neutralize the symbolic constraints of their behaviour, fails to explain the origin of this behaviour. The author suggests that a good start for this explanation would be to explore 'the relative strength of the culture of competition and the normative restraints on it among different groups and different organizational segments of society' (ibid.: 434–5).

Availability of criminal opportunities and the knowledge of the techniques necessary to commit offences may account for both the motivation of this behaviour and its diffusion throughout an industry. For example, it has been suggested that, unlike street crime, fraud is not an 'equal opportunity crime', 'and to the extent that there is disadvantage or discrimination by class, gender, ethnicity, or religion in occupying particular roles, the opportunities for particular types of fraud are correspondingly restricted (Levi, 1987: 2–3).

Finally, explanations of white-collar and corporate crime are also located within the analysis of technological and bureaucratic development. The development of non-natural persons, such as corporations, is said to provide the backcloth against which powerful offenders operate (Coleman, 1982). The growth of corporate actors, it is argued, causes a structural change in society where 'natural persons' play an increasingly insignificant role. Corporations become pre-eminent actors: they substitute functionally for a natural person, can act in a unitary way, own resources, have rights and responsibilities. Natural persons can now gain mobility, as the fixed function in which they previously operated is taken over by functional units: corporate bodies. Continuity of functions is therefore no longer provided by individual persons and their skills, but by these growing corporate bodies. The changing distribution of roles among natural and corporate actors leads to new relationships of power. According to Coleman (1982), these relationships produce four different kinds of actions whose nature and characteristics vary according to the actors involved. Actions performed by two natural persons constitute the first type, and are those to which we have all been socialized. The second type is characterized by actions in which two corporate bodies are involved. The third and fourth are those actions in which the two parties are a person and a corporation who perform respectively the role of subject or object. Unlike the other types of actions, these imply relationships which can be defined as asymmetric. In these relationships, one of the actors is endowed with very large resources compared with the other party. For example, a non-natural actor is in a position to control the conditions in which their relationships with natural actors take place. They also hold more information regarding the nature of their relationship and the way in which this can be altered. Coleman's analysis suggests that this asymmetry provides the backcloth against which powerful offenders should be studied and their crimes analysed. According to the author, the 'irrelevance' of persons favours the increase of opportunities for corporate bodies to offend against them.

White Collars and Men of Honour

In the preceding review of definitions, characteristics and causations of white-collar and corporate crime I have touched on a number of points upon which I shall now try to enlarge. This exercise will clarify the kind of offending upon which this study is focused and will also provide a broad analytical context for the following chapters.

There is one point which, in Sutherland's analysis, seems beyond question among many authors: that *white-collar crime is organized crime*. Both types of crime are collusive in nature, are performed in formal structures, and enjoy the connivance of administrators or legislators. On the other hand, Sutherland himself excludes from his celebrated definition all offences committed by other 'organized criminals' who lack respectability and high social status. In other words, white-collar crime *is* organized crime but not conventional organized crime. I believe that this demarcation produced a number of problems in criminological analysis whose reverberations are still strongly felt. Since Sutherland's formulation, the study of corporate and organized crime have proceeded separately, thus forming two distinct branches of criminology. As a consequence, experts of white-collar crime know little about conventional organized crime and vice-versa. This separation is by now strongly established and constantly reproduced. It is now perpetuated less on grounds of the diverse nature and characteristics of the two types of crime than by courtesy of the subdivisions within criminology as an academic discipline.

In the initial pages of this chapter I pointed out that there is a selective attitude among criminologists *vis-à-vis* Sutherland's work. This allows many scholars to focus their analysis on Sutherland's specific contribution in the field of white-collar crime while taking their distance from the author's general theory of crime. I believe that this fragmentation of Sutherland's thought is partly responsible for the separation mentioned above. Once the anti-positivist assertion that both poverty and wealth may cause crime is ignored, inevitably the study of white-collar and corporate crime becomes independent from that of organized crime. Many prefer to distinguish the former from the latter because only poverty is among the accepted causes of crime. It comes as no surprise that organized crime is still analysed against the background of poverty or relative deprivation, an approach that will be challenged in the next chapter. Neither is it surprising that white-collar and corporate crime, in turn, are treated as isolated, almost embarrassing issues which, as Nelken (1994a) notes, complicate any general explanation of the crime phenomenon. I believe that this separation, which is the result of successive elaborations of Sutherland's analysis, is also embryonically present in that analysis. It is also embedded in the unspoken belief that illicit acts committed by the élite are only 'quasi-criminal offences': they do not describe the overall immorality of the perpetrators, whose lifestyle is deemed otherwise commendable (Norrie, 1993). When the same acts are performed by members of conventional organized crime they are instead criminal: their immoral background and lifestyle, in other words their extra-juridical characteristics, taint all the behaviours they adopt.

An example of how Sutherland's legacy is somewhat uncritically received is provided by subsequent definitional distinctions included in some classics of criminology. Quinney (1970) distinguishes between 'crime in business' and 'the business of crime'. The former type includes embezzlement, misrepresentation in advertising, restraint of trade, fraudulent appropriation of public funds, illegal tax exemptions, patent infringements, fee splitting, fraudulent damage claims, and misrepresentation in the labelling and packaging of foods and drugs. The latter type includes activities that are organized for the explicit purpose of achieving economic gain through crime: numerous kinds of rackets (extortion of money and services from various businesses), the illegal control of other illegal activities (gambling, prostitution, and drug trafficking), and the illegal control of legitimate businesses (financial institutions, trade unions). Despite the general statement that the emphasis on work and success has created a way of life that can make criminals of us all, Quinney maintains a rigid distinction between crime in business, defined as occupational crime, and the business of crime, identified as organized crime. The statement that crime as business enjoys a symbiotic relationship with legitimate business is supported by a general consideration: 'The motives behind organized crime are the same as those so highly valued in our mythical free-enterprise system, such as the belief in economic success and respect for business' (ibid.: 179).

This vague similarity between corporate and organized crime is as much as many criminologists are prepared to concede. It is my contention that the two types of crime share more than the pursuit of success and financial gain. To paraphrase Sutherland's statement, organized crime *is* also white-collar crime. Let us discuss this point.

From his study of a number of large corporations, Sutherland's general conclusion is that the ideal businessperson and the large corporation are very much like the professional thief (Sutherland, 1956). Their violations of law are frequent and persistent, they do not lose status among their associates when violating laws. 'In this respect, also, they are akin to the professional thieves, who feel and express contempt for police, prosecutors, and judges. Both professional thieves and corporations feel contempt for government because government interferes with their behaviour' (ibid.: 95). Sutherland concludes that, being like professional thieves in a number of respects, businesspeople are participants in organized crime. They nevertheless differ from the latter, the author argues, by their greater interest in status and respectability: they think of themselves as honest men, not as criminals. I believe that this kind of rationalization, or technique of neutralization, is very common both among criminal businessperson and street criminals. Research conducted by Baumhart (1961), for example, suggests that many white-collar criminals tend to regard their colleagues as 'more criminal' than themselves, even when admitting to serious offences. 'If I am unethical, what is he?' is a common displacement of guilt. This is also used among conventional criminals. Although it may sound paradoxical, a similar technique of neutralization was used by Salvatore Riina, one of the leading figures of the Sicilian Mafia. When questioned about the morality of his killings, he said that those were nothing if compared with the killings of children perpetrated in Bosnia. (*La Repubblica*, 23 December 1993).

There is a link between conventional organized crime and a wide range of activities being carried out within a market economy. These activities, along with the illegal fashion in which they are performed, display a distinctive entrepreneurial character. 'When viewed apart from traditional assumptions about lower-class and immigrant groups, the *events described as "organized crime" become part of a much wider problem that includes major segments of white-collar crime as well*' (Smith and Alba, 1979: 37; my emphasis). Illicit entrepreneurs can be bankers, wholesalers, retailers, and power brokers, although the names by which they are defined are respectively loan sharks, smugglers, fences and bribe takers. Smith and Alba (1979) argue that the analysis of both corporate and organized crime should focus on entrepreneurship rather than criminality, a shift that may better describe behaviour patterns as a product of market-place dynamics. In drawing a number of common traits shared by the two types of crime, the authors also mention how illicit entrepreneurs avoid the imposition of regulatory power through corruption, a device which parallels the legitimate entrepreneurs' use of lobbies and other political devices which, indeed, include corruption. More specifically, once organized crime is understood to be rooted in the market-place, similarities among a wide range of events, which are commonly seen as distinct, can be recognized. Many events described as corporate crime possess an equally entrepreneurial character as typical organized crimes such as bookmaking, smuggling, and loan sharking. 'They reveal a degree of organized, concerted action among a large number of individuals engaged in illicit endeavour similar, in behavioural terms, to that of traditional organized crime' (ibid.: 38).

A better appreciation of both white-collar and organized crime is possible if a single conceptual perspective is adopted to examine them. This avenue is followed by Smith (1980), who applies the same economic categories to both corporate crime and criminal enterprises. A similar path is taken by

Albanese (1982), who identifies 'What Lockheed and La Cosa Nostra have in common'. In the Lockheed case, the corporation was found to have made illicit payments in order to secure sales abroad. Those charged claimed they did it because their competitors did it as well. It was the only available way of competing with them. La Cosa Nostra admitted, through the words of Joe Valachi, that the purpose of the organization was protection from rival gangs in operating illegitimate business. In the Lockheed case, 'payments to foreign officials were necessary to establish a "favourable climate" for selling aircraft overseas. For Valachi, it was the bribery of public officials to gain protection for illegal goods and services' (ibid.: 231).

The first hypothesis informing the perspective of this book is, therefore, that white-collar and corporate crime are variants of organized crime. As Quinney argues, the two are symbolically linked by virtue of a shared set of values but, as we have seen, they may also exhibit similar characteristics in terms of the complex structures in which they operate. Furthermore, as Smith and Alba suggest, similarities can be seen in their impact on and significance for society at large. Finally, both illicit activities can be examined by recourse to economic and organizational theories, an avenue that will be followed in the central part of this book.

The elements sketched so far may not appear sufficient to treat corporate and conventional organized crime as similar events requiring similar tools of analysis. However, the addition of yet another element may make the similarity of the two types of crime more plausible. This regards the techniques utilized by both 'corporate' and 'organized' offences. Shapiro (1990: 347) argues that definitions such as organizational/corporate or occupational crime, which delimit the conceptual terrain drawn by Sutherland, perpetuate a fundamental problem: 'They confuse acts with actors, norms with normbreakers, the modus operandi with the operator.' Crimes cannot be defined by the characteristics of their perpetrators, even if among these characteristics the variable 'respectability' is included. Respectability itself may, in fact, possess diverse meanings according to the social groups and actors using the term. The focus on offenders hinders the understanding of the deviant acts and the techniques utilized to perform these acts. These techniques may in a sense be socialized, they may be transmitted by corporate offenders to organized crime or vice-versa. 'Offenders clothed in very different wardrobes lie, steal, falsify, fabricate, exaggerate, omit, deceive, dissemble, shirk, embezzle, misappropriate, self-deal and engage in corruption or incompetence' (ibid.: 358).

The second point informing my perspective is therefore that corporate and organized crime often share the same illegal know-how and should be jointly analysed irrespective of the social characteristics or background of the perpetrators. This is perhaps the best way to be consistent with the original motive inspiring Sutherland's seminal work. The author created the concept of white-collar crime in order to include the offences of the élite in criminological analysis. But, as Shapiro notes, Sutherland's breakthrough is at risk of causing the opposite effect, that of 'segregating the rich and the poor and removing intensive inquiries about those of privilege from mainstream criminology' (ibid.: 363).

A related point regards the question whether the beneficiaries of corporate and organized crime are individual or collective actors. The emphasis on the act and the techniques making the act possible may allow one to sidestep this dilemma. As these techniques are learned by different groups, they may also be individually applied by isolated persons in these groups. An important consequence of this is that a definition such as 'crimes of the powerful' may lose part of its intrinsic value, especially if that definition implies the powerlessness of the victims. Identical offences may be committed by powerful people against vulnerable victims and by socially powerless persons against powerful victims. For example, once the technique of defrauding the European Union is learned, this can be applied by a number of actors including corporate bodies, middle-range businesses, conventional organized crime, joint ventures of these, isolated clerks or groups of unemployed. Here, one of Sutherland's hypotheses seems to be invalidated. His notion of crime as a learned behaviour is confined to a process occurring within a specific group. Thus, white-collar criminals learn rationalizations and techniques which are instrumental for the perpetuation of their own specific occupational illegalities. Conversely, we now witness a situation where rationalizations and techniques cross the boundaries of specific occupational groups and are learned by a diversity of enclaves and individuals. In the light of all this, analyses of corporate crime revolving around the notion of social asymmetry also become insufficient. These analyses, in fact, imply that offenders are always more socially powerful than their victims.

Finally, the reason for a joint analysis of corporate and organized crime is part, as it were, of a tautology. In a number of cases, some of which will be analysed in Chapter 6, corporations and conventional organized crime commit offences jointly. They form short- or long-term partnerships, they exchange services and mutually enhance their entrepreneurial activity (Ruggiero, 1992a; 1993a). Incidently, the demarcation between corporate and organized crime, which persists among many scholars, is viewed as increasingly blurred by agencies. As Levi notes, changes in this demarcation can be appreciated, 'in the growing involvement of professional and organized criminals in sophisticated fraud, and the increasing use of financial institutions to launder vast quantities of money from fraud' (Levi, 1987: 15). Hinting at the parts of the upperworld intersecting with the activities of organized crime, Levi mentions undertakings such as money laundering, illegal dumping of toxic waste, and financial fraud. In this light, even *criminal corporations*, namely those businesses where criminals deliberately exploit the appearance of legitimate business, are superseded by new types of corporations. These operate in the grey area where overlaps are found 'between white-collar crime and clear-cut kinds of crime, such as organized crime, [which] has so far been relatively neglected' (Nelken, 1994a: 376). The nature and operations of these enterprises are to be understood within the context in which the licit, semi-licit, and overtly illicit economies are constantly developing points of contact, common interests and strategies. Together, they form what Centorrino (1990) terms 'bad' economies.

I can finally return to the definitional aspects which I have previously left aside. My repeated use of 'white-collar and corporate' crime alludes to the circumstance that these behaviours may be adopted by a variety of individuals and groups, and that my analysis is focused on these behaviours rather than on their perpetrators or beneficiaries.

2 Criminal Enterprises

In the previous chapter I highlighted the customary separation between the study of white-collar and corporate crime on the one hand, and that of organized crime on the other. This separation, which was embryonically present in Sutherland's writings, has undergone a process of crystallization, to the point of shaping two distinct subdisciplines within criminology. Students of corporate crime, therefore, may come across illegal acts which are usually carried out either by or in conjunction with organized criminal groups, but may be unable to include them in their field of study. The categories adopted, along with the thorough but circumscribed understanding of corporate subcultures, will often prevent them from doing so. Conversely, students of organized crime, who frequently focus on what are deemed the typical subcultures which give rise to this kind of offending, will be disoriented when faced with criminal groups becoming corporate actors or their partners in crime. Nevertheless, an economic and organizational analysis of both types of offending may reveal many similarities between the two. This route will be followed later. Moreover, the examination of the common techniques used and the partnerships between them may even suggest that the conceptual distinction between corporate and organized crime has no basis. This chapter is concerned with the study of conventional organized crime and the way in which, in many instances, Sutherland's original distinction is either accepted or accentuated.

Sutherland's work maintains an anti-institutional flavour due to the author's purposeful attempt to bring the study of the 'crimes of the powerful' into mainstream criminology. His argument that both wealth and poverty may cause crime represents an implicit critique of the criminal justice system, which instead emphasizes offences caused by poverty. This critique also encompasses criminologists who seek their exclusive source of theoretical inspiration in the criminal justice system. Sutherland's lesson constitutes the starting-point for criminologists whose research transcends the domain of conventional crime – particularly so for students of crime as behaviour that meets with harsh informal and institutional reaction only when associated with low socio-economic status.

Definitions

Unlike Sutherland, many students of organized crime are usually not inspired by the same polemical drive, nor do their contributions aim at establishing new paradigms. Moreover, their view of the criminal justice system is often influenced by their over-reliance upon this system as a source of information for their study. Participant observation and ethnographic research into organized crime are rare and dangerous. All too often social scientists rely on 'either government pronouncements of organized crime's history, which are typically self- (and state-) serving, or work from exceptionally poor, often undocumented, secondary sources' (Block, 1991: ix). For this reason, the criminal justice system ends up playing a crucial role in the evaluation of that kind of crime, its impact and severity, and its very definition.

Abadinsky (1990) notes that there is confusion and eclecticism as to what exactly constitutes organized crime. There is also a tendency to avoid the problem of its definition, as if the obvious need not be defined. In a statement issued by the US President's Commission on Organized Crime, it is stressed that, while there is acceptance and recognition of certain acts as criminal, there is no standard awareness as to when a criminal group is to be regarded as organized. 'The fact that organized criminal activity is not necessarily organized crime complicates that definition process' (PCOC, 1986: 25). Descriptions range from 'two or more persons conspiring together to commit crimes for profit on a continuing basis' to more detailed accounts of what these crimes are: the supplying of illegal goods and services, predatory crime, violent crime, and so on (Abadinsky, 1990).

A number of North American agencies have often suggested that organized crime is formed by one single, albeit segmented, wide group which, because of its hunger for money and power, is alien to and threatens the society of the United States (Kefauver Committee, 1951; Fijnaut, 1990). The content of this definition, which was coined during the late 1940s, was maintained unaltered in following descriptions. According to a definition dating back to 1967, for example, 'organized crime is a self-perpetuating, continuing criminal conspiracy.... It is a society that seeks to operate outside the control of the American people and their governments' (Short, 1991: viii). Thus, the alien conspiracy theory was reiterated after almost two decades. This theory was endorsed by Donald Cressey (1969), who included it in one of his most famous books. Cressey also applied to the 'crime families' the notion of bureaucracy, whereby organized crime was described as hierarchically structured, characterized by formal rules and consisting of individuals with specialized and segmented functions within the hierarchy. A few individuals and families were therefore deemed to centralize and coordinate all organized criminal activities (Haller, 1992).

This interpretation exposed Cressey to criticism for the adoption, or indeed for the very coinage, of concepts which were elaborated within strictly institutional contexts (Albini, 1971). Cressey was accused of providing the official agencies with intellectual legitimacy while conferring scientific credibility on their definitions (Smith, 1991). Moreover, such definitions were based on a very selective attitude on the part of the institutions themselves, which chose to disclose certain judicial material while protecting a large mass of events with official secrecy (Calder, 1992). A credulous sociology, as it has been defined, was led to believe in the big conspiracy: The Organization. This sociology, 'innocent of such notions as informal organizations and patron–client networks, fixed the sociological frame of organized crime around conspiracy' (Block, 1991: 10). However, after years of field research, Chambliss (1978: 9) concluded: 'I do not believe that organized crime is run and controlled by a national syndicate with a "commission" or "board of directors" who have a feudal-like control over underlings spread across the nation.'

Many elements in the above institutional definition are present in criminological literature. In 1994, Europol indicated that its main task was to tackle organized crime in the countries of the European Union. Criminologists were invited to contribute research and analysis on the basis of a pre-established legal definition of what organized crime is (Statewatch, 1994). Is it a criminology, as Calder (1992) suggests, sanctioned by state categories?

While bearing these controversies in mind, I suggest that the best-known definitions of organized crime entail larger flaws than their being inspired by official agencies. These definitions can be classified in the following manner. Some hinge on strictly quantitative aspects: the number of individuals involved in a criminal group is said to determine the organizational degree of that group (Johnson, 1962; Ferracuti, 1988). Organized crime is said to differ from conventional crime for the larger scale of its illegal activity (Moore, 1987). Some others focus mainly on a temporal variable, that is on the time-span during which illegal activities are conducted. The death or incarceration of a member of organized crime, for example, do not stop the activities in which they are involved. Ianni (1972) seems to rely on both the quantitative and the temporal variable. He describes a complex web of kinship tying families together through alliances and intermarriages, a web strengthened by an equally complex pattern of godparent–godchild relationships. The author describes crime families as being linked together into a composite clan. 'Some clans obviously form compact, interlocked regional groups with frequent intermarriages cementing the alliances; all are related by some common interests' (Ianni, 1972: 172). He concludes that this clan-like organization makes criminal groups seem very similar, a circumstance that has led observers to maintain that organized crime is a highly structured, national or even international conspiracy.

Criminologists who focus attention on its structural characteristics observe that organized crime operates by means of flexible and diversified groups. Such a structure is faced with peculiar necessities due to its condition of illegality. Firstly, the necessity, while remaining a 'secret' organization, to exert publicly its coercive and dissuasive strength. An equilibrium is therefore required between publicity and secrecy that only a complex structure is able to acquire. Secondly, the necessity to neutralize law enforcement through *omertà* (conspiracy of silence), corruption and retaliation. Finally, the need to reconcile its internal order, through specific forms of conflict control, with its external legitimacy, through the provision of occupational and social opportunities (Cohen, 1977).

Frequently, definitions of organized crime revolve around the concept of 'professionalism': its members, it is suggested, acquire skills and career advancement by virtue of their full-time involvement in illegality. Mannheim (1975) only devotes a dozen pages of his voluminous treatise to organized crime. The reason for this may perhaps be found in his preliminary general statement, where it is assumed that all economically oriented offences require a degree of organization, or at least necessitate forms of association among persons. In this light, the term 'organized crime' should be applied to the majority of illegal activities.

Other authors prefer to concentrate on the collective clientele of organized crime. This is therefore identified with a structure involved in the public provision of goods and services which are officially defined illegal (Zincani, 1989). Organized criminal groups, in other words, simply fill the inadequacy of institutional agencies, which are unable to provide those goods and services, or perhaps officially deny that demand exists for them (Martinoli, 1985). The contribution of McIntosh (1975) is to be located in this perspective. She notes that organized crime is informed by a particular relationship between offenders and victims. For example, even the victims of extortion rackets often fail to report the offenders, less because they are terrified than 'because they see the extortionist as having more power in their parish than the agents of the state' (ibid.: 50). It may be added that the victims may also recognize their 'protector' as an authority which is more able than its official counterpart to distribute resources and opportunities.

The definitions examined so far have a number of elements in common. Firstly, they refer exclusively to one particular variant of organized crime, namely the Italian–American Mafia. Secondly, they are only concerned with the illegal activities carried out by organized crime. This neglects other variants which bear characteristics similar to the Mafia-type organized crime on the one hand, and some distinctive traits of their own on the other.

Moreover, the neglect of the legal businesses in which organized crime is involved obscures the fact that, once 'gone legal', organized crime may become very similar to white-collar or corporate crime. The only aspect distinguishing the former, it has been suggested, is a vowel at the end of the offender's name (Edelhertz and Overcast, 1993). Arguably, some variants of organized crime undergo an evolution which brings them to a number of successive stages. These may describe a typical relationship that criminal groups establish with the licit economy and include a predatory, a parasitic, and finally a symbiotic stage. Other forms of organized crime may still or always will be unable to undergo a similar evolution (Peterson, 1991). A more complete definition, I believe, should also include these 'pariah' forms of organized crime.

The descriptions mentioned above also share another central element: they are, to varying degrees, related to the notion of 'professionalism'. This seems to allow for an original approach to the subject-matter, because such a notion alludes to a plausible parallel to be drawn between organized crime and the organization of any other industrial activity. However, one crucial aspect which characterizes the crime industry is neglected. This is that the crime industry itself cannot limit its recruitment to the individuals who constitute its tertiary sector or middle management. In order for the parallel with the licit industry to be validated, it has to be stressed that organized crime also needs a large number of unskilled criminal employees. Professionalism and unskilled labour seem to cohabit in organized criminal groups, and their simultaneous presence should be regarded as a significant hallmark of organized crime. The validity of this hypothesis will be explored in Chapter 5 through the case studies of specific criminal industries.

Among the authors who stress the importance of the variable 'labour' in the definition of organized crime is Gambetta (1992). The author emphasizes how organized crime is dependent on a range of employees whose skills and work stability vary considerably. Unfortunately, his analysis is only devoted to the Sicilian Mafia and mainly focuses on conventional crime performed by this organization. While neglecting the above-mentioned stages in the evolution of organized crime (predatory, parasitic and symbiotic), Gambetta claims that the Mafia is still (and merely) a service-providing organization. Among the goods provided, trust and protection are singled out as paramount. These, which should be supplied by the state, may under certain circumstances become the preserve of private entrepreneurs, namely organized crime. This type of crime is therefore an industry for the supply of private protection and the distribution of trust to economic actors who would otherwise be unable to interact safely. In the case of the Sicilian Mafia, for example, its strength as an industry for the supply of protection and trust is deemed a consequence of traditional popular distrust of the official agencies, and foreign domination before them. It should be noted that this definition alludes to aspects concerning the causation of organized crime, which is therefore regarded as a counter-power replacing the authority gap left by an ineffective state. But with this definition we are now entering the domain of the aetiology of organized crime, which will be dealt with separately in the pages that follow.

The Aetiology of Deficit

The definition suggested by Gambetta shows how attempts to locate organized crime within criminological theory can be hindered by a cumbersome legacy. This consists of explanations revolving around notions of 'deficit', deficiency and inadequacy. These notions tend to associate all antisocial behaviours with a condition of disadvantage, be it economic, cultural or psychological.

In this respect, during the course of a whole century, the aetiology of organized crime only moved a few steps forward. Some early positivist tenets, when updated with new linguistic expressions, seem to survive intact in our time. For example, when Lombroso discussed organized crime, he suggested that 'tradition' plays a crucial role in its perpetuation. Lombroso (1971: 389) argued:

> It seems to me that the high persistence of some wicked associations such as the Mafia, the Camorra and brigandage depends first of all on their long-term existence, in that the continuous repetition of our acts transforms these acts into a custom and therefore into a norm.

This argument sounds very familiar, as it echoes some contemporary analysis which explains the persistence of organized crime by resorting to the variables 'backwardness' or 'archaism'. Other comments made by Lombroso on the subject sound even more familiar: for example, that the perpetuation of organized crime is also due to the lack of stigma in the very concept of 'Mafioso'. The author notes that the Mafiosi are not regarded as individuals belonging to a distant and censurable social universe: in the local popular culture 'they are not associated with immorality, nor do they elicit contempt' (ibid.: 390). It would be interesting to assess to what extent these assumptions were transmitted to a score of criminological theories including, for instance, subcultural theory. Moreover, it is noteworthy that Lombroso, when trying to explain the extraordinary long-term prosperity of organized crime in Italy, indicates a strong causality in what he terms the 'inadequate governments, which do not rule according to justice, and in a sense make it necessary and useful that people exercise and implement their own justice' (ibid.: 390). We are here in the domain of well-known theories according to which organized crime thrives where the state is absent or has an authority deficit.

Also in the anomic tradition we find a set of notions which persist, deservedly or otherwise. In the celebrated elaborations of Durkheim, some particular forms of division of labour are described as 'anomic'. The author argues that:

> One might be tempted to reckon as irregular forms of the division of labour criminal occupations and other harmful activities. They are the very negation of solidarity, and yet they take the form of special activities. But to speak with exactitude, there is no division of labour here, but differentiation pure and simple. The two terms must not be confused. Thus, *cancer* and tuberculosis increase the diversity of organic tissues without bringing forth a new specialisation of biological functions. (Durkheim, 1960: 353; emphasis added).

The author never wrote about organized crime, although we can assume that this type of crime is to be included in those incompatible forms of antisocial activity whose damage goes beyond the functional level. In this respect, the distinction Durkheim makes between division of labour and differentiation is illuminating. The former, he stresses, brings vital forces together, whereas the latter, in its criminal variant, causes disintegration, like microbes and indeed *cancer*.

I believe that the nucleus of a series of well-known theories can be detected in Durkheim's argument. Among these are, first of all, so-called control theories, which appear to be experiencing an unexpected return. For example, at the Organized Crime Division of the Chicago Police Department the fight against 'the mob' is inspired by the assumption that 'deviant acts result when an individual's bond to society is weakened' (Lombardo, 1991: 11). This denies that organized crime may expand its activity when its bonds with accepted society are instead strengthened. In turn, Durkheim's metaphor of cancer is still among us, as it is obsessively utilized in journalistic jargon, and recurs in judicial and academic language, though often as an involuntary quotation. Ironically, this metaphor was also put forward by Tommaso Buscetta, a Mafia turncoat, when he declared: 'In the interest of society, my children and all young people, I intend to reveal all I know about this *cancer* which is the Mafia, so that the new generation may lead a more humane and dignified life' (Arlacchi, 1994a: 3).

In Merton's extension of anomic theory, deviant adaptations of the 'innovative' type are found exclusively among the lower strata of the social structure. The dominant culture, it is argued, make incompatible demands upon those who occupy these strata. 'On the one hand, they are asked to orient their conduct toward the prospect of large wealth ... and on the other, they are largely denied effective opportunities to do so institutionally' (Merton, 1968: 200). Notions such as 'relative deprivation' emerge in Merton's analysis, although the author is far from suggesting that this notion be applied to the explanation of white-collar and organized crime. It is the lower strata of society, he emphasizes, that are pressurized towards crime.

Deficit categories, although in a different form, are also devised by the Chicago School theorists, who in a sense anticipate Merton's elaboration. An important theory emerges from the Chicago School, namely 'social disorganization' (Downes and Rock, 1988). This crucially attributes the emergence of organized crime to the decline of informal social control. According to this theory, the degree of organization of illegal structures (be they youth gangs, groups of pimps, gambling syndicates or others) is dependent on the degree of disorganization of society. In other words, their organization is a function of the distance which separates them from other social groups (Thrasher, 1927; Shaw, 1930; Shaw and McKay, 1972). Sociological studies conducted in Chicago's 'delinquent areas' unveiled micro-societies of immigrants which were perfectly organized (Whyte, 1943). Deviance, in this perspective, endorses a surrogate social order, a vicarious system which is nevertheless a social system in its own right. In this system, it is perfectly logical that a gangster is not met with disapproval (Landesco, 1969). He is a product of his surroundings in the same way in which the good citizen is a product of his environment. Therefore the problem, as indicated by Whyte, is not the lack of organization within those particular micro-societies, but the lack of meaningful relationships between these enclaves and society as a whole.

Finally, among the analyses offered by sociocriminological literature, subcultural theories should be mentioned (Cohen, 1955; Coward and Ohlin, 1960). Derived from a combination of Merton's structural anomic theories on the one hand, and in debt to Sutherland for their emphasis on the learning dimension on the other, these theories seem to constitute an inexhaustible source for students of organized crime. Criminal groups are said to adopt criminal solutions to resolve their status problems. They adhere to a delinquent subculture which can provide them with accessible opportunities. Cohen (1990) has reiterated this argument more recently, and his repeated use of the phrase 'criminal subculture' neither signals his critical reappraisal of the concept nor indicates willingness to update his definition of organized crime.

Cloward and Ohlin are still frequently cited when both organized crime and the drug phenomenon are discussed. In their celebrated categorization (delinquent, conflictual and retreatist subcultures), organized crime goes under the heading of 'delinquent subcultures', its main motive appearing to be of an economic nature. Subcultural theory has been criticized because it applies with particular force to exponents of one specific class. 'It may be termed differential magnification, the tuning of the analytical lens to an almost exclusive degree on the "subordinate" cultures, with a corresponding neglect of the "dominant" or "subaltern" cultures' (Downes and Rock, 1988: 164).

To summarize, it is noticeable that the interpretation of organized crime shows an extraordinary continuity in time. For over a century its aetiology has been based on categories such as tradition, absence of the state, pathology and lack of control, relative poverty, and delinquent subcultures. All these categories fall, to different degrees, within a *paradigm of deficit* whereby the causes of crime originate in a deficiency, be it one of control, of socialization, of opportunities, of rationality, and so on (Ruggiero, 1993a). Categories such as 'low self-control', to which we referred in the previous chapter, also fall within this paradigm. 'We do believe that there is no need for theories designed specifically to account for gang crime, organized crime, or professional criminals. The theory of crime and self-control is capable of accounting for the facts about "organized" crime' (Gottfredson and Hirschi, 1990: 214).

However, such formulas can hardly explain the types of organized crime which have developed over the last decades in many European countries. Organized illegal activities seem less the result of poverty, underdevelopment or lack of self-control than of its opposite: affluence, development and the control of resourses. The *paradigm of deficit* seems therefore to remain prevalent only in that it provides an irreplaceable ideological device. Social disadvantage, lack of socialization, control deficit and so on are suitable analytical tools only when one tries to depict organized crime as a distinctive form of social pathology. On the other hand, these tools are ineffective when this type of crime is explained with reference to 'ordinary' relationships among people and within the 'normal' conditions of the economy.

Social disorganization theorists focus their analysis on the internal relationships of organized groups, hence the emphasis on units such as 'crime families' (Godson and Olson, 1995). These authors neglect the fact that, in order to reproduce itself, organized crime is bound to establish some external relationships with society at large. The nature and strength of these external relationships may explain more than genealogical trees or clan-type structures can. In this perspective, organized crime can be interpreted as a coalition which, in the research conducted by Chambliss (1978: 9), consists of 'politicians, law enforcement people, businessmen, union leaders, and (in some ways least important of all) racketeers'. Cloward and Ohlin (1960:

166) themselves were aware of this aspect of organized crime, although perhaps they failed to draw a logical conclusion from it. In a sense, they belied their belonging to the 'subcultural school' of thought when they described typical criminal careers. Apprentice criminals, they argued, pass from one status to another in the illegitimate opportunity system, and as they do so, develop a set of relationships with members of the legitimate world. 'Unless [they] can form these relationships, the possibility of a stable, protected criminal style of life is effectively precluded' (ibid.: 166). In other words, organized crime can reproduce itself less because crime families maintain their close-knit structures and distinctive subcultures than because they dissolve within both the dominant social structure and culture. In fact, the more they do so, the more their criminal opportunities may increase. In other words, new skills may be acquired as licit and illicit activities observe a process of mutual enhancement. This aspect was highlighted by a report by the Pennsylvania Crime Commission (1993), where concerns were aired at the 'benign attitudes' displayed by local communities towards racketeering groups. These attitudes were chastised not so much for fostering distrust in the legitimate governmental processes as for permitting racketeers to grow powerful enough to enter into the official economy. 'Infiltration of legitimate business', in other words, was feared as a synonym for more possibilities to engage in crime.

Many of the controversial issues outlined so far stem from the difficulties met by students of organized crime. As Block (1991) puts it, the study of organized crime has been fascinated by conspiracy theory, a fascination which leads to the depiction of monolithic, impenetrable, culturally hermetic groups of criminals. He also suggests that the term 'organized crime' should be abandoned altogether in favour of the term 'illegal enterprises'. This approach is implicitly adopted by scholars analysing organized crime, and crime in general, as an economic activity. It is to the contribution of these scholars that I now turn.

Criminal Enterprises

According to Becker (1968), crime is an economically important activity or industry, notwithstanding its almost total neglect by economists. This neglect, he argues, probably results from an attitude that illegal activity is too immoral to merit any systematic scientific attention. Becker seeks to formulate a measure of the social loss caused by crime and to find the optimal levels of expenditures that minimize this loss. In turn, the optimal expenditure is to be understood as the ideal amount of enforcement, which depends, among other things, on the cost of detection, apprehension and criminal conviction of offenders, the cost of punishment, and the responses of offenders to changes in enforcement. Inevitably, this type of approach enters into the domain of criminological theory, and suggests that 'a useful theory of criminal behaviour can dispense with special theories of anomie, psychological inadequacies, or inheritance of special traits and simply extend the economist's usual analysis of choice' (ibid.: 170). Lest readers be repelled by the apparent novelty of an economic framework for the analysis of crime, Becker reminds us that 'two important contributors to criminology during the eighteenth and nineteenth centuries, Beccaria and Bentham, explicitly applied an economic calculus' (ibid.: 209).

Economists note that the basic premise of sociological work on crime is that criminals are somehow different from non-criminals, and the major research consist of the ways in which criminals differ (Rubin, 1980). Assuming a rationality to human behaviour, Rubin argues, potential criminals should also be acknowledged as being endowed with principles guiding the rationality of their action. The choice of action for criminals depends on the value of alternative uses of time, a choice that also engages law enforcers. In other words, all actors involved in the crime sector of the economy 'are consciously or subconsciously weighing the costs and benefits of their actions and making explicit choices among alternatives' (Andreano and Siegfried, 1980: 4). Those involved in illegal activity rationally maximize their own self-interest subject to the constraints they face in the marketplace. 'Thus the decision to become a criminal is in principle no different from the decision to become a bricklayer or a carpenter, or, indeed, an economist' (Rubin, 1980: 13).

Other economic definitions distinguish between two main types of offences: acts of consumption and acts of production (Stigler, 1970). The former could be exemplified by ignoring speed limits while driving to a party. Therefore, consumption offences hinge on merely recreational aspects. The latter could be illustrated by all activities aimed at gaining income. For those who engage in 'production offences', the normal rules of occupational choice will hold. They will weigh prospects, returns and costs of specific criminal activities, and compare these with other criminal activities as well as legitimate ones. 'The costs of injuries to a professional athlete are comparable to the costs to the offender of apprehension, defence, and conviction' (Stigler, 1970: 530). Criminals are faced with details regarding their occupational choice which do not substantially differ from those of licit occupations. For example, they may have to consider which location offers maximum potential income, and therefore, like salespersons, move from area to area. They may consider whether infrequent large-scale crimes yield more returns than frequent small-scale ones. Finally, they may have to plan or save for periods of illness, unemployment, and eventual retirement.

Incidently, some criminal occupations result in frequent periods of inactivity due to frequency of apprehension, whereas: 'certain occupational roles require youthfulness by definition, and thus enforce unusually early retirement' (Polsky, 1967: 103).

What market characteristics determine whether a criminal activity becomes organized? As Schelling (1967) notes, the car industry is characterized by large firms, whereas machine-tool production is not. If the economic principles operating in the upperworld also apply to the activities of the underworld, explanations should be found as to why, for example, gambling, extortion and contraband require large firms and a higher degree of organization. The first explanation rests on overall costs and some element of technology that make small firms more costly than large ones. Schelling identifies the lower limit to the size of a firm in the need to keep equipment and skilled personnel fully utilized. The second explanation concerns the prospect of establishing monopolistic conditions. Monopolies allow for the rise of prices at which goods and services can be sold. On the other hand, monopolies often result in the overall reduction of output due to the absence of competing firms. But the increase in profit margin will compensate for this. Cartels or mergers can lead to monopolies, as can intimidation. The three options are equally available to firms.

With Schelling's work we are entering into a crucial aspect of the debate on organized crime. This regards the 'preferability' of structured large-scale illicit activities as opposed to dispersed disorganized ones. The author observes that the larger the firm, and especially the larger its market share, the more will formerly 'external' costs become internalized. External costs are those falling on competitors, customers and others outside the firm itself. Violence, for example, could be regarded as one such external cost. Thus, members of organized crime may have a collective interest in restricting violence so as to avoid the disapproval of the public and attention from the police. Ideally, their task would be to reduce violence to a minimum. On the other hand, individual (professional or unskilled) criminals have little or no incentive to reduce the violence connected with their crime. Schelling suggests an analogy with the whaling industry, which has a collective interest in not killing all whales, while individual whalers may not consider the future of the industry as a whole when trying to maximize their own catch. A large organization, he argues, can afford to impose discipline, holding down violence if the business is crime, holding down the slaughter of females if the business is whaling. In this light, even episodes of 'accommodation' that organized crime sometimes reaches with institutional agencies or individual members of them may be regarded as attempts to restrain dangerous practices and limit violence while delineating spheres of influence.

Schelling's observations about 'compromising with organized crime' include the awareness that corruption of public officials entails a price for society to pay. This is exemplified by frustration for the criminal justice system and a general lowering of standards of morality. Instead, successive analyses of this issue tend only to emphasize the social 'preferability' of organized crime as opposed to disorganized crime while omitting the evaluation of the moral costs involved. Buchanan (1980) bases his 'defense of organized crime' on the distinction between goods and 'bads'. Monopoly in the sale of ordinary goods and services, he contends, is socially inefficient because it restricts output or supply. It also permits vendors to increase prices and therefore concentrate profits. This widely shared belief suggests that efforts should be made to limit monopolies and favour competition instead. However, 'if monopoly in the supply of "goods" is socially undesirable, monopoly in the supply of "bads" should be socially desirable, precisely because of the output restriction' (ibid.: 395). The validity of this argument, in Buchanan's analysis, is exemplified by prostitution. In spite of legal prohibitions, for many buyers prostitutes are 'goods' in the strict economic sense. Monopoly organizations providing these goods are preferable to competitive ones because they restrict the total output. On the other hand, a competitive situation will result in firms imposing 'external diseconomies' on one another. In sum, the overall social costs of a number of firms competing in the provision of the 'good' prostitutes would inevitably grow. More prostitutes would be available, a variety of appealing settings and markets would be set up for the sale of these goods, and diseconomies associated with conflictual and even violent competition would follow. The replacement of competition by monopoly would have the effect of internalizing such diseconomies. Buchanan concludes his analysis by stressing how self-interest can be made to serve social purposes under the appropriate institutional arrangements. Official agencies should therefore discourage competition among illicit firms and translate the self-interest of organized crime into a reduction of the social damage caused by crime in general. 'It is not from the public-spiritedness of the leaders of the Cosa Nostra that we should expect to get a reduction in the crime rate but from their regard for their own self-interests' (ibid.: 407).

Rubin (1980) notes that illegal activity conducted by organized crime lacks the coercive aspects of other types of crime. Individuals are not forced to buy the goods and services provided by organized criminal groups, a circumstance which encourages us to analyse these activities with tools derived from industrial organization, the branch of economics dealing with firms and their behaviour in markets. In this perspective, organized crime is not an ordinary criminal enterprise, its behaviour in markets being usually inspired by a degree of monopoly power. 'It is likely that this monopoly is in dealing with other criminal firms, rather than in dealing with ultimate consumers' (Rubin, 1980: 18). An important distinction emerges from this analysis. Like many authors, Rubin identifies organized crime with one variant, or perhaps one specific function only, of this type of criminality. Nevertheless, his description accounts for a useful identification of a particular aspect of some criminal organizations. Some variants of organized crime can be viewed as firms holding monopoly power in the provision of goods to other criminal firms. Among these goods, the most important is capital. 'Thus a criminal firm can lend money to a heroin importer and not itself deal with the heroin at all; the price charged for the loan will be high enough for the lender to make most of the profit in heroin importing' (ibid.: 18). Another good provided by one monopoly firm to another may be protection, which takes the form of taxation imposed on criminal activity.

Rubin also notes that monopoly restricts output and raises prices, a circumstance which in the case of the provision of illegal goods suggests the preferability of organized rather than disorganized forms of crime. The examples given by the author pertain to the domain of victimless crime, among which is gambling. After arguing that many illegal goods are illegal because society decides 'that they are wrong', Rubin concludes that if gambling were 'provided by a monopoly, then in fact we will have less gambling than if the activity were provided by purely competitive criminal firms' (ibid.: 19). Therefore, if we want less crime, one way of achieving this goal might simply be to allow the activity to become monopolized. Again, it is assumed that with the development of organized forms of crime some of the costs of criminal activity become 'internalized'. Conversely, external costs falling on society at large are exemplified by an individual hijacker who might kill a bystander to eliminate a potential witness, even though criminals as an occupational group would suffer from public outrage and increased police activity. In this sense, society might 'contract out' some of the regulatory functions to criminals themselves, 'encouraging them to stick to less damaging kinds of crime' (Reynolds, 1980: 43–4).

Discussions concerning the preferability of organized crime are based on the premise that forms of criminal activity exist which can indeed be termed 'organized'. This term usually implies monopoly or cartel domination of one illicit firm in the market-place. We have already discussed how official accounts of organized crime were responsible for the propagation of this view. According to many official accounts, all illicit activities are centrally planned and tightly controlled: they are part of a general plot hatched by a committee or commission. This structure is deemed crucial for the establishment of monopolies, which is regarded as a natural evolution of organized crime. Monopolies, in turn, are said to imply coercion, arising from superior violence and control of corrupt law enforcers. However, Reuter

(1983) suggests that the major sources of revenue for organized crime are not as strictly organized as official agencies make us believe. In his examination of bookmaking, numbers and loansharking, he refutes the notion that one group controls these markets through violence and a monopoly in corruption. The high costs required for the suppression of competition make these markets populated by small firms, many of which are marginal and ephemeral.

To conclude this overview, it is worthwhile mentioning one author in particular who takes issue with the economic approach to the study of crime, although adopting an economic approach himself. Gordon (1980) terms as orthodox economic analysis the arguments presented above. He argues that crime represents a rational response to the conditions of competition and inequality fostered in capitalism. In his view, white-collar, organized and 'ghetto crime' should be explained with the same analytical tools, the difference between them being part of an illusory effect caused by the criminal justice system's response to them. Gordon asserts that we cannot realistically expect to 'solve' the problem of crime without a radical redistribution of power in society. 'Radicals therefore argue that nearly all crimes in capitalist societies represent perfectly *rational* responses to the structure of institutions upon which capitalist societies are based' (ibid.: 103). In sum, the author assumes that offences of many different varieties constitute functionally similar responses to the organization of capitalism, for all crimes help provide a means of survival in a society within which survival is never assured. People are said to respond quite reasonably to the structure of economic opportunities available to them. Starting with powerless criminals, the author contends that only rarely can these offenders be regarded as raving, irrational, antisocial lunatics. The legitimate occupations available to them would typically pay low wages, offer relatively demeaning assignments, and carry the constant risk of lay-off. In contrast, many kinds of crime 'available' in the ghetto 'often bring higher monetary return, offer even higher social status' (ibid.: 103). In much the same way, organized crime is regarded as a perfectly rational economic activity. Demand for illicit goods and services is said to structure the rationality of the economic activities in which organized crime engages itself. It is important to note that the author also considers corporate crime as a rational response to life in capitalist societies.

> Corporations exist to protect and augment the capital of their owners. If it becomes difficult to perform that function one way, corporate officials will quite inevitably try to do it another... . In the context of the perpetual and highly competitive race among corporations for profits and capital accumulation, each response seems quite reasonable. (ibid.: 104).

A number of important aspects emerge from this brief review. As I have already highlighted, the use of economic tools for the study of crime permits us to abandon notions of social or individual pathology and, at the same time, allows us to concentrate on the behavioural traits that criminals share with all other actors. I shall return to this aspect in the Conclusion to this book.

It could be suggested that an economic approach renders definitional questions of organized crime more easily answerable, while providing a pointer for the distinction among different variants of this type of crime. Therefore, if all criminal enterprises share a need for capital to invest and demand for the goods they provide, not all of them will provide goods and services to other criminal enterprises. Furthermore, as we have seen, an economic approach contributes to the understanding of the degree of organization that the running of a criminal enterprise requires. In Reuter's analysis, this approach leads to the very rejection of the term 'organized crime'. I shall return to this aspect later in this book and suggest that organized and disorganized crime are two forms of criminal business which do not necessarily exclude each other. In fact, as the example of the drug business will attempt to show, organized and disorganized crime feed on each other with the result of making both more remunerative.

It should be borne in mind that the analysis presented so far is confined to the examination of conventional criminal activities. In other words, although crime is regarded as work and criminal groups as enterprises, this analysis assumes that the proceeds of illegal business are only reinvested in further illegal ventures. The remaining pages of this chapter are devoted to the examination of licit activities carried out by criminal entrepreneurs. It should be understood that the choice to invest criminal proceeds in the licit economy is not an irreversible one, as criminal entrepreneurs may intermittently shift profits from the criminal to the official economy and vice versa.

From Crime to Business and Back

According to Block (1980), there are two main types of criminal syndicate. One is the 'enterprise syndicate', which operates exclusively in the arena of illicit businesses such as prostitution, gambling, contraband and drugs. The second he calls the 'power syndicate', which is predominantly engaged in extortion as a form of territorial control rather than enterprise. The Sicilian Mafia is often described as belonging to the second type, as its overriding aim is purported to be the control over the environment and the people that are part of it (Catanzaro, 1994). It is my contention that the two types of organized crime cannot be so easily separated. Enterprise syndicates, to use

Block's phrase, may be forced to invest their proceeds in the licit economy because there are limits to the expansion of illicit markets. The amount of money accumulated in the drug economy, for example, may not always find investment opportunities in the same economy or in other illicit ones. The very instability of the demand for illicit goods may render it necessary that some illicit capital seeks valorization opportunities in the mainstream economy. Secondly, so-called power syndicates may well find entry into the licit economy as an additional source for the growth of their power. If their aim is the control of the territory and the people who are part of it, the provision of occupational opportunities in that territory will certainly boost their control and power.

When analysing the licit enterprises originating from illicit revenues, difficulties arise due to a subtle moral imperative. This suggests that a distinction *must* be drawn between this kind of business and the 'clean' economy. Consider Arlacchi's (1983) study of organized crime and his definition of the 'Mafia enterprise'. Drawing on Schumpeter, the author extends the attributes of licit businesses to businesses set up by the Mafia. These are: an innovative aspect, an element of rational calculation and, finally, an irrational and aggressive aspect which lies in the 'animal spirit' incorporated in the accumulation of wealth. Despite this neutral and somewhat scientific approach, the author seems uneasy when it comes to distinguishing the enterprises originating from 'dirty' money from ordinary 'clean' ones. After reading his analysis, some questions remain. What really denotes the former? What makes them pathological? In what way do they constitute an obstacle to the development of the official economy? Arlacchi believes that key answers to these questions lie in the following characteristics. The Mafia enterprise, he argues, practises unfair competition and discourages the development of natural market forces; keeps wages low; is endowed with large financial resources which unfairly protect it from competition.

Now, these elements hardly typify licit enterprises created with criminal proceeds. They in fact belong to many small and mid-range licit firms which are the result of industrial decentralization. Think of the small industrial units connected with their mother factory. These units may operate both on the same domestic territory where their main factory is located or in offshore territories where labour is cheaper and more disciplined. Indeed, their existence prevents competition in that these units are closely controlled by larger industries of which they are also exclusive suppliers. Although located outside the main factory walls, they are to be considered in-house suppliers. They are financially supported by the main industries, which also provide them with fixed capital in the form of machinery. The low degree of conflict in these small units, and the consequent low wages, are due to the limited number of workers they employ and the virtual ban on union rights: in a sense, they are beyond legality. Furthermore, these decentralized productive units seem to have acted as a model for other non-industrial organizations, as characteristics of flexibility and the virtual ban on union rights now seem to extend to large parts of the tertiary sector. The attempt to attribute these characteristics only to enterprises set up by criminal entrepreneurs sounds, therefore, like a moralistic artefact. This attempt contains less a condemnation of the above characteristics than an indictment of the criminal entrepreneurs who adopt them. In sum, these businesses end up being defined on grounds of who owns them and how the money to start them was found. In this way, some businesses are deemed criminal simply because they are run by criminals or former criminals. Again, as discussed in the previous chapter, the definition of a behaviour as crime is largely based on the curriculum vitae of those who adopt it, rather than on the nature of that behaviour.

I suggest that legal businesses originating from illegal proceeds be regarded as a subsidiary sector of organized crime. These businesses are akin to subsidiaries and suppliers which operate in conjunction with the large legal industries. In both cases, in fact, conditions of semi-legality prevail and benefits are brought back to the parent firms which own them.

According to other interpretations, the presence of enterprises originating from criminal proceeds hampers the development of a genuine entrepreneurial spirit. This is believed to be the case in areas which are not fully developed, where organized crime is said to play a devastating role for its 'rigid protectionism, for wasting resources, and repressing entrepreneurial, intellectual and productive energies' (Dalla Chiesa, 1983: 19). Criminal entrepreneurs are said to remain criminals even when 'co-opted' into the licit economy, to keep resorting to violence and to maintain a strong sense of belonging to their previous ambience (Falcone, 1991; 1992). While engaged in the official economy, they may still be strongly associated with violent gangs and extortionists. They may therefore utilize the power of intimidation of their previous associates to discourage competitors or, through extortion, to financially penalize them. Licit entrepreneurs who intend to conduct business in territories controlled by criminal entrepreneurs may therefore incur additional costs for their activities. They may be discouraged to sell their goods and services at competitive prices, thus passing these additional costs on to their clientele. Waste and the repression of entrepreneurial energies are said to follow.

I believe that it is difficult to establish whether the presence of organized crime contributes to the waste and the repression of productive energies or whether the previous existence of the two favours the development of organized crime. In many European countries, in fact, some areas are traditionally relegated to underdevelopment by the domestic economic structure in which they are located. These areas are expected to provide only labour and consumers, a limited role which derives from their historically determined 'lack' of entrepreneurial spirit. If forms of organized crime take shape in these areas, these may be regarded as a consequence of the absence of entrepreneurial spirit rather than an obstacle to its growth. As for selling goods at prearranged, non-competitive prices, it is hard to claim that this practice typifies criminal entrepreneurs, as it is a well-known practice to licit ones under the name of 'price fixing'. In this respect it could be argued that, once involved in the official economy, criminal entrepreneurs may adopt already established practices rather than impose them on others.

According to another argument, licit businesses originated from crime hamper economic development while failing to accomplish the natural task of all investment, namely the production of value (Centorrino and Signorino, 1993). Capital produced by illegal entrepreneurs may, in effect, become stagnant because not reinvested, or may 'dissolve' in order to evade taxation. Illegal capital, in other words, is said to suffocate production in that it tends to translate into inert wealth, or into mere status. A variant of this argument suggests that all illegal capital, be it produced through crime or simply concealed for tax evasion purposes, should be compared with money transferred abroad (Reuter, 1984). This is said to slow down economic growth, as does an excess of imports over exports.

Authors who argue in this fashion usually draw upon notions of classical economy. But it is exactly in classical economic terms that this argument is flawed. There always exists a part of inactive capital which is not utilized for the production of value, which was estimated by John Stuart Mill in 1844 as being around 50 per cent. Waste, therefore, does not exclusively characterize criminal enterprises and entrepreneurs. 'This is anyway the habitual situation of a very substantial part of all capitals of the world.... The number of producers and customers who practice a short-term rotation of their capital is indeed very low' (Mill, 1844).

Relatedly, criminal entrepreneurs, whether engaged in licit, illicit or in both economies, are attributed an egoistic rationality as opposed to an entrepreneurial collective rationality. Anarchy versus harmony? Again, authors who endorse this argument usually refer to classical economic theory, in particular to Marxist theory, where this distinction is far from being so neat. Marx suggests that all entrepreneurs constitute separate universes in their own right but, at the same time, reproduce and incorporate all elements of the system of which they form a part: 'The reciprocal action of capitals one upon the other generates the necessity that they behave like capital; it is indeed the apparently independent action of single capitals and their clashing without rules which pose their general rule.'

When entering into the licit economy, criminal entrepreneurs are alleged not only to continue their illegal activities, but also to retain the characteristics of violence and intimidation which distinguish them. As specialists of violent social regulation, their presence in the licit economy is said to 'corrupt' this economy and to 'convert to violence those who hold entrepreneurial aspirations and abilities' (Catanzaro, 1988: 154). By spreading violence in the licit economy, criminal entrepreneurs make it necessary for 'clean' entrepreneurs who intend to remain in business to become their allies. 'The everyday presence of violence prevents impersonal and effectively neutral trust relationships. Where violence is paramount, interpersonal ties must necessarily be strong, intense and affectively connoted' (Catanzaro, 1994: 273).

This argument raises a number of issues. It is true that organized crime directing its proceeds towards the licit economy may still hold its power of violent intimidation. On the other hand, it seems more likely that its entry into licit business would be favoured by contacts with the official political or economic world. Once these contacts are well established, the costs of violence may exceed the benefits it brings (Reuter, 1983). Violence, in other words, may only be an important tool for organized crime in its phase of 'primitive accumulation', namely in the phase which precedes its involvement in the licit economy. When this involvement begins, accommodation rather than conflict may become more productive, especially if contacts with the official political and economic world are to be maintained. Even a seasoned gangster such as Meyer Lansky is believed to have eschewed violence after an initial phase of accumulation of funds: he paid his taxes and cheated no more than the average legitimate entrepreneur (Lacey, 1991).

Organized crime operating in the licit economy may have further reasons to abandon violence and intimidation, along with traditional aspects which are usually associated with its market behaviour. These are that, in transparent markets, such behaviour 'would be immediately noticed and the criminal entrepreneur would be ousted' (Becchi and Rey, 1994: 30). Only in markets where unorthodox tools and illegal behaviour are already widespread can criminal entrepreneurs go unnoticed. But, in these cases, do criminal entrepreneurs socialize 'clean' ones to illegality, or are they socialized to an already illegal economy? This question leads to a final, inevitable conclusion. When organized crime establishes connections with the licit economy, it undergoes a learning process whereby its criminality will increasingly resemble white-collar and corporate crime. In the licit economy, criminal entrepreneurs will frequently find aspects of their own previous activity, or they will acquire skills to be used if intending to go back to it. Undertaking a licit entrepreneurial career, in other words, may become part and parcel of their criminal career, the boundaries between the two being extremely blurred.

In conclusion, there seems to be a moral imperative whereby criminal activities *must* be regarded as having a completely different logic from other economically motivated activities. As I have already argued, this mirrors a well-established distinction between organized crime and corporate crime, whose original formulation goes back to the work of Sutherland. In this respect, it has been noted that definitions such as 'differential association' and white-collar crime have produced a disputable shift in the interpretation of both corporate and organized crime. Let us briefly look at the way in which organized crime was viewed before these definitions were coined. The first governmental attempt to study organized crime in the United States dates back to 1929–31. This was conducted under the auspices of the National Commission on Law Observance and Enforcement (Smith, 1991). According to this commission, *events* rather than *persons* could be identified as organized crime. Corporate and organized crime could therefore be studied jointly, by emphasizing the logic by which both operated. Conversely, Sutherland's definitions were utilized to shift that emphasis: people rather than events were focused upon. In this way, 'Once the businessmen were segregated into a new category with a catchy heading of "white-collar" crime, the gangsters were left as the sole and indisputable occupants of organized crime' (ibid.: 144).

Economists who have studied crime have in a sense triggered a shift back from persons to events. Some authors, for example, have studied professional and financial crime and found strong similarity between the two. 'Strong similarities exist as the legitimate world of politics, banking, law, accounting and appraising took on the style of professional criminals' (Hagan and Benekos, 1992: 3). In order for this shift to be complete, the concepts of entrepreneur, enterprise and organization should be revisited. Through these concepts, more similarities may emerge between licit and illicit economies, and relatedly between corporate and organized crime. It has been argued that there is a paradoxical relationship between legal and illegal enterprises, which is that the seeds of the illegal business are sown in legal business enterprises (Block and Chambliss, 1981). Before examining cases in which there exists a *de facto* partnership between licit and illicit entrepreneurs, the next chapter will deal with the notions that may help to explain this paradox more clearly.

3 Merchants, Entrepreneurs and Organizations

The history of entrepreneurs is tormented and eventful, in a sense reflecting the rough existence experienced by merchants and traders before them. Their activities can be studied as a succession of breakthroughs which, initially condemned, slowly gained acceptance within the prevailing sensibility of the time. In the Middle Ages the list of officially proscribed activities included all trades which were not aimed at collective well-being. The nature of these trades varied according to the region, but prohibition, imposed by the Church, was inspired by a number of broad principles. Prohibited trades included, first of all, commerce geared to purely individual earnings, or *lucri causa* (Le Goff, 1977). On Sundays, 'servile occupations' or *opera servilia* were also proscribed, these being only accepted when devoted to the ecclesiastical hierarchy and thus to God. A distinction was in operation between overtly illicit and sinful acts, such as prostitution and usury, and those 'vile occupations' or *vilia officia* which were regarded as despicable. The latter acts, if not illicit or sinful, raised contempt in that they infringed prevailing taboos. Among others, the following were met with contempt: butchers, innkeepers, minstrels, jesters, wizards, alchemists, physicians, surgeons, notaries, soldiers (surprisingly), and obviously merchants. Le Goff (1977: 55) provides a longer, though not comprehensive list which, he notes, would otherwise have to include all medieval trades: 'fullers, weavers, saddlers, dyers, confectioners, shoemakers, gardeners, decorators, barbers, fishermen, childminders, land wardens, customs guards, exchange brokers, dressmakers, perfumers, tripe sellers, millers'.

Many of these prohibitions derived from taboos inherited by the Middle Ages from primitive societies. Firstly, the taboo of blood, which was directed against butchers, surgeons, barbers and bleeders but also professional soldiers. 'In the Middle Ages our societies, bloodthirsty though they may have been, seemed to oscillate between delight and horror for the bloodsheds they provoked' (ibid.: 55). Secondly, the taboo of impurity and dirt, which addressed fullers and dyers but also cooks. This aversion can be found, not without surprise, even in St Thomas Aquinas who located dishwashers at the bottom of the occupational hierarchy for their incessant contact with filth. Thirdly, and most importantly, the taboo of money, which played an important part in the resistance of a society based on a natural economy against the invasion of a monetary economy. All merchants would be despised for their horrid relationship with money and for the *professional sin* of their trade: avarice. The condemnation of usurers was also prompted by their infringement of Christ's precept of fraternity among humans – or at least among Christians – whereby lending need not imply hopes of restitution: *Inde nihil sperantes*.

Two important aspects in the work of merchants made them contemptible. Firstly, Christians must emulate God, whose Creation should inform their daily work: thus peasants create crops while artisans transform matter into tools and objects. Merchants, it was felt, do not create or transform anything, abstract value being the aim of their dealings. Secondly, the earnings of merchants and usurers rely on the exploitation of time, their goods and finances being valorized through deferral. This is a sacrilege: time belongs to God.

History, according to Le Goff, is also a process whereby disenfranchised groups gain acceptance through both material achievement and simultaneous ideological devices. Despised in the year AD 1000, some traders occupy a high rank during the years of the Renaissance. Usury, for example, was able to move freely in the Christian conscience when the invention of Purgatory made it a venial and redeemable sin. Christians were thus able to save their money and their lives – their eternal lives, it should be understood (Lefevre, 1902; Le Goff, 1987). However, what should be noted here is the somewhat deviant origin of many trades, particularly those more closely connected to innovative forms of enterprise. It seems that entrepreneurs bear an original sin which, according to the specific devices offered by different contexts, is either 'purged' or removed, and sometimes just attributed to some of them with the exclusion of others. The history of entrepreneurs themselves coincides with the history of this removal or displacement.

Redemption through Risk

Initial mention of the French word *entrepreneur* goes back to the sixteenth century, when it designates those who recruit mercenary troops on behalf of princes, municipalities or leagues. During the eighteenth century the definition is used in three different contexts. It is applied to individuals who undertake the building of weaponry, roads and bridges after being commissioned by governments. In agriculture, entrepreneurs are landlords either from the aristocracy or the new bourgeois class, and apply the new technologies to the land to make it more productive. In manufacture the term indicates those who engage their capital in the production of goods destined for the market (Gallino, 1975). The German *Unternehmer* and the English *undertaker* had a similar meaning, and, while the former is still in use in contemporary terminology, the latter, which ironically now mainly applies to funereal matters, was eventually replaced by the French version in the sociological and economic lexicon.

A characteristic of entrepreneurs is commonly that of 'being prepared to buy goods and labour and to run the risks of loss due to the uncertainty of prices' (Gallino, 1975: 369). The dimension of risk was central to the study and definition of the entrepreneur in past centuries. Building contractors, for example, would undertake the construction of a bridge without knowing precisely the cost they would incur. Similarly, a rural entrepreneur would buy labour, seeds and tools while remaining uncertain about the quality and quantity of the produce, and also of the prices at which this would eventually be sold. Incidently, note how this qualitative character of risk, which is aimed at redeeming in moral terms the activities of entrepreneurs, has been recently replaced by risk seen in a quite different sense. Risk and uncertainty no longer describe the condition of, but the potential social loss from, entrepreneurial activity. The very term 'risk' is now referenced to the extent to which the community as a whole can bear the consequences of entrepreneurial activity.

However, uncertainty and risk describe a marginalized condition, a somewhat deviant position *ab initio*, as opposed to inherited status and automatic income characterizing the aristocracy. The work of Knight (1921) focuses primarily on these attributes, which are related to the capacity to initiate and co-ordinate a productive process. Like Purgatory, these attributes render entrepreneurs venial sinners, but also make them particular types of sinners. One is tempted to define them as altruistic perpetrators, in that risk and uncertainty are incurred with a view to mobilizing other people's initiative and participation. The two attributes, therefore, define a social role, a function which promotes work and helps circulate and produce goods, and therefore a function which transcends individual benefits.

The redemption of entrepreneurs occurs against the background of what constitutes the 'normal' condition of their activity. I am talking about competition, whose ethics has been much discussed. In his analysis of the ethics of competition, Knight (1935) attempts a preliminary definition of biological, human and social needs, and concludes that the idea of a distinction between these and economic wants must be abandoned. Behind all these needs, he argues, 'is the restless spirit of man, who is an aspiring rather than a desiring being; and such a scientifically undescriptive and unsatisfactory characterization is the best we can give' (Knight, 1935: 34). Economics are therefore the only all-inclusive science of conduct, and it is disputable whether this view requires supplementing with an ethical view of values. The same author stresses that the nature of values and standards is similar to that of desires, which are 'not describable because not stable, growing and changing by necessity of their inner nature' (ibid.: 39). There should be no rules for the judgement of values, because risk and uncertainty in themselves suffice in allowing the ethical stretching of values. Good judgement is the only limit. We shall see how the categories suggested by Knight can be fruitfully utilized for the description of some types of corporate crime.

It would be an exaggeration to claim that Knight's argument is an implicit incitement addressed to entrepreneurs to bend rules and engage in all sorts of illicit activities. The author, in fact, likens the behaviour of entrepreneurs to that of a good player in a game. What is required here is the acceptance of the game and its rules. Economics and competition are therefore part of a game and, as Knight concedes, the winners may well be 'generally speaking industrious, resolute, proud, covetous, methodical, sensible, unimaginative, insensitive and ignorant' (ibid.: 66). On the other hand, among the losers there may well be a considerable fraction of the most noble and sensitive characters. But everyone is compelled to play the economic game and be judged through their success in playing it, while questions regarding the very nature of the game are futile and do not usually bring victory.

Speculators and Confidence Men

Issues regarding entrepreneurial sense of guilt are dealt with magnificently by Weber. The spirit of entrepreneurs, he argues, is consistent with the rationality of emerging economic activity, and is an extension of the form of rationality simultaneously emerging in the religious realm. 'Substantive rationality cannot be measured in terms of formal calculation alone, but also involves a relation to the absolute values or to the content of the particular ends to which it is oriented' (Weber, 1976: 185). In his classical text, the absolute values under scrutiny are those of the Protestant ethics which have a particular 'elective affinity' with the spirit of capitalism. As we shall see, Weber also expresses some misgivings when envisaging forms of irrationality stemming from the very rational set-up of enterprises and bureaucracies. However, his solution to the ethical problems linked to the characteristics of entrepreneurs proves unsatisfactory in the eyes of subsequent authors, who often return to the subject.

Entrepreneurs are not simply pious and thrifty: these qualities may only explain the particular variety of entrepreneurs in the English Industrial Revolution. Internationally, they are also exceptional individuals, as they are the expression of a particular type of psychological disposition. This is provided by their position 'on the margins' of society, a position which functions as a stimulus towards economically daring activity (Sombart, 1915). Surely, Weber himself identifies a vague sense of marginalization in the Protestant sects as a consequence of their persecution, and within this 'sectarian marginalization' he also locates the birth of entrepreneurs (Weber, 1977). However, there is a tangible shift of emphasis in other authors like Sombart, who seem to equate marginalization both with the inherited culture of a group and with outright deviance, an argument which perhaps allows for more interesting developments. In Sombart's view, the beliefs included in Puritan and Quaker religious teaching do not account for the birth of an enterprise spirit in, say, Germany, France or Italy:

> The component parts of the capitalist spirit vary very much so that their origins will vary also. Some of the factors in that spirit may be what are termed 'instinctive passions' – acquisitiveness, activity, the desire to plunder your neighbour. All successful undertakers have always had a goodly dose of these instincts. (Sombart, 1915: 195)

To Sombart, the 'desire to plunder your neighbour' is exemplified by the speculator, a character which is both devious and proper, peripheral and central to the entrepreneurial spirit. Speculators possess a new power, the 'power of suggestion', and this alone enables them to realize their plans. Instead of exerting overt might or fear, they set hope.

> [The speculator] sees visions of giant undertakings; his pulse beats quickly like a person's in a fever. ... His soul may be said to be in a condition of lyrical enthusiasm. And the result of all this? He carries others along with him, who help him to realize his plan. (ibid.: 92)

Sombart's speculators form an important section of entrepreneurs, namely those who involve other individuals in their dreams, those one might say who do not take all risks on themselves (as Knight suggests), but decentralize risk among those they mobilize. They marshal energies by depicting realms of gold and showing the marvels they can produce, the blessings their enterprise will bring to the world. Never mind the means adopted, Sombart insists, if only the end is achieved. What is important is attracting people's attention, appealing to their curiosity: 'The speculator's work is done, he has reached his desired heaven, when large numbers of people are thrown into a state of feverish restlessness, ready to provide the wherewithal for the completion of the speculator's undertaking' (ibid.: 93).

These particular types of entrepreneurs seem to perform the simultaneous roles of employer, inventor, and demand stimulator. One feels the echo of modern advertising, but also that of seductive financial advisers. These characters resonate with Melville's confidence man, who is the quintessence of economic adventure and characterizes the epic deeds of the new 'American frontier' (Melville, 1984). Also Melville's con man promises enormous revenues to those who risk their money in the adventures he engineers, while to those who have no money to risk he just offers an ordinary but 'rewarding' occupation. Some cases of corporate crime such as bankruptcies remind one of this double nature of the entrepreneur/speculator, whose illicit practices seem to be justified by the fact that they keep up employment.

Insider Deviants

The history of entrepreneurs is indeed the history of their persecution. Both inside and outside accepted society, their behaviour is a joint product of the way in which they are perceived and treated, and their reaction to this. Entrepreneurial talent is not distributed randomly throughout the population in any given country. In Sombart's analysis, marginalization and deviance play an important role in producing entrepreneuriality, although the origin of the two characteristics is not thoroughly explored. Successive studies try to identify common traits shared by entrepreneurs by focusing on specific social groups of origin, rather than specific psychological dispositions.

Hagen (1962) pinpoints an important element which seems to belong to 'high achievers' in general. Individuals or groups who are looked down on, he suggests, will tend to create a reassuring atmosphere among themselves so that they can overcome or discount the exclusion suffered. Every little achievement, for example, will be met with disproportionate commendation and with collective joy, which are likely to inculcate an increasing need for further achievements. Exclusion, described by Hagen as 'derogation', may therefore become a source for the development of talents which lead to innovation. Hagen notes that almost every society displays social derogation of some groups and that the responses elaborated by these groups often lead to enterprising attitudes and innovations which are then spread to society at large. In seventeenth- and eighteenth-century France, for example, economic development was the result of the religious beliefs and the marginalized condition of the Huguenots. 'The Huguenots were middle- and upper-class townspeople, but they were barred by their religion and perhaps also by their bourgeois attitudes from membership in a close association with the king's court' (Hagen, 1980: 222). In Russia, so-called Old Believers, who did not adapt to the revision of the official Church ritual, seceded and were persecuted. They became prominent in the accelerating economic growth which occurred in Russia during the last half of the nineteenth century. Analogous patterns are found by Hagen in India, where the marginalized community known as the Parsees provided a number of entrepreneurs out of proportion to its size and social weight. The economic rebirth of Japan and the subsequent Restoration of 1868 were largely due to the entrepreneurial spirit of the lower grades:

> A survey of 196 corporate executives and individual business entrepreneurs of the period between 1868 and the early twentieth century shows that a very large percentage came from the outer clans – those the Tokugawa had held in a socially inferior position for two and a half centuries. (ibid.: 223)

What these entrepreneurs seem to share is not so much their condition as aliens, as their being 'eccentric' with respect to the ruling groups. They are natives who previously occupied a respectable position in their society, but were later expelled from the relatively privileged milieu in which they were a part. They are looked down upon for a period of time before making a comeback by means of innovative activities (Kerr et al., 1964). Their common condition, in many countries, lies in their relationship with the official religion, which is one of dissent. The reaction of the ruling groups to their dissent makes them deviant of a particular sort, in that they still harbour memories of high status of the past. Being both outside and inside the official order makes them experiment with new undertakings and economic explorations. They are tantalized by power, to which only partially they have access. Nevertheless, they do have a degree of access to resources, because they are not outsiders, and are therefore able to establish relationships with other groups who control resources. Furthermore, they do not fear to fail, as their being inured to ostracism protects them from disapproval in case they do. They are 'inside deviants' to whom a wide range of possibilities and practices are open, some of which are unacceptable or not acceptable as yet in the eyes of the official ruling groups. They are opportunity perceivers, and the ambiguity of their behaviour is necessary for a real process of innovation to take place.

Hermes and Innovation

This ambiguity characterizes a distinguished member of the Greek pantheon: Hermes, regarded as the patron of the upwardly mobile Athenian merchant entrepreneurs (McClelland, 1961). Hermes makes a lyre out of a tortoise that he finds in the doorway of his cave. He invents wicker sandals in order not to leave footprints on the road. 'He not only wants to get ahead in the world; he gets real pleasure out of the schemes he devises for doing so' (ibid.: 302). He exhibits the most vivid characteristics of entrepreneurship: the capacity to innovate. Always on the move, he starts out into the world to get ahead the moment he was born. 'He makes his technological innovations and pursues his career in a spirit of restless energy in which there is much motion and little waste of time' (ibid.: 303). Hermes produces change and avoids repetition, while his very expressive movement is restless: he is wing-footed, a messenger of the gods and the patron of travellers. But the infant Hermes is also a thief: as soon as he is laid in his cradle he jumps up and goes looking for Apollo's cattle, which he steals. He lies to the point of persuading Apollo to let him keep the cattle. He is dishonest: on closer examination, his sandals are in fact worn backwards in order to deceive those who follow him after being cheated. He is an innovator and at the same time the trickster hero, 'physically weak but smart enough to defeat powerful rivals' (ibid.: 302). His image is perhaps a reflection of how the rising entrepreneurs were perceived: both envied and scorned, an ambiguity that can also be attributed to their deviant status.

Hermes the entrepreneur belongs to one of Hagen's ostracized groups, as he is the product of a casual relationship between Zeus and Maia. He reacts to ostracism with his 'need for discovery and invention – which means invention also in the sense of deceit' (Kerenyi, 1958: 10). His temple in Rome is adjacent to the ancient market-place, while in Pompeii he appears on the threshold of shops in *Via dell'Abbondanza*, wearing a cloak and holding a bagful of coins. True, Weber's entrepreneurs are innovative but they are also self-restrained, as their religious creed prompts a selection of the acceptable means to achieve and pursue goals. However, as we have seen, this selective process is almost sidestepped by subsequent analysis, where innovation preserves its ambiguous traits intact. Economic innovation and deception are almost one and the same.

Creative Destruction

Schumpeter's definition of entrepreneurs is among the most celebrated; it also offers important hints for the examination of the boundaries between licit and illicit economies. The entrepreneurial characteristics identified by Schumpeter are closely related to the variable of innovation. This variable is also crucial among physiocratic economists for the distinction between landowners passively following tradition and landowners more inclined to adopt new technologies (Gallino, 1975). Only the latter are granted the definition of entrepreneurs by the physiocrats, a tenet which must have inspired Schumpeter's analysis. Let us summarize it.

The economic process is an evolutionary one, by nature 'a form or method of economic change [that] not only never is but never can be stationary' (Schumpeter, 1961a: 82). The fundamental impulse that sets and keeps the economic engine in motion derives, according to Schumpeter, from new consumer goods, new methods of production or distribution, new markets, new forms of industrial organization. The author resorts to a biological concept to illustrate the process of industrial mutation. This, he argues, 'incessantly revolutionizes the economic structure *from within*, incessantly destroying the old one, incessantly creating a new one. This process of Creative Destruction is the essential fact about capitalism' (ibid.: 83). By development, therefore, only those changes should be understood which arise from within the economic structure and are the result of precise entrepreneurial initiative. Schumpeter does not deny the mutually enhancing nature of demand and supply. Nevertheless, he does not believe that needs arise spontaneously and then force the productive apparatus to satisfy them:

> It is, however, the producer who as a rule initiates economic change, and consumers are educated by him if necessary; they are, as it were, taught to want new things, or things which differ in some respect or other from those which they have been in the habit of using. (Schumpeter, 1961b: 65)

This subjective, almost voluntaristic aspect of entrepreneurial activity needs emphasizing, as it forms the core of Schumpeter's thinking around both development and innovation. Development emerges when productive factors are arranged in new combinations which appear discontinuously. In this concept the following five cases are covered. The introduction of a new good or a new quality of an already existing good. The introduction of a new method of production: 'that is, one not yet tested by experience in the branch of manufacture concerned, which need by no means be founded upon a discovery scientifically new, and can also consist in a new way of handling a commodity commercially' (Schumpeter, 1961b: 66). The opening of a new market. The conquest of a new source of supply of raw materials or half-manufactured goods. The carrying out of 'the new organization of any industry, like the creation of a monopoly position (for example through trustification) or the breaking up of a monopoly position' (ibid.: 66).

As mentioned above, it is the subjective dimension of the new combinations which needs emphasizing here, the economic system itself being incapable of bringing automatic innovation. In fact, it is in the nature of the economic process to tend towards a static equilibrium, and therefore to extinction, were it not for entrepreneurial innovative action (Samuelson, 1981). The aspect of *discontinuity* also deserves a brief comment. It is not necessary that new combinations or innovation be carried out by the same entrepreneurs who control the productive or commercial process which is displaced by the new one. New combinations may be introduced by new firms: 'in general it is not the owner of the stage-coaches who builds railways' (Schumpeter, 1961b: 66). Here Schumpeter seems to overlook the fact that some firms may instead both control old productive and commercial processes and introduce new combinations. In other words, new firms building railways may maintain their old ownership of stage-coaches as well. Discontinuity, in this sense, can apply to the very same firm, which is simultaneously conservative and innovative. New combinations can therefore be discontinuous not only in a temporal but also in a spatial sense, as they may occur within the same structure where traditional combinations continue to operate. I shall explore the possibility of applying these notions, and the concept of innovation itself, to the episodes of organizational deviance examined later.

The strength of Schumpeter's economic analysis has not been fully utilized by sociologists of deviance and criminologists. Arlacchi (1983), for example, argues that the 'Mafia enterprise' innovates by introducing new productive combinations offering them a competitive edge with respect to other enterprises. However, he warns, the difference between the innovative entrepreneur in Schumpeter's terms and a Mafia entrepreneur lies in the effects caused by the two types on economic development, the former contributing to and the latter hampering it. In the previous chapter we discussed these aspects and criticized this position. What should be noted here is that the very nature of Schumpeterian innovation is not fully appreciated. Only capitalists who innovate are defined as entrepreneurs by Schumpeter, and only their activity may avoid the growth of social and cultural conditions inimical to the very survival of capitalism (Bottomore, 1981). The collapse of the economic order is identified with the persistence of a 'circular flow', a stagnant condition devoid of an innovative drive. Entrepreneurs or innovators, therefore, deviate from mainstream behaviour, and theirs is a voluntaristic struggle against the whirl of conformity:

> While he swims with the stream in the circular flow which is familiar to him, he swims against the stream if he wishes to change its channel. What was formerly a help becomes a hindrance – what was a familiar datum becomes unknown. (Schumpeter, 1961b: 79–80)

In this perspective, to claim that economic categories such as Schumpeter's can only apply to the behaviour of law-abiding individuals or groups seems reductive. Santino and La Fiura (1990: 89–90), for example, argue that:

> The exclusive consideration of the licit market, which is peaceful by definition, can be explained ... above all by the more or less conscious neglect of a reality that could not be included in the schemata of theorists, which proves the validity of the motto: *economics is what economists do*.

This is not completely correct. In the sociology of deviance, the reappearance of the term *innovation* proves that the hints provided by some economists can at times be fruitfully developed with a view to the study of illicit economies (Merton, 1968). This may be particularly true when sociologists of deviance using this term imply the two Schumpeterian concepts which underpin innovation: the subjective determination of those who innovate and the creative destruction inherent in their behaviour.

The Murky Objectivity of the Firm

Schumpeter's view of the entrepreneur retains an aspect of free choice which is central to innovation and therefore to the survival of the economic system as a whole. However, the author seems to be aware that the character of the entrepreneur itself is destined to be displaced by depersonalized firms. His distinction between 'capitalist' and 'entrepreneur' alludes to the fact that those financing and therefore owning innovation do not coincide with those who put it in place. This distinction, which appears in successive analyses of the firm, highlights the separation between ownership and control (Scott, 1989). The emerging class of managers exercises a fiduciary role on behalf of the interests of the owners and, it is assumed, the interests of the community at large (Chandler, 1977). Here, subjectivity and innovation become more difficult to detect. Where should one search for individuals 'swimming against the circular flow'? The structure of the firm becomes increasingly complex, responsibilities are decentralized, while the very human components and goals of production are not easily definable. Is the hybrid nature of entrepreneurs, who stride across conformity and deviance, translated into the vagueness of corporations? In the analysis of the firm some broad distinctions feature prominently. Some frameworks emphasize the market character, or the exchange, contractual nature of the firm. Others emphasize its hierarchical, or planned, or authority-infused character. Some authors argue that firms are driven mainly by efficiency, others that they are informed mainly by considerations of control, in particular of its members (Putterman, 1986).

In corporations adopting illicit practices, these elements are not mutually exclusive. This is due to the fact that illicit activities constitute in themselves diversification, which is carried out simultaneously with licit activities. It has been argued that multi-product firms may require some of the above-mentioned elements in certain sectors of their activity and other elements in others (Teece, 1982). By the same token, these firms will adopt some of those elements when conducting licit activities and some others when engaging in illicit ones. In some cases, for example, they may rely on hierarchy, in others on efficiency or control, depending on whether their practices are official or shadowy. We shall see examples of this.

Enterprises without Entrepreneurs

We have seen that the ambiguity of merchants and entrepreneurs is commonly associated with their social origin and their peripheral, eccentric position with respect to the official religion. Deviants *ab initio* because of their creed, they undertake initiatives which vindicate their merits and seek redemption in the eyes of the ruling groups which exclude them. In this process, they are able or forced to bend the rules inspiring the conduct of accepted society. For this reason they are precisely identifiable: their deviance is manifest in the very innovative practices they put in place. These practices, which are initially condemned, then end up establishing new rules that become widely accepted. The firm, in turn, allows for the disappearance of identifiable individuals and innovators along with their respective responsibilities. It also permits the disappearance of those aspects of subjectivity and voluntarist action which are central in Schumpeter's analysis. The ambiguity of rules seems now to characterize the firm as a whole, while the boundaries dividing acceptable and unacceptable conduct become increasingly uncertain. In particular, this occurs when corporations, as Schumpeter feared, make entrepreneurs and their initiatives redundant.

Burns (1963) posits two ideal types of firm: the one *mechanistic*, adapted to relatively stable conditions, the other *organismic*, adapted to conditions of change. The latter inherits Schumpeter's notion of innovation, and its structure is meant to respond to new and unfamiliar problems which arise continually. Their solution cannot be fragmented or apportioned among specialist roles within a clear division of labour. Demarcation of functions, and therefore of rules, becomes difficult. This process is not only the result of inbuilt mechanisms of firms, but also of a different relationship between demand and supply. It is the very relationship between the two which becomes insecure, as consumers oscillate between spontaneous needs and needs guided by marketing promotion. Examples of organismic firms will be provided which offer illicit goods or services, and which show a similar insecurity in their relationships with consumers. It could be objected that the examples provided below do not belong to the current panorama characterized by the disappearance of entrepreneurs and the emergence of professional managers. However, it is important to note that the growth of corporate and monopolistic firms perhaps did not make middle-range and small firms obsolete, nor did it sanction the demise of Schumpeterian innovators. Many of these still take the initiative within small units which are often linked to larger ones. From these they inherit, or to these they transmit, an innovative spirit. In this light, episodes of deviance occurring in smaller firms may well describe how larger ones find it more appropriate to displace, outside their more visible settings, practices mirroring the professional sins of the old merchants. In many cases, therefore, it appears as if ambiguity and flexibility of rules are nowhere to be found within larger firms: instead, these set up smaller units where rules are not only flexible and ambiguous, but can be suspended altogether.

Merchants, entrepreneurs, and competitive, corporate or monopolistic firms are specific economic subjects on whose characteristics one may draw to sketch analogous characteristics with which corporate and organized crime present themselves. However, these subjects form only a fraction of a wider variety of organizations. In order to ascertain whether other common characteristics exist, other organizations should also be examined. The following overview of organization theory may serve this purpose.

Approval or, at least, Non-disapproval

In a simplified definition, organization theory is the body of thinking which addresses itself to the problem of how to organize (Pugh, 1990). More precisely, it is the study of the structure, functioning and performance of organizations, and the behaviour of groups and individuals within them. 'The subject has a long history which can be traced back, for example, to the Old Testament when decentralisation through the appointment of judges was undertaken to relieve the load on Moses, the chief executive' (Pugh, 1990: ix).

Classical theories of organization are said to be wider in scope than their more modern counterparts. Their analyses are placed in precisely identifiable contexts and linked with the social structure as a whole. Their broad historical perspective makes them all-inclusive: in other words, the study of organizations coincides with that of the social system. In dealing with the problems of bureaucracy and bureaucratization, for example, classical theories are 'fully aware that such problems can only be understood when the societies within which they arise are studied dynamically, in their historical development and change' (Mouzelis, 1967: 35).

Given their wider scope, classical theories of organization seem to mirror the complexities, dilemmas, tensions and ambiguity of society at large. In this regard, the work of Max Weber is commonly interpreted as the most successful attempt to focus attention on rational types of organization: administrative systems and precisely identifiable bureaucracies. Weber's approach is therefore regarded as a fruitful reorientation towards organizations in themselves, their internal structure and functioning, a reorientation which allegedly sidesteps or supersedes wider social dilemmas, tensions and ambiguities. However, the depiction of Weber's analysis as a static one, centred on the increasing rationalization which prevails in both organizations and human relationships, is not completely correct. Dilemmas and ambiguities are alluded to in his writings where they emerge here and there in the form of pessimistic admissions. Weber (1947) stresses that organizations are inspired by a body of abstract rules which guide the pursuit of a corporate group. These rules are said to be located within the limits laid down by legal precepts 'and following principles which are capable of generalized formulation and approved in the order governing the group, or *at least not disapproved in it*' (Weber, 1947: 330; emphasis added).

This statement conveys a much less static view than that usually attributed to the author. Weber seems aware of the blurred boundaries between approval and disapproval of the principles governing organizations. He seems also to imply that processes are in place which may achieve acceptance for practices previously deemed unacceptable, in a constantly dynamic landscape. A similarly dynamic notion is conveyed by Weber's account of how ideal officials are to conduct their office. The author identifies a 'spirit of formalistic impersonality' guiding the behaviour of officials. This spirit presents itself *sine ira et studio*, without hatred or passion, devoid of affection or enthusiasm. Norms, therefore, indicate duties without regard to personal considerations, their amorality being a guarantee for the rational and effective running of offices. But on a number of occasions, Weber seems to detect a 'substantive irrationality' in the outcome of what seem to be entirely rational norms. It has been noted that Weber can offer no analysis of how and why this transformation of rationality into irrationality takes place, 'all he can do in his early work is despair that it should be so' (Clegg and Dunkerley, 1990: 41).

Subsequent analysts of organizations abandon Weber's despair and try to highlight how irrationality, ambiguity and the constant shifting of rules and targets constitute the very strength of organizations. It is within this analytical framework that a definition of corporate and organizational crime could be located.

Dalton (1959), whose book is based on long-term participant observation in a number of firms, describes the uncertainty surrounding both the internal set-up of organizations and their prevailing objectives. This is the result of perpetual struggles carried out by groups and individuals within organizations in the name of their narrow interests. The cliques and struggles which inform organizational life are not only hidden from outside observers, they are also 'scrupulously and skilfully camouflaged so that the resulting policies appear to be in harmony with the official ideology and the organizational codebook' (Mouzelis, 1967: 159). Shifting alliances, contingent interests and a permanent climate of antagonism account for the day-to-day activity of organizations, whose final goals are as indefinite as the outcome of the power struggle within them.

Advocates of this analysis tend to stress the mystifying aspects of organizations, in that they hide behind their stated goals of general interest the interests of the more influential cliques within them. Therefore, analysis should avoid reifying organizations by focusing on impersonal needs and goals. Organizational activity should instead be regarded as the outcome of motivated people attempting to resolve their problems (Silverman, 1970). As a consequence, organizations are not monadic units; rather, they generate a plurality of conflicting goals which are the result of the diversity of their members (Fox, 1966). This point was put forward some 40 years before by Gouldner, when he specified the ends of different people, or the typical ends of different strata within organizations:

> Such refocusing suggests these ends may vary, are not necessarily identical or salient for all personnel, and may in fact be contradictory, a conclusion which will in no way startle students of industry, however much students of administration have systematically neglected it. (Gouldner, 1954: 21)

Mouzelis (1967) and Wells (1993) also argue that societal values, which allegedly inform the activity of the organization as a whole, in fact constitute a source of legitimation for specific groups within the organization and their limited interests. In other words, decision-making practices diverge considerably from those posited by advocates of formal and instrumental rationality (Reed, 1993). Organizations do not select options nor do they assess the effects of choices on the basis of systematically collected information. Practices often stem from piecemeal information, intuition and partial technical knowledge, while sectional interests are masqueraded as the general good (Reed, 1993).

This hypothesis will be tested in the cases of organizational deviance examined in Chapter 4. However, in the cases discussed below, as we shall see, the distinction between sectional interests of cliques and organizational general interests will be more blurred than other commentators suggest.

Dispersed Social Agencies

Priorities for managerial action are often related to the clear definition or redefinition of the *objectives* of their organization. As Thompson (1982) notes, it is bemoaned that the objectives of the company are not clearly understood either by those who occupy the lower strata of the organization hierarchy or those who are supposed to guide them. According to a common assumption, organizations are required to resemble well-oiled mechanisms inspired by a single dominant objective or a cluster of non-contradictory objectives. 'The military analogy can be strong here – all the sub-units or elements are commanded with respect to a coherent and unambiguous aim' (Thompson, 1982: 235). Most organizations are in fact heterogeneous, non-unitary, dispersed and fractured units: 'there is no "one thing" called the firm, the essential characteristics of which can be found, analysed and verified' (ibid.: 236). Organizations are composed of 'places' where individuals may pursue partial objectives, hamper change, and identify new partial objectives. These are unlikely to be organized rationally under a single dominant objective. The reverse is likely to be the case, because competencies and partial objectives which are pursued within the different 'places' of the organization are ungenerously kept and guarded. The role of management, in this context, is to try to reconcile these conflicting interests and objectives. The agency of direction 'acts more like a "reconciling chairman" than a leading commander with a series of already articulated objectives and a geared-up series of elements organized or in the process of being organized "rationally" to achieve that task' (ibid.: 237). Compromises and alliances form the rule rather than the exception, in a panorama where negotiation among actors forming the organization is incessant.

Ambiguity and multiplicity not only characterize organizational goals, but also a specific dimension which is commonly taken for granted when the functions of organizations are examined. This is the dimension of profit maximization, a widely accepted objective of organizations in classical economics. Given that organizations and their goals display a diversity of characteristics and configurations, the very goal that we term 'profit maximization' may also be appreciated and pursued in a variety of ways. The concept of profit itself varies, according to different theoretical perspectives and different accounting techniques or procedures. 'How can there be an essential and unambiguous objective of maximization of profit ... if there is no clear agreement on what profit actually is' (Thompson, 1982: 240).

Many different items could be included under the heading 'profit', some of which may be evaluated by means of a direct monetary equivalent while some others may not. Organizations may diversify their activities and, while pursuing revenues in one unit, aim at empire-building or non-monetary growth in another. In turn, some organizations or sectors of them may be concerned with stability, continuity, conservation of power and other issues which do not immediately translate into financial benefits (Wells, 1993).

A number of cases listed in the following pages will be grouped under a similar heading. These regard episodes of organizational misconduct, in particular the police, not directly linked to the pursuit of illicit income, but rather to the enhancement of power, status and other abstract gratifications. Here, episodes of administrative deviance could also be grouped whose objective is less profit maximization than the illicit appropriation of its equivalent in terms of time.

Who Benefits?

It is not easy to classify the variety of existing organizations. If even profit-making is not acceptable as a universal common denominator, categories such as *benefit* may instead offer the advantage to broaden the definition of organizational goals beyond the purely financial domain. This route is tested by Blau and Scott (1963), who suggest a typology based on the criterion *cui bono?* – who benefits? 'Using this criterion, four types of organizations [are] distinguished: mutual-benefit associations, business concerns, service organizations and commonwealth organizations' (ibid.: 58). In these types of organizations the prime beneficiaries are respectively: its members or participants, its owners, its clients, the public at large (Clegg and Dunkerley, 1990).

As we shall see, in deviant organizational behaviour an inherent attempt can be detected to confound the identification of 'who benefits'. In deviating from officially stated practices, for example, 'business concerns' or 'mutual associations' may try to present themselves as service or commonwealth organizations. The act of deviating itself may be justified because it is assumed to benefit less the perpetrators than the clients or the public at large.

Cases in which the category 'who benefits' is confounded occur in the so-called hidden or black economy. Here, the lack of safety regulations and union rights, and as a result lower salaries, reflect lower costs of goods or services produced. In these cases, while the prime beneficiaries are the owners of the organization, these often claim that clients benefit as well because of the lower prices they are offered. Moreover, the employees of such organizations may also be persuaded that they benefit too, in that the salary they receive, even if very low, at least staves off the absolute deprivation of unemployment. This optical illusion, whereby deviance actually initiated by the élites miraculously appears to benefit the underprivileged, also occurs in other deviant practices. In administrative and political corruption, for example, the fact that a 'corrupt exchange' takes place seems to put all participants in this exchange on the same level, regardless of their respective gains, to the point that there appears to be no victim (Ruggiero, 1994).

The shift of the variable 'who benefits' also occurs in illegal arms production and trafficking, where the violation of rules seems to benefit both the owners and leading members of the organization and their employees. The latter maintain their jobs by courtesy of their employers' crimes. Other aspects of the illegal arms trade will be examined in Chapter 6.

The Technology of Foolishness

Two main elements are said to characterize organizations and their leading members. The first is defined by Etzioni (1964: 108) as *worldliness*, and 'requires an empirical reference, a reality testing, found only in this world'. The second is identified as *asceticism*, which requires a commitment to long-term achievements rather than short-term goals. A psychological quality underpinning a larger variety of features which are needed for rational organizational work is, according to Etzioni, 'a high tolerance for frustration and the ability to defer gratification' (ibid.: 109). Hence the emphasis on education, punctuality and neatness which characterize Etzioni's 'organization man'.

This approach is disputed by other authors who argue that uncertainty characterizes organizations, not only with regard to their objectives but also the human and professional relationships within them, and their relationship with the external dominant values. This uncertainty alludes to the incomplete rationality of organizations which can be traced back to Weber's thought. As stressed above, the author lamented the re-emergence of irrationality, and feared that the very *raison d'être* of organizations ran the risk of decline. Further, if the goals of organizations change in a perpetually mobile landscape, so do the ways in which goals are pursued.

One important strand within organization theory takes issue with the very concept of rational choice as a focus for interpreting and guiding human behaviour (March, 1990). This concept rests on the faith that human beings make choices by evaluating alternative and potential outcomes of their action. If the evaluation is conducted correctly, and all relevant information gathered properly, the most appropriate choice inevitably follows. This view implies that goals are pre-existent, that consistency is necessary, and that both are embedded in strict rationality. March suggests that organizations should supplement the technology of reason with a *technology of foolishness*. 'Individuals and organizations need ways of doing things for which they have no good reason. Not always. Not usually. They need to act before they think' (ibid.: 335).

The notion of foolishness should convey that of playfulness, which in turn entails a temporary relaxation or suspension of rules. This temporary absence of rules may favour the exploration of new possibilities, so that new, alternatives rules may eventually be identified. Consistency is also suspended while, as March suggests, a sort of transitional hypocrisy is to be adopted. Organizations, in other words, are required to ignore the increasing gulf between the values they officially adopt and their actual behaviour. Only by means of this inconsistency may new values emerge and new behaviours be adopted. In a sort of moral limbo, organizations should therefore delete their memory: forgetting past rules and goals is a guarantee for the discovery of new ones.

These definitions will be utilized when describing examples of both conventional organized crime and corporate crime. As we shall see, the involvement of traditional criminal groups in the drugs economy may well fit the logic and technology of foolishness, as perhaps does the involvement, if episodic, of corporate bodies or individual licit entrepreneurs in conventional crime.

Dark and Grey Sides

Organizations are often interpreted as monolithic structures whose internal set-up and goals are clearly visible. There is a dark side of organizations which is commonly identified in the 'terrible process whereby technical means are applied to the most immoral of ends' (Reed, 1993: 4). This view, however, seems to rely too heavily on apocalyptic notions of technology, while overlooking the social processes which accompany technological innovation. Surely, a pessimistic perception of technology can be easily shared when one looks at the élite which control it and the way they apply it. But the identification of a dark side of organizations purely focused on technological development echoes somewhat nostalgic attitudes towards times past, when presumably a more rudimentary technological patrimony allowed for only limited abuse. Rather, abuse may be regarded as a potential but permanent feature of organizations. Its nature may change alongside new opportunities offered by development. However, past models did not reduce chances of organizational abuse or deviance, they only provided different frameworks in which abuse and deviance could take place.

A further implication of the 'dark side' hypothesis seems to be that organizations control in a somewhat secretive manner both the goals and the ways of pursuing them. This hypothesis presupposes a mono-directional concept of power, which is perhaps beyond the scope of this book to refute. Perhaps the identification of a 'grey side' of organizations may allow for a clearer interpretation of abuse and deviance. Nothing 'terrible', therefore, but routine procedures which are both secretive and public, licit and illicit, in a constant redefinition of boundaries and acceptable practices. The definition of 'grey side' also suggests that deviance is far from mono-directional, as it implies the participation of various actors, including sometimes those who benefit less or not at all from deviant acts. Again, consider those phenomena which are found in the hidden economy, but also in corrupt exchange, which may be initiated by those who benefit most but end up by being accepted by those who benefit less or are even damaged most. An example of how organizational procedures may be both secretive and public, and how the grey sides of organizations may foster more opportunities than their dark ones, will be provided in Chapter 6, where the arms trade is discussed.

Mock Organizations

Rules governing organizations may simply be a dead letter, in that under normal circumstances they may be ignored by most of their members. Gouldner (1954) gives a nice example of what he terms 'mock bureaucracies' in his study of a gypsum mine. Here, the no-smoking rule provides a typical pattern of this type of bureaucracy: rules, posters calling for their enforcement, and the threat of inspections are all there 'but in the ordinary day-to-day conduct of work, this bureaucratic paraphernalia [is] ignored and inoperative' (Gouldner, 1954: 187). Mock bureaucracies or organizations may include the paradoxical feature whereby deviation from rules is status-enhancing and conformity is status-impairing.

Elements of mock bureaucracy are to be found in both traditional illegal groups and licit organizations. In the former, for instance, rules covering internal loyalty and the nature of activities permitted to members are systematically violated. In some cases, the status of those who violate the rules is indeed enhanced, in a process whereby a bad reputation produces advantages for those who bear it. Examples of this type occurring in traditional organized crime will be provided.

Operative Goals and Official Goals

According to an important distinction proposed by Parsons, every system or organization relies on both a *normative order* and a *factual order*. The former refers to a given set of ends, rules or other norms. 'Order in this sense means that the process takes place in conformity with the paths laid down in the normative system' (Parsons, 1982: 98). But the breakdown of a given normative order may result in an order in the factual sense, that is, a situation where organizations and the system in which they operate reproduce themselves despite the apparent 'chaos from a normative point of view' (ibid.: 98).

Perrow's more specific analysis of organizations introduces the concept of 'operative goals' in contrast to 'official goals'. The latter constitute the general purpose of the organization as presented in statements and documents issued by key executives. The former 'designate the ends sought through the actual operating policies of the organization; they tell us what the organization is actually trying to do' (Perrow, 1961: 856). The contrast between these two types of goal mirrors the multiplicity and conflicting nature of organizational goals in a general sense. As Perrow indicates, organizations are never stable. Goals may be pursued in sequence or simultaneously, some may be conservative and some innovative, while quality may be emphasized in one area and quantity in another. This apparent tension between goals is a sign of health, as is the differentiation of subunits within a large organization. 'Despite inevitable costs, such tension helps ensure ready channels for changes in goals, when appropriate' (Perrow, 1970: 174).

It should be noted that the gap separating official and operative goals is determined by the environment in which organizations operate. Operative goals, in other words, are to be interpreted as provisional practices or tests with a view to their becoming officially accepted. Unorthodox goals and practices are faced with problems of legitimacy in the environment in which they take shape and in society at large. Perrow seems to stress the 'control' aspect of the environment, which supposedly exerts variable degrees of restraint on organizational goals. The examples he provides are in this respect very clear. About the tobacco industry he argues, 'On almost any scale a titanic battle is being waged to certify the legitimacy of this output' (Perrow, 1970: 99). The automobile industry too, he claims, 'has periodically been questioned as to the legitimacy of producing mobile weapons which are "unnecessarily" lethal, (ibid.: 99). In this view, the environment seems always to constitute a threat to organizational activity.

However, the environment may represent instead both a 'threat and a resource', and legitimacy varies according to the prevalence of the two.

Changing values in society, a renewed cultural climate and shifts in the political set-up may act as resources for legitimacy. Some organizational goals may indeed find support in the environment, although they had previously found none. The formation (or superimposition) of an 'enterprise culture' in a number of European countries is a case in point. This culture may modify, for example, both the nature of operational goals of organizations and the way in which they are perceived. It may also alter the opportunities for organizational deviance and its shared perception.

Enterprise Culture

The attempt to establish an enterprise culture follows both a material, technical process and a more ideological one. The former process is commonly identified in governmental programmes of economic reform whereby the production of goods and services is increasingly removed from the state and assigned to the private sector. In this way, industrial and tertiary sectors which were previously subject to protective and restrictive rules are said to become 'deregulated' as they enter the domain of the free market. The second process is related to the spread of the notion that what was previously perceived as a right must increasingly be regarded as a commodity. Citizens, in other words, are led to redefine themselves as clients, consumers, customers of their own citizenship. Both these processes accompanying the promotion of an enterprise culture imply the development of specific features on the part of those concerned. 'Here one finds a rather loosely related set of characteristics such as initiative, energy, independence, boldness, self-reliance, a willingness to take risks' (Keat and Abercrombie, 1991: 3).

Organizations involved in constructing an enterprise culture are enticed into taking on a commercial spirit and even adopting a related vocabulary. However, this transformation also entails a series of experiments of unpredictable effects that the term 'deregulation' seems to account for only partially. Deregulation should perhaps be understood less as an abandonment of rules than a potentially infinite broadening of them. Following the definitions provided earlier, it could be suggested that the promotion of an enterprise culture encourages the growth of a factual as opposed to a normative order, dispersed as opposed to monadic interests, operative as opposed to official goals. At the same time, this culture may cause substantial shifts in the principles inspiring organizational behaviour and, as Weber postulated, alter the way in which these principles are approved 'or at least not disapproved of'.

All of this may perhaps provide the backcloth against which the illicit activities of both corporate actors and organized criminal groups can find new definitions.

4 Work as Crime

In this chapter a number of specific cases will be discussed in which corporate crime can be observed against the background of the theory of the enterprise and organization theories. Categories and definitions sketched in the previous chapter will be applied to precise episodes occurring in a number of European countries. This exercise is not intended to provide a 'theory' of corporate and white-collar offending, but is meant only to serve descriptive and definitional purposes. As Cressey (1989: 49) stressed, 'It is not reasonable to identify the causes of crimes that are said to be committed by organizations', not least because such an investigation should encompass both organizational norms and the motives of individual actors who comply with or violate them. These causation concerns are not part of the present book, as will be briefly discussed in the conclusion.

As already emphasized, the selection of the following episodes is based on the attempt to identify typologies rather than to single out the most sensational cases. The selection is also driven by the desire to cover a range of European countries as evenly as possible, rather than focusing on countries where corporate and white-collar crime are more widespread.

Some of the categories and definitions discussed in the previous chapter may apply to more than one of the cases examined. Perrow's distinction between two sets of organizational goals, for example, lend themselves to universal application. Arguably, all organizations could simply be described as possessing official goals, which are included in public statements and documents, and operative goals, which designate the ends sought through the actual operating policies of the organization (Perrow, 1961). But this type of universalistic analysis would leave us with vague descriptions and would unjustifiably prevent any attempt to draw typologies. The use of subcategories, which are inscribed in the crucial distinction suggested by Perrow, may therefore be preferable. Nevertheless, one should be aware that some of the descriptions presented below do retain a degree of vagueness, as even the use of more detailed subcategories leaves the analysis blurred. Attempts to typologize behaviour can hardly avoid this limitation. Moreover, both the types of offence under examination and the categories that I deem useful for their description are equally blurred. In other words, the theory of the enterprise and organization theories themselves reflect the difficulty of drawing boundaries – between acceptable and unacceptable practices, morality and immorality, legitimacy and illegitimacy.

Purgatories Abroad

The case below illustrates aspects of the history of entrepreneurs which have been sketched in the previous chapter.

Case 1

In many European countries it is very common for enterprises to establish branches abroad in order to sidestep domestic legislation and evade tax. Taxation or safety controls may be more 'liberal' in other parts of the world. In Finland, for example, research found that this practice is rife because, by establishing branches abroad, enterprises can take advantage of tighter bank secrecy operating in other countries (Laitinen, 1993). Finnish enterprises tend to choose countries where the requirements concerning registration are less strict than in their own country. In this way, for example, the real names of the owners of a company, and the international network in which the company itself operates, may be hidden. The reason why this is widespread in Finland is attributed to the particular segmentation of the state functions in the country:

> In the different branches of the administration, each sector ... jealously guards its privileges against the other. It can be said that there is a 'taxation state', a 'trade state', and a 'police state', each of which operates in its own area. A precondition for effective control is tight co-operation of these three segments of the state. This is, however, often prevented by security regulations. (ibid.: 8–9)

Adequate legislation might succeed in overcoming this administrative segmentation and reduce the opportunities for tax evasion. Frequently, however, the very political apparatus which is expected to introduce such legislation overlaps with the economic world to which this legislation would apply. In 1993, around 80 per cent of all cabinet ministers were also members of management boards of economic enterprises, or had been so during the period 1950–86. According to the Finnish Ministry of Justice, tax evasion accounts for about 7 per cent of the gross national product.

* * *

According to Lefevre (1902) and Le Goff (1987), entrepreneurs are characterized by a deviant core which is part and parcel of their activity. They bear an original sin which they constantly attempt to purge or displace, but can only rarely completely remove. Entrepreneurs transferring entire sectors of their businesses elsewhere seem to export that deviant core abroad, namely in countries where their original sin can be purged. Moreover, in this purgatory theirs may not even be regarded as sins, but perceived as good deeds. The country hosting businesses from abroad may see important economic opportunities arising from them. It may also happen that entrepreneurs exporting that which in their own country would be regarded as a crime may instead appear as benefactors in the host country.

As we have seen, *who benefits*? has been identified as a crucial variable for the understanding of organizational goals (Blau and Scott, 1963). A typology based on this variable permits us to distinguish between the prime beneficiaries of different types of organizations: their members, their owners, their clients, or the public at large (Clegg and Dunkerley, 1990). In deviant organizational behaviours such as that presented above, there is a customary attempt to present those behaviours as benefiting the host country rather than primarily the perpetrator. This miraculous reversal of *who benefits?* also occurs when dangerous production is transferred to countries lacking strict safety regulations, or where it is assumed that health risks are warranted by the benefits brought.

Disasters such as Bhopal can be read within this logic (Pearce and Tombs, 1993). When toxic gas leaked out of the Union Carbide plant, no emergency response system was in place. Environmental health and safety took a back seat to development in India (Cassels, 1993). In this respect, consider also the sale to Third World countries of the Dalkon Shield intra-uterine contraceptive (Grabosky and Sutton, 1989). The risk to women from developing countries was justified by the argument that 'any contraceptive device was better than none, especially since birth rates were so high in Third World countries' (McMullan, 1992: 15).

Some car manufacturers also seek Purgatories abroad. For example, they may fail to apply the legally required safety devices to their product, and decide to export productive operations elsewhere (Mokhiber, 1988). Here, the likelihood of being seen as benefactors might exceed that of being considered corporate offenders. As further examples of 'deviance displacement', some firms move entire productive cycles in countries where salaries are lower and trade union rights non-existent. However, firms do not necessarily have to cross international borders, as a similar displacement can frequently be effected within their own national territory. Examples of enterprises opening up smaller units within their own country are numerous, with industrial restructuring and decentralization often fostering the hidden economy and illegal work conditions (Aglietta, 1979; Garofoli, 1983; Gallino, 1985; Lipiez, 1987; Bagnasco, 1990). Nor does this displacement of illegality only take place within the traditionally productive sector of the economy. Consider the financial sector: when 'shady advisers' are faced with expulsion from the investment scene of one country, they head for other countries where investors' compensation schemes are non-existent (Atkinson, 1994).

Risk and Ethics

As anticipated, a number of categories and definitions derived from organization theory and the history of entrepreneurs may simultaneously apply to the cases considered. For example, the entrepreneurial practices described above can also be analysed by referring to the notion of 'redemption through risk'. Many firms venturing into unknown territories may easily claim that risk and uncertainty determine the degree to which ethical values are stretched. Knight's work on this issue should be borne in mind. The author equates human needs with the relentless 'spirit of aspiring rather than desiring' (Knight, 1935). The economic sphere is the ideal domain of this spirit, which eludes all ethical judgements. Therefore 'aspiring', which entails risk and uncertainty, allows for the dilatation of acceptable practices. This notion, which may help to analyse the examples mentioned above, may perhaps better apply to the following case.

When the barrier between the two Europes collapsed, great opportunities arose for Western investment. But often the nature and techniques of Western penetration in the former Communist countries differed completely from those observed by investments in the West. Indeed, the process of turning the former Communist economies into free-market economies posed risks and uncertainties, due to the lack of a free-enterprise spirit and infrastructures in those countries. As a consequence, an important resource was lacking, namely 'trust', which is indispensable for market transactions to take place. The following case exemplifies how the risk associated with venturing in unknown territories was counterbalanced by stretching moral and legal rules.

Case 2

In 1989, most of Hungary's farming co-operatives were dismantled and the land privatized. With privatization, the price of particularly fertile areas rocketed. Large parts of such areas are located along the border with Austria, where Hungarian farmers cannot afford to buy the land on which they have worked for years. Prices were also pushed up by Austrian firms which bought up farmland illegally (Hooker, 1994). Theoretically, non-Hungarians are not allowed to buy land in Hungary, but the law is easy to get round. The land is sold at state auctions, and foreign purchasers find it easy to strike a deal with front Hungarian persons who formally buy for them. The sum given to these front persons would only buy up to some five acres (two hectares), too little for local farmers to survive. Many of them are therefore forced to leave the countryside and seek jobs either in Hungarian towns or, ironically, in neighbouring Austria. Foreign purchasers find real bargains in Hungary, as prices are less than half what they would be elsewhere. Moreover, environmental restrictions are lax and no quotas on production are in place.

A lawyer based in Budapest argued that the Hungarian authorities know very well that these illegal deals are taking place, but are reluctant to stop it for fear of retaliation by the Austrian government, which could, for example, introduce stricter legislation to reduce Hungarian migrants. Not surprisingly, illegalities occur even within this illegal procedure. The same lawyer described such illegalities as follows:

> My client was promised a certain sum of money by an Austrian company. Like many others he acted as a front person who was in fact buying the land with someone else's money. When the deal was concluded, the company only gave him half the sum promised, relying on the fact that he was not in a position to report to the police what had happened. But he did, because he was encouraged by a large number of other people who had the same experience.

These cases are becoming so frequent that none of those who illegally acted as mediators for foreign buyers are likely to be prosecuted, while new legislation is being discussed to prevent such illegal purchases from happening. However, by the time the legislation is introduced, large parts of the most fertile farmland in Hungary will be owned by individuals and companies based outside the country.

* * *

Similar cases were denounced by Treuhand, the agency presiding over the privatization process in former East Germany. The agency was forced to stop selling businesses in 1993 because too many illegal transactions conducted by West European firms were uncovered (*La Stampa*, 26 July 1993).

As we have seen in the cases discussed so far, illegality may be exported to areas where certain procedures are not regarded as illegal. But illegality can also be 'imposed' on countries which supposedly benefit from it. This logic seems not only to underpin business transactions between West and

East European countries, but also between developed and developing countries in a more general sense. See, for example, the case of Western companies distributing baby food in the developing world. According to a report released by the International Baby Food Action Network, seven Swiss companies, including Nestlé, breached United Nations health guidelines on the distribution of milk powder (The *Guardian*, 10 September 1994). These companies ignored the World Health Organization's advice that breastfeeding is preferable to milk powder unless clean water is absolutely guaranteed. As clean water may not always be available in many developing countries, firms are required to put health warnings on milk powder packets. Not only did the seven Swiss firms fail to do so, they also launched misleading advertising campaigns about their products, and as a promotional measure they provided developing countries' hospitals with free packets lacking the required health warning.

There are analogous cases in the sale of goods whose consumption in the producing countries is in decline due to public awareness of their damaging effects. Rules which limit the consumption of such goods are usually in operation in developed countries, with companies having to seek elsewhere the buyers they lose. Cigarettes are among such goods, with new plants being built in former Communist countries and the Third World, where no rules are in place as regards the amounts of damaging substances contained in cigarettes, and nor are *ad hoc* health prevention programmes particularly developed (Hall, 1992).

In 1989, the United States Trade Representative Panel held a session to consider a tobacco industry request that the USA impose sanctions on Thailand if it did not agree to drop restrictions on the import of US tobacco. 'Such US government actions had already rammed tobacco down the throats of consumers in Japan, South Korea, and Taiwan' (Chomsky, 1992: 123). This narcotrafficking operation had its critics, among which were the American Heart Association and the American Cancer Society. A representative of the latter said: 'When we are pleading with foreign governments to stop the flow of cocaine, it is the height of hypocrisy for the United States to export tobacco' (ibid.: 123). With respect to European manufacturers, it is unknown what kind of pressure they put on buying countries, and the sort of negotiations taking place, in a climate that manufacturers themselves define as cutthroat competition (Hall, 1992). Among European companies winning against their competitors is the BAT group, which earmarked a £133 million investment in Uzbekistan's tobacco industry. The operation included building a cigarette factory in Samarkand and helping to develop tobacco-leaf processing plants. The group no longer sells cigarettes within its national territory, but its factory in Southampton (England) exports around the world, including Eastern Europe. Moreover, the light type of cigarette that would sell in the West would be too expensive to produce in developing countries, a circumstance which leads the group operating abroad to produce heavier varieties of cigarettes (Cowe, 1994).

One of the ways in which European countries may impose their goods on developing countries is via aid programmes. Here the variable risk, which in other cases alone permits the exemption from ethics, is strengthened by the 'humanitarian' nature of the operation. European Community aid grew 50.7 per cent in monetary terms between 1988 and 1992, disbursing in 1993 about £27 billion (Vidal, 1994). Critics argue that aid is skewed and that it hardly reaches poor countries, let alone poor communities and people. The choice is often prompted by political criteria, and falls on countries loyal to developed countries. This is exemplified by Egypt and Jordan almost quadrupling their share of aid in the wake of the Gulf war, and Iraq facing a health crisis, with more than 300,000 people dying as a result of medical shortages during the three years of United Nations trade sanctions (ibid.). Commercial criteria can also apply: for example, the willingness of the governments receiving aid to sign contracts with those granting aid. Significant amounts of funds go to countries such as Turkey, Tunisia and Jordan, which are not officially classified as poor or needy, but are willing to establish commercial partnerships with the 'donors'.

In some cases aid is specifically linked to contracts that the receiving country agrees to sign. In this respect, it is worth mentioning the case known as the Pergau Dam affair. The British National Audit Office exposed the misappropriation of £234m of overseas aid: the suggestion was made that the aid was linked to the sale of goods, including arms, and the building of a special forces base in Malaysia (Blackhurst, 1994). The use of public interest immunity orders in Britain may protect this case from full disclosure for a long time. The matter is currently the object of a Foreign Affairs Committee inquiry, which has to establish whether millions of pounds of British taxpayers' money, earmarked for the world's poorest countries, was given to Malaysia as a 'sweetener' instead. Allegations of bribes to Malaysian officials given by British companies form part of the inquiry (Durham and Nelson, 1994). *The Observer* of 6 February 1994 reported:

> The British Government has always claimed the Pergau aid was not linked to arms. However, George Younger, who was Defence Secretary when the deal was negotiated, has admitted 'a verbal undertaking was given by somebody – not myself – to link the aid to the defence project. There was pressure from the Prime Minister's side to be pals.'

The World Development Movement, which investigated and exposed the case, produced evidence that:

> The granting of provision funding for the Pergau project represents a serious breach of the Overseas Development Administration's stated priorities. Many of the concerns raised by the National Audit Office and the Public Accounts Committee in the Pergau case form a repeating pattern in projects funded under the Aid and Trade Provision which highlights its inherent weaknesses. The Pergau project was funded only because aid policy was subordinated to other commercial and foreign policy priorities – including securing a major arms order from Malaysia. There are significant grounds for deep concern that links between government-to-government discussions of aid funding and military equipment contracts may not have been isolated to the Pergau project, or even just Malaysia. (World Development Movement, 1994: 2)

A member of one of the local groups affiliated to this movement added:

> These projects have very poor economic, social, technical and environmental records. They are not properly assessed because commercial confidentiality prevents the release of key documents, or because of time pressures due to the rush to bid for a contract. None of these projects have specific goals relating to direct poverty relief.

Deception and development, as in Sombart's (1915) entrepreneur/speculator, are in this case one and the same.

Opportunity Perceivers

If the cases sketched above revolve around the need to sell, those described in this section are the result of the need to buy. Unbalanced commercial relationships also prevail in these cases, as they involve wealthy countries on the one hand and needy countries on the other. Entrepreneurs who engage in such commercial undertakings remind us of Hermes, the mythological Greek character embodying the traits of both the merchant and the thief (McClelland, 1961). As we have seen, Hermes travels extensively, being endowed with winged feet. His incessant movement allows him to act as an innovator in one place and as a trickster in another. He is dishonest with some, but at the same time he honestly provides services to others. Similarly, the entrepreneurs considered in the following cases conduct their business legally in their own country, but act illegally abroad. This ambiguity is also found in Schumpeter's analysis, where the author describes opportunity perceivers and innovators. It is the subjective, voluntaristic aspect of entrepreneurial action which characterizes Schumpeter's innovators, who initiate change and subsequently educate consumers. They rearrange the labour process in an innovative way, expand markets or, as in the following case, conquer new sources for the supply of raw materials.

Case 3

In 1991, a team of financial investigators were engaged in the monitoring of up-market Milan boutiques. Initially, their investigation was aimed at identifying luxurious shops located in the historic centre of the city which failed to provide customers with the obligatory receipt for each item sold. A number of customers had reported, in particular, that shops where leather goods were retailed failed to issue receipts. The public prosecutor for this case explained:

> The financial police started to double-check the declared income of a number of shops. The indications of customers proved correct, because most shops retailing leather goods and other items made of animal skin appeared to have declared suspiciously low profits. These shops were visited by agents, who posed as customers and found that only cheaper goods were displayed in the shop windows. Once inside the shops, they were offered other items whose price was extraordinarily high. What they came across, after a while, was much more than cases of tax evasion. They found a chain of shops which retailed handbags and belts and only served a selected clientele. The skin of which these items were made could come from protected species. The investigation tracked the distributor of these goods. They found a company by the name of *Italrettili*, which manufactured belts, shoes and handbags. The warehouse of this company was raided, and alligators' skins were found. Further investigations proved that this company had a representative based in the area of Pantanal, the wildlife-rich zone between Brazil and Paraguay, from where the skins were illegally imported. The local representative hired hunters, who were poor farmers, and we presume that they were very poorly paid. Obviously no record was found of these 'employees', nor of the goods imported.

Experts suggest that more than one million caiman alligators are killed every year for the skins that will become shoes and bags for wealthy Westerners. The defendants in this case justified the illegality of their business by invoking the pressing demand for the goods they sold – an argument which could well be used by illicit drug traffickers.

* * *

Returning to Schumpeter's analysis, his notion of discontinuity comes to mind, though in this case discontinuity does not describe two different entrepreneurs utilizing traditional and innovative combinations respectively.

Discontinuity characterizes the same firm, which introduces innovation and at the same time retains aspects of the old commercial process. The Italian employees of this firm were properly registered and paid, while those abroad were not. The firm was conservative at home, and innovative abroad.

A similar case was uncovered in Britain in 1994. A study commissioned by the Overseas Development Administration, after pressure from the World Wide Fund for Nature and Friends of the Earth, showed that hundreds of tree species faced extinction due to excessive logging. The report was presented at a seminar in Cambridge attended by timber companies. They agreed that the data should not be published because it could be misused, and could harm the sale of wood 'mistakenly' listed as endangered (P. Brown, 1993). Members of Friends of the Earth to whom I spoke claimed that the government backed the timber companies, and therefore the report was suppressed. Later in 1994, three British timber companies were prosecuted in Brazil for illegal logging. They were accused of logging mahogany within the forbidden area of 22,500 square miles (58,275 square kilometres) of Indian reserves in Amazonia. To the embarrassment of Britain's Timber Trade Federation (TTF), the companies were on the list of 22 approved suppliers who had signed a declaration that they would not trade in illegally logged wood (Tickell, 1993). The certification scheme for timber companies launched by the Federation was a response to previous criticisms by environmentalists, but doubts always remained over verification procedures. Britain is said to import about half of Brazil's mahogany exports, although the quantity of the wood imported illegally is unknown. Environmentalists claim that, looking at the existing demand, it is unthinkable that this could be satisfied by only exploiting permitted areas (Friends of the Earth, 1992; 1993).

Both literally and metaphorically, these episodes illustrate Schumpeter's analysis of innovation as 'creative destruction' (Schumpeter, 1961b).

Conflicting Goals?

Organizations are said to be inspired by conflicting goals, as the ends of the different strata of individuals within them may differ. A number of authors mentioned in the previous chapter draw a distinction between organizational internal cliques and organizations in their entirety. These may have a plurality of goals as a result of the diversity of their members, and sectional interests may be disguised as general interests (Gouldner, 1954; Fox, 1966; Mouzelis, 1967; Silverman, 1970; Reed, 1993; Wells, 1993). These notions have serious implications when episodes of organizational deviance are examined. Clinard (1983) found that middle-management executives tend to ascribe to their chief executive officers a leading role in setting the corporate ethical tone. 'Over half of the interviewees went even further, believing top management to be directly responsible for the violation of government regulations' (ibid.: 133). Although few of Clinard's interviewees reported any personal involvement in unacceptable conduct, they argued that pressures from top management may result in illegal behaviour. However, when such behaviour is detected, each group participating in corporate activity may lay the blame on the other, with the consequence that ethical or legal responsibility becomes difficult to apportion. The case presented below is an illustration of such difficulty.

Case 4

One of the biggest drug companies in Europe admitted that some of its staff had been using sales techniques banned by the industry's code of practice. The company cannot be named because, at the time of writing, criminal investigation is in course. Five employees were dismissed for irregularities concerning the handling of company funds and falsification of records. The funds were used for activities such as holding meetings or events (dinner parties and the like) with general practitioners, though with little or no medical content. The company said it had never condoned or tolerated unethical conduct from its sales personnel. However, one of the dismissed employees said:

> Not only were many senior managers aware of the breaches of the code taking place. Some of them would also encourage these unethical practices with very clear innuendoes. They would start by describing their own predicament for the pressure put on them from the top. Selling, selling, selling, at all costs. Even if our prices were higher than our competitors', doctors had to be persuaded in one way or another to prescribe our drugs. I have heard a manager hinting at leisure cruises in the Mediterranean which were intended to put doctors and sales personnel together. Conference and scientific workshops would have been part of the cruise, of course, but all expenses would have been covered by the company.

This cruise never took place, but each member of staff had budgets of up to £20,000 for what is called 'hospitality'. The code says that only 'moderate hospitality' can be offered to doctors, and gifts have to be restricted to small items such as pens or notebooks.

* * *

This case may validate the notion that organizations have conflicting goals, and that goals reflect the specific aims and roles of different groups within them. But this notion also seems to act as a safety-belt for organizations seeking to blame their internal cliques for unethical behaviour, while retaining their ethical image intact. In Case 4, top managers fired the staff allegedly involved in unethical behaviour, while these staff accused top managers of having inspired their behaviour. Both could claim to be the prime victims of such behaviour. Some of the authors discussed in the previous chapter argue that sectional interests of cliques are frequently masqueraded as the general interest of organizations (Mouzelis, 1967; Reed, 1993; Wells, 1993). In the case examined above it is difficult to detect the difference between these two types of interests and which of the two inspired the illegal practices in question.

A similar case involved European-based multinational Fisons, which suspended one of its regional managers on allegations that the employees he supervised had tried to bribe doctors to use its products. Fisons had admitted to running a scheme involving patient treatment cards that led to a cash payment to doctors of £10 for each new patient prescribed the group's asthma product (Counsell, 1993). However, after suspending the scheme, the company claimed that it had never encouraged personnel to bribe doctors or use similar selling techniques. Again, it is not easy to establish whether companies do promote such techniques or genuinely condemn them. Moreover, in the case of Fisons it is hard to assess whether the sacking of personnel was the result of people external to the corporation exposing such techniques or the result of the organization's independent action. Again, this would suggest that the distinction between the goals of internal cliques and those of organizations in their entirety is more blurred than some authors imply.

The following case is yet another illustration of this.

Case 5

In November 1993, an estimated 1000 people were infected with the HIV virus by contaminated blood in Germany (Gow and Tomforde, 1993). UB Plasma, a company providing blood to hospitals, was closed down and four of its employees arrested. Investigators found that in 1987 an anonymous UB Plasma employee had warned the health authorities of infected blood reaching the market, but that those warned had failed to act. Due to the international nature of the blood market, this was not merely a German issue. UB Plasma products had been bought by countries ranging from Sweden to Saudi Arabia, Greece, Italy, France, Switzerland and Austria. Members of the Association of Haemophiliac Patients accused companies of buying blood from poor countries such as Romania, where donations are often motivated by despair. A member of this association said: 'The blood is not checked, because the screening process is too expensive.' One firm based in Hamburg was accused of recruiting local heroin users, a high-risk group, who were paid the equivalent of £10 a shot. The high demand for blood in Germany was said to be one of the reasons for systematically cutting corners and costs, while the market is said to attract many fly-by-night companies.

* * *

This was described as a tale of greed and incompetence, and was said to reveal the inadequacy of the law and supervisory procedures in such a sensitive commercial arena (Gow and Tomforde, 1993). The law only requires that plasma producers be inspected biannually, which, according to haemophiliacs, leads to merely cursory examination of procedures and personnel. The German Association of Haemophiliac Patients also stressed that the recruitment of personnel was careless and pressure was put on staff in terms of performance. Premiums were attached to the quantity of samples collected by individual staff, a circumstance which inevitably pushed them to cut corners. Again, when episodes such as these occur, managers may always blame employees for disregarding the correct procedure and the safety rules and tests. Typically, as Conklin observed, supervisors may blame staff for violation of the law 'even when their own orders clearly indicated that it would be necessary to violate the law to achieve a goal' (Conklin, 1977: 64).

This case bears similarities with the French 'blood scandal' in 1985. In both cases the companies were not charged with causing bodily harm or manslaughter, but with negligence and deception about the property of the product they sold. In the French case, haemophiliacs complained that blood samples had been collected in prison institutions, which was estimated to be the origin of 40 per cent of the contamination. They also accused both the director of the National Blood Transfusion Organisation and the director of the National Health Laboratory of knowing of the contamination but failing to denounce it for fear of raising 'public hysteria' (Greilsamer, 1992; Nouchi, 1993). Developments in the French 'Bloodgate' indicated that in a ministerial meeting which took place on 9 March 1985 the introduction of an American blood-screening test was postponed in order to give French firm Diagnostic Pasteur the opportunity to devise its own test and monopolize the French market (Erhel, 1994). Fresh investigations in this case are currently targeting three ministers of health who were in office in the mid-1980s. As in the German case, both were convicted for 'deception regarding the quality of the product sold' and 'failure to assist persons in danger', because they knew of the contamination (Bantman, 1994).

Ethical Diversification

Organizations which decentralize illegality are simultaneously conservative and innovative, in both Schumpeter's and Merton's terms. In the previous chapter I mentioned the ironic reappearance of the term 'innovation' in the sociology of deviance. This celebrated term, which was borrowed from the theory of enterprise, denotes the behaviour of lawbreakers who adhere to officially shared goals but find illegal ways of achieving them (Merton, 1968). The case regarding the pharmaceutical industry which is described below could be located within this Schumpeterian and Mertonian framework.

The pharmaceutical industry is said to be characterized by more serious criminal conduct than any other industrial sector in the world economy (Braithwaite, 1984). Of the 20 largest American pharmaceutical companies studied by Braithwaite, 19 had been involved in bribery episodes during the decade preceding the completion of his study. Many of these companies had vice-presidents 'responsible for going to jail', in the sense that if criminal conduct were uncovered they would be held responsible. 'After a period of faithful service as the vice-president responsible for going to jail, they would be rewarded with promotion sideways to a safe vice-presidency' (Braithwaite, 1993: 14). However, in the following case it is the decentralization of illegality which primarily characterizes the conduct of the pharmaceutical companies involved. The directors of these companies admitted that a sort of ethical diversification allowed them to act differently according to the context in which they operated. They were thus able to be innovative, in both an entrepreneurial and a criminal sense.

Case 6

In 1993, the Italian Minister of Health was arrested for taking bribes from a number of pharmaceutical companies. Glaxo, the multinational British company, was among the companies involved in the investigation (Semier and Lynn, 1993). Executives at the Italian subsidiary of Glaxo were arrested, as were the managing director and chairman of Smith Kline Beecham in Italy. Judges also proved that some drugs had been recycled and renamed, before being sold at higher prices. Officials issuing drug licences were involved, including medical academics, the president of the EC Commission for pharmaceutical products, and a member of the World Health Organization's pharmaceutical commission (Radice, 1993). One of the judges conducting the investigation said:

> There was official record of the monies paid to cabinet ministers, because this money had been given through the association of the pharmaceutical industry in Italy. The money was deposited in bank accounts of medical associations and university foundations managed by renowned doctors. These doctors, who were in charge of issuing drug licences on behalf of the government, would keep their share and give the remaining money to officials working in the Health Ministry. Politicians sitting on the committee which establishes the prices of drugs received personal cheques from pharmaceutical companies. The fact is that a number of companies paid two or more officials in order to have the prices of their drugs raised. But these officials ignored the fact that their colleagues were also receiving bribes. I interrogated a number of general directors of these companies whose mother company was based abroad. They were very co-operative with interviewers. One of them said that he knew the way of doing business in Italy was different, and he just thought he had to adapt.

Sins without Sinners

As we have seen, the ascent of the firm led to the gradual disappearance of precisely identifiable innovators and individual entrepreneurs, along with their respective responsibilities. If Le Goff describes the history of merchants as a succession of efforts to purge the original sin upon which commerce is based, the history of the enterprise seems to aim at the complete disappearance of that original sin. The examples in this section testify to the phenomenon whereby some organizational practices cannot be ascribed to any particular individual. Because organizations are 'dispersed social agencies' or 'fractured units', practices and responsibilities are diffuse (Thompson, 1982). Corporations may lack precisely identifiable decision-making structures, because these structures instead may allow for sudden diversification, while the enhancement of non-hierarchical decision-making practices may put all members in a position to act when contingencies arise. This 'dispersion' is also reflected in the allocation of responsibility for organizational illegal conduct. The fragmented layout and the minute division of labour and distribution of responsibility which characterize modern organizations render their activities opaque (Clarke, 1990). Moreover, in these contexts, responsibility does not imply individual faults, because organizations are devoid of emotional traits or moral concerns: as Wolf argued, they do not have a soul (Wolf, 1985; Wells, 1993). Again, if Le Goff was concerned with the way in which traders purged their souls, the concern of contemporary organizations seems that of jettisoning their souls.

Case 7

In January 1994 the European Parliament was faced with a detailed report by a number of its members regarding shipping abuses within the European Community. Abuses of international regulations to ensure the safety and seaworthiness of ships were described in detail in the report. One of the European Members of Parliament who contributed to the report explained that safety certificates were issued without inspections taking place. Sometimes these certificates were faxed to vessels thousands of miles away. He added:

> Although all ships have safety certificates, our inquiry found that approximately 30 per cent of ships are substandard, with oil tankers being the most dangerously unsafe. In order to cut costs, many owners do not repair their ships; in particular, they do not treat corrosion, which is extremely dangerous. Safety equipment is often defective. Some shipping classification societies sell safety certification without having seen a ship. More than 1200 lives were lost at sea in 1991. It was impossible to identify precise individual responsibilities for these deaths. The number of ships destroyed by fire, explosion or other accidents was the highest since 1983. Many incidents are caused by poor safety, although there is reason to believe that accidents also occur because they 'are cheaper' than repair works. The fact is that owners have three options: sell their vessel, repair them, or *lose* them somehow, and therefore get the money from their insurance company. The last option is the most advantageous.

* * *

As this MEP emphasized, oil tankers are particularly at risk, which is partly the result of low oil prices. Oil companies impose freight rates, thus discouraging shipowners to renew and diversify their fleets. As a consequence, flags of convenience are increasing greatly, with European companies adopting Liberian or Panamanian flags to avoid safety requirements and therefore costs:

> Analysis of the world's biggest oilspills between 1967 and 1984 shows that 66 per cent involved flags of convenience or Greek-registered tonnage. Almost a third of the world's tanker fleet is now under convenience registry. Between 1987–92 the Liberian fleet grew 7 per cent, Panama 15 per cent, Cyprus 30 per cent, the Bahamas 120 per cent and Malta 500 per cent. Yet these countries do not have the resources to enforce safety standards. (The *Guardian*, 9 January 1993)

Similar examples of sins without sinners are found in the leisure industry. Among the most tragically notorious is the Zeebrugge disaster.

Case 8

On 6 March 1987 the *Herald of Free Enterprise*, a ferry owned by Townsend Thoresen, was due to leave the Belgian port of Zeebrugge and return to Dover, from where she had arrived in the morning of the same day. Many passengers were on a cheap day trip to Belgium offered in a popular newspaper promotion.

> The ship swung round, its bow doors still open but out of the sight of the captain and the other officers on the bridge. At 18.20 it passed the inner harbour breakwater and began to accelerate towards the open sea. When its speed was between 15 and 18 knots, water began to enter the car deck through the open doors. Water entered at a rate of 200 tons every minute. At 18.25, exactly 23 minutes after its departure, the ferry turned right round and rolled over on to a sandbank less than a mile from the harbour. Only its starboard half remained above the water. The rest of this huge ship was submerged, leaving its 80 crew and 459 panic-stricken passengers to fight for their lives. (Crainer, 1993: 11).

The relatives of the 193 victims formed the Herald Families Association. Apart from the prime function of helping the people affected to come to terms with the tragedy, the Association campaigns to raise awareness around the issue of corporate responsibility. According to the association, ship owners do not take action on safety unless they are forced to do so. A member said:

> Safety reduces competitiveness. If one company invests a lot on safety and its competitors do not, these competitors will produce more profits, and consequently attract more shareholders. Few are prepared to take the risk of prejudicing profit by spending on safety. They spend their time watching what their competitors are doing. Business remains, to a large extent, a reactive occupation.

Another member of the Association added: 'In this way, when tragedies such as these happen, they can always blame their competitors or the particular business in which they operate, rather than taking their own responsibility'.

In an unusually strong report, the public inquiry into the disaster found serious flaws in the company's management. Warnings and suggestions from captains had been ignored or rejected. Procedures and roles on board were vague and confusing. Some of the shore managers were unsure of what their jobs actually entailed, and put captains and crews under pressure to operate as speedily as possible. The report concluded: 'Cardinal faults lay higher up in the company. From top to bottom, the body corporate was infected with the disease of sloppiness' (Crainer, 1993: 2). In 1987, a coroner's court returned a verdict of unlawful killing. Members of the crew and directors of the company were charged with manslaughter. The decision to prosecute seemed to mark an important step forward in the development of the principle of corporate accountability. But the court acquitted the defendants, because the case was deemed unsustainable. The father of one of the victims argued that this case shows how wide is the gulf between the public's perception of justice and the legalistic interpretation of it. He added:

> We feel that people in positions of leadership sometimes don't want to know what is going on in their organization, because if they did know they might be held accountable – perhaps their lawyers are advising them in this way. Others simply do not understand how they should properly exercise their duty of responsibility or that their standards are reflected in the acts of those below them in the corporate ladder.

* * *

In Britain, despite 19,000 deaths related to company faults in the last 20 years, no company has ever been convicted of manslaughter (Slapper, 1994). In larger companies the partial responsibilities of different managers or directors cannot be aggregated (Bergman, 1991). In this sense, recommendations that directors and managers need to have a clearer idea of what their jobs entail may sound naïve. 'In too many cases it appears that the very vagueness of their duties enables managers to avoid facing up to direct responsibility' (Crainer, 1993: 4). A similar vagueness also denotes the very notion of corporate liability (Norrie, 1993; Young, 1993). Criminal liability requires that a damaging act occurs, that a damaged party be visible, and the harm sustained measurable (Edelhertz and Overcast, 1982). It also requires intentionality as regards the damage caused. *Mens rea* denotes the mental state, the subjective element making the allocation of guilt possible (Williams, 1983). The virtual 'invisibility' of corporate victims makes the allocation of guilt even more difficult. This is so because often the damaging effects of corporate offences are only appreciated in spatial and temporal contexts which are different from those in which the initial offences took place. In other cases, instead, the victims of corporate offences may even be unaware of having been victimized.

Incursions into Illegality

Faith in human choice entails a number of tenets. First, that choice is based on a careful evaluation of the alternatives and information available. Second, that the process of making choices can be improved by using the 'technology of choice'. As I mentioned earlier, critics of this faith posit the need to supplement the technology of reason with a technology of 'foolishness'. In order to discover new opportunities and goals, organizations are said to require some idea of 'sensible foolishness'. 'Which of the many foolish things that we might do now will lead to attractive value consequences?' (March, 1990: 335). Examples of sensible foolishness are provided by licit businesses periodically adopting illegal practices: insider dealing is one such example (Bosworth-Davies, 1993). This illegal practice may be a one-off or a periodical undertaking, and indeed its 'sensible foolishness' does not contradict the technology of reason normally inspiring those who perform it. Corporate tax evasion could be another example, this behaviour being an intermittent foray into illegality which enhances the availability of funds and therefore boosts the possibility of new licit undertakings. Widespread entrepreneurial tax evasion in Germany is a case in point. This involves the transfer of part of the profits to Luxembourg, a practice which became all the more common since the 'coupon tax' was introduced in Germany in 1991. The tax, which exacts 35 per cent of dividend income in excess of DM6000 'prompted Germans to transfer around DM100bn into Luxembourg-based mutual funds between mid-1991 and November 1993' (*The European*, 28 January/3 February 1994).

However, examples, of licit entrepreneurs engaging in more conventional crimes are also examples of how technologies of foolishness can be put in place. The case of two Italian small entrepreneurs financing a kidnapping because in urgent need of cash is one such example (*La Stampa*, 6 May 1990). These behaviours should be understood in contexts where illegal supplementary incomes are made available which offer legal capital the possibility of a rapid valorization (Ruggiero and Vass, 1992). In this respect, the existence of 'illegal islands' has been hypothesized which allows licit entrepreneurs occasional or intermittent incursions into the criminal arena and the related access to rapid profits (Coco and Serra, 1983). In the case I have chosen to highlight in this section, a German entrepreneur evidently found 'illegal islands' insufficient for the achievement of his purposes. After a number of incursions into the illegal arena, he planned the ultimate offence of his career. This entrepreneur, who employed some 2000 individuals, committed the country's biggest post-war fraud. He could be likened to Melville's con man, whose illegal exploits allow for the expansion of employment opportunities.

Case 9

Mr Schneider had a degree in economics and was Germany's largest property developer. He was trusted by banks and financial institutions, and before going into hiding he owed them more than the equivalent of £3 billion. He disappeared with his wife after withdrawing £200 million from a number of deposit accounts and telling his staff he was going to Tuscany for a short break (Gow, 1994). A public prosecutor based in Frankfurt said:

> Fraud proceedings were launched not so much because of the number of jobs at stake, but as a result of pressure on the part of powerful creditors. Among the victims are both banks and trade creditors, some of which have only recently discovered that they were the victims of Mr Schneider's fraud. The fact is that this large developer built an empire which was in large measure hidden behind a tangled web of companies. Some of these companies were short-lived, and disappeared or merged with others overnight. Some companies of the empire were set up only for the purpose of receiving loans. For this reason, creditors found it difficult to track the assets of Mr Schneider, and some didn't even know that the companies they were dealing with belonged to him.

A private investigator employed by one of the creditors said that the speciality of Mr Schneider was the redevelopment of historic buildings, and that with the reunification of Germany this type of business experienced an unprecedented boom. Examples were given of historic properties purchased in Leipzig. However, the private investigator said:

> This type of speculation has been possible because the major banks shared with Mr Schneider the enthusiasm related to property investment in former East Germany. Banks sense that big business can be carried out there, and as a consequence they may lay excessive confidence on clients who invest in East Germany. They may cut corners in asking for collaterals, and also go along with the unorthodox practices of their clients because they may eventually have their share of benefit. For example, developers investing in East Germany hold on to refurbished sites and make sure that prices are inflated before reselling. Banks accept this and even calculate the inflated price of these properties as a collateral for further loans. In Mr Schneider's case, fraud was the result of his own greed but also the result of his victims' greed.

The Deutsche Bank, the biggest lender to the property developer, announced it would carry out an in-depth internal review, 'a serious admission of failure by a bank whose lending policies were once held up as exemplary' (*The European*, 29 April/5 May 1994). Controversy over the Deutsche Bank's role in the affair revolved around the bank allegedly ignoring the financial problems of the developer, and ignoring a complaint against him regarding a fraudulent application to finance a development in Frankfurt. Deutsche's chairperson was reported to have said: 'On the one hand the banks are too smart, crafty, greedy, altogether cut-throats. On the other hand, they act *foolishly* and naïvely when faced with fraudsters, phoneys and other good-for-nothings who ought to be uncovered immediately' (The *Guardian*, 20 May 1994, emphasis added).

* * *

In an unintended reference to March's theory, aspects of 'foolishness' were alluded to by commentators on this case. The offender's 'foolishness' characterized what is likely to constitute the epilogue of his entrepreneurial career. In the following case, however, foolishness and rationality were intertwined, as the entrepreneurs involved combined their incursions into illegality with otherwise routine licit practices. The case was reconstructed through communication with a Dutch private investigator and additional information drawn from his autobiography (Hoffmann, 1990).

Case 10

As an introduction to this case it should be borne in mind that a number of European countries subsidize the export of certain goods in order to boost sales abroad and sustain levels of employment within their own territories.

> The export of wire mesh for reinforcing concrete buildings attracted a subsidy in West Germany. After a comparatively short period following the introduction of a subsidy on this product, the Dutch market was flooded with extraordinarily cheap wire mesh. Dutch suppliers were puzzled as to how it could be offered at a price so low it was actually below production costs. (Hoffmann, 1990: 78)

A Dutch private investigator was hired to find out the reasons for this low price, because the product also simultaneously qualified for a subsidy from the Netherlands government. He said: 'The most convenient and therefore likely way of transporting the wire from Germany to Holland was by barge, and we started our enquiries by following the River Rhine and its tributaries from the Dutch border'. After the identification numbers of barges were recorded, these were compared with the numbers of later loads shipped to the Netherlands from Germany, and also with barges sailing in the opposite direction, from Holland to Germany. The numbers were the same.

> The German supplier was shipping the product to the Netherlands and collecting his subsidy. The Dutch trader shipped the same mats back to Germany and

> collected his subsidy – and had sent them back on the same barge which brought them in originally. The same shipment went back and forth between Germany and Holland several times and on each occasion the traders at each end claimed their export subsidy. After several journeys the mesh began to look a little shabby, so was sold in the Netherlands at greatly reduced prices which accounted for the low price which had puzzled Dutch suppliers in the first place. (Hoffmann, 1990: 78)

Non-profit Organizations

As we saw in the previous chapter, maximization of profit is not the essential and unambiguous objective of organizations (Thompson, 1982). Non-monetary growth, empire-building, conservation and enhancement of power may be included among other organizational goals. The following is an example of organizational deviance which is not immediately translatable into monetary profit, and shows how the very notion of profit maximization may be appreciated and pursued in a variety of ways.

Case 11

In one of the rare Amnesty International reports devoted to Western European countries, the French police was accused of being responsible for a shocking pattern of shootings and killings (Amnesty International, 1994). The report selected 11 cases in the period between February 1993 and September 1994 to illustrate 'reckless and illegal use of force', often victimizing many juveniles of non-European origin (Webster, 1994). Time and again, officers were said to ignore their own guidelines on the use of arms, and the French government was asked to rectify shortcomings in police training and practice. The report followed protests by French human rights groups concerned with the record of Mr Pasqua, appointed as interior minister in April 1993. During his previous appointment to the same office (from 1986 to 1988), the police force was accused of 14 illegal killings. In April 1993, three young men were murdered in separate incidents, only days after Mr Pasqua had been appointed.

> A 17-year-old Zairian was killed in a police station in Paris. An inspector shot him through the head while he was questioning him about a suspected petty theft. The inspector reportedly claimed that he had merely wished to intimidate him with the gun. (Amnesty International, 1994: 2).

Foreigners and young people were said to be 'preferred targets'. The report also referred to other cases of police brutality, which were said to have a distinctive racist element. Among the most serious cases were the killing of unarmed passengers in suspect cars and unarmed men in failed robberies.

> Amnesty International sought information from the authorities about progress of investigations. The organization wrote to the Ministers of the Interior and Justice regarding its concerns over deaths in custody, shootings and allegations of ill treatment by police. No replies have been received from the authorities. (ibid.: 2).

* * *

Similar cases which continue to occur in the majority of European countries could be included in this section. For example, the European Committee for the Prevention of Torture, charged with examining the treatment of people deprived of their liberty, found that most countries practised forms of torture and ill treatment of people in custody (Cassese, 1994).

I have chosen to include these episodes under the heading 'non-profit organizations', even though the police and other law enforcement agencies do engage in profit-making deviance. The selection is driven by the attempt to highlight the organizational nature of this type of offending, organizational factors in these cases playing an important part in determining how individuals act (Kramer, 1982). Arguably, these forms of deviance benefit the organization as a whole rather than its members, as they are aimed at solving performance problems and at saving labour. To clarify this point, episodes involving enforcement agencies cutting corners in their practices should be considered. Examples include planting weapons and drugs, fabricating evidence and serious miscarriages of justice. See the case of a densely populated London area, where the local Community Defence Association denounced 40 cases of serious police misconduct which resulted in 14 officers of the same station being sentenced to more than two years (HCDA, 1991; 1992). Although officers of the same police station were also convicted for drug offences which indeed brought profit, the 'labour-saving' aspects of their misconduct also deserves attention. There are ways of thinking which permeate organizations and are crucial for their method of operating. As regards the police, this way of thinking, which is said to permeate their structure, their education and their training, was defined as 'targeting' (Mansfield, 1994). 'Targeting essentially means that police concentrate on the individuals or families, groups of people or even whole communities who they think are most likely to be responsible. It is a kind of labour-saving short circuiting' (ibid.: 11).

A similar, very serious case which occurred in Spain could be seen in the same light. This regarded the formation of special investigative units contributing to the fight against the ETA group. The units operated in France, where many Basque militants found refuge, and where particularly brutal 'labour-saving' practices were denounced. These included torture, fabrication of evidence and even murder (Giacopuzzi, 1994; Kontrolpean, 1995).

These episodes also reveal another important component of many organizations. This can be described as the provision of unofficial incentives attached to non-prestigious or downright unpleasant occupations. Some organizations offer those who accept unattractive positions within them the opportunity to gain a hidden quantum of remuneration in a non-monetary form. This may imply a degree of flexibility on work time or, in some cases, abuse of power. The latter applies to the episodes mentioned above. But the police behaviour which has been described resonates with analogous cases involving similar hidden incentives. For example, some public employees in Italy find compensation for their meagre salary and the low status of their occupation by practising a rotary system of unchallenged and thoroughly organized absenteeism. This practice is so largely tolerated that one could regard it as part of the unwritten incentives attached to civil service occupations, which would otherwise be completely shunned. The same principle is said to apply to other, more prestigious occupations, within a *total reward system* which includes both official benefits and hidden incentives. 'The fiddled benefits obtained, far from being the exceptional activity of the minority, are an integral aspect of all the occupations they include' (Mars, 1994: 3).

Mocking One's Own Principles

Mock bureaucracies are defined as sets of rules which, albeit officially central for the governing of organizations, are in fact a dead letter (Gouldner, 1954). Available examples seem to entail less trivial episodes than the no-smoking rule with which Gouldner typified the pattern of this type of bureaucracy. Price fixing, rigged contracting, dishonest advertising and insider dealing are among the violations performed by individuals and organizations which vehemently advocate the principles they themselves violate. These individuals or organizations seem to mock not only their own internal rules but also the very set of values upon which their power and status are based. Among these are the principles governing fair competition.

A case which entered the literature on corporate crime regards a colossal price-fixing operation involving two of the largest electric corporations in the USA (Geis, 1968). Cases of dishonest advertising involving large European organizations also exemplify this type of offending. For example, the National Westminster Bank was fined in connection with misleading advertising for a business expansion scheme it was promoting (*The Financial Times*, 2 August 1993). The advertisement urged the purchase of shares which falsely promised an annualized return of nearly 30 per cent. Another example is the fine levied by the European Commission on steel firms in France, Germany, Spain, Britain, Italy, and Luxembourg for 'a very serious, illegal price-fixing' (Palmer and Bannister, 1994). The Commission imposed a total fine of more than £80 million.

In similar cases it is not rare for the managers punished to justify their anti-competitive practices by appealing to the exigencies of free enterprise (Conklin, 1977).

Industrial espionage is another example of how the paladins of the free market perhaps do not actually believe in such freedom. The sales director of Volkswagen was proven to have taken with him important information concerning the future plans of General Motors, a company by which he was previously employed (*Le Monde*, 11 August 1993). He was accused of systematically transmitting secret documents detailing GM's future plans, including car models, production, and purchasing strategy. He did so before, during and after moving to Volkswagen (The *Guardian*, 3 September 1993). A case of espionage which deserves to be highlighted occurred in Spain. Although arrests have been made for this case, investigation is still under way at the time of writing, which is the reason why the public prosecutor I interviewed required anonymity.

Case 12

Six former members of the military intelligence service, including a general, were arrested for illegal phone-tapping. The public prosecutor investigating this case said:

> These men had been hired by a media magnate who had received threats from the Basque separatist movement. After leaving the army they had set up a private investigative agency, and the material we have found proves that they specialized in phone-tapping. Their clients were companies and businessmen who carried out espionage on one another. When employed by the media magnate, whom they were supposed to protect from terrorist attacks, they also tapped his phone. They sold information about him to other clients and information about other clients to him. The investigation of this case generated a 'bugging psychosis' because all powerful people were scared of either being bugged or accused of bugging their competitors or enemies. However, the amounts of tape-recorded conversations that we found proved that this security firm did not limit its job to what was commissioned to them. In a sense they went independent as to whom and when to phone-tap. Evidence of insider dealing on the stock exchange was found. Moreover, this firm committed

> illegalities even within the illegal job they were doing. A lot of the information they gathered was used for extortion purposes, with the illegal trading and dealings they discovered being held as a blackmail.

* * *

Other examples where the rules officially inspiring free entrepreneurship are treated as 'mock bureaucracies' concern public tendering and contracting. In a report published in 1994, the British Committee of Public Accounts found that all too often the principles of free competition were completely ignored. Examples included the Wessex Regional Health Authority, which contracted services without proper advertising. 'The Authority also allowed a secondee from IBM to advise them on the purchase, without competition, of an IBM computer for £3.3 million, at a time when it could have been purchased for £0.5 million to £1 million less' (Committee of Public Accounts, 1994: xiii). In the same report the cases of corporations based in Milton Keynes were mentioned which encouraged their staff to form private business ventures to undertake work for the corporations under contract.

> By 1987, these ventures had undertaken work worth a total of some £37 million. The limited competition involved in setting up the ventures virtually guaranteed a substantial amount of contract work to those involved; the reliance on 'discreet approaches' to selected firms was unsatisfactory; and publicizing the privatization programme more widely might have secured better value for money, including a wider choice of professional skills. (ibid.: xiii)

Mocking the principle of free entrepreneurship and hampering the freedom of market forces is also epitomized by insider dealing. Unorthodox use of the most important resource for those who operate in the stock market, namely information, is at the basis of this type of offence (Ashe and Counsell, 1993). Insider dealers have also been described as individuals who 'replace trespass with trust, burglary with self-dealing' (Shapiro, 1984). A well-known British example of trading based on an imbalance of information, resulting in one party to the transaction having an advantage over the other party and the public in general, is provided by the Guinness affair.

> The charges involved theft, false accounting, Section 151 of the Companies Act 1985 – which prohibits the purchase of a company's shares with its own money ... and conspiracy to contravene the Prevention of Fraud (Investments) Act 1958, which prohibits the creation of false markets. (Levi, 1991a: 258)

Ideally the price of shares fluctuates according to the performance of companies, that is, their current and prospective profits. But this idyllic free floating market is influenced by news, suppositions and announcements which may be the patrimony of all or only some of the operators. Moreover, news, suppositions and announcements may be fabricated or falsely divulged. For example, a company whose profits are declining may be in the process of being taken over. If a formal announcement of a bid is made, the price of shares will leap and the bidder will have to offer a higher price to take over the company. But the announcement may be informal and false, with the result that the price of shares will increase despite the absence of a prospective purchaser (Bowen, 1994). As already stressed, the typical notion that underpins the accepted definition of insider dealing relies on the illegitimate use of information regarding takeover bids, whereby those who possess this information can buy shares and then wait for the price to leap, and sell when the takeover is accomplished. Examples of this kind are numerous in all European countries. In Britain 104 cases of insider dealings have been reported since 1987. Only 33 were prosecuted and only 16 resulted in a conviction (*The Times*, 15 January 1994). Among those convicted was former Conservative MP Keith Best, who was given a four-month sentence in 1987, and was recently appointed to a government-funded post, as the director of the Immigrants Advisory Service (Donegan, 1993).

The case I should like to highlight occurred in France.

Case 13

In September 1993 seven financiers were given a two-year suspended sentence for fraudulent share dealings regarding the Pechiney–Triangle affair. Confidential information concerning the takeover of Triangle by Pechiney brought a £3 million profit (Greilsamer, 1993). Among the purchasers of the shares were businessmen funding the French Socialist Party, and among those investigated was Mr Beregovoy, who was finance minister between 1988 and 1992. The prosecutor gathered evidence of the offences committed while investigating alleged illegal funding of political parties. He came across this case while drawing a map of the connections between politicians and financiers. He likened insider dealing to sectarian conspiracy, where the tangled network of friendships, partnerships and family bonds provide the structure for this offending to take place. He added:

> The problem with this type of offence is that it is based on the use of no other arm but information. This is *per se* not an offensive weapon, and its circulation is impossible to control. One of the defence lawyers in this case rightly suggested that the stock exchange thrives exactly on this weapon, which consists of rumours, unexpected news, unchecked suppositions and intuitions. Information,

> in his view, is always hypothetical, in the sense that insider dealers may simply hypothesize that a takeover is going to occur. The buyer is never provided with evidence, let alone a written and signed document assuring that the value of shares will leap. Insider dealers, in other words, may be regarded as individuals who sell consultancy, basing themselves on their own private opinion. We were able to prosecute because this 'consultancy' work involved a number of people who were too closely related. We traced some funds which were given to a political party, and then discovered that the 'donor' was a financier who had realized large profits on the stock market. The identification of middlemen, sellers and buyers was therefore relatively easy. True, the whole plot came to our attention because a Lebanese middleman was involved. His defence lawyer claimed that, by the way the investigation was carried out, to be rich and Lebanese constituted enough evidence of guilt. The truth is that our investigation may have initially focused on this defendant, but then the prosecution was only possible after the connections of this gentleman with French financiers and politicians had been unravelled.

* * *

To flout one's own principles is not a characteristic of entrepreneurs and financiers. As I mentioned in the previous chapter, mock bureaucracies are also found in conventional organized crime. A sensational example of this was provided by a turncoat of organized crime *par excellence*, the Sicilian Mafia. Mocking the 'rules of honour', in the confession of Tommaso Buscetta, was one of the most important rules allowing internal cliques within the organization to expand their power. Among those mocked were the rule requiring that killings be agreed within the regional 'commission', and the rule prohibiting men of honour to engage in drugs trafficking and distribution (Arlacchi, 1994a). As noted in the previous chapter, the cliques mocking organizational rules may paradoxically enhance their status by doing so. Those groups within the Mafia which violated the 'code of honour', in effect, did gain power and widespread respect within the organization. But with this example we are in the realm of conventional organized crime, which will be examined in the following chapter. As I have argued throughout, the analysis of this type of offending can also be conducted against the background of organizational theory and the theories of the enterprise.

5 Crime as Work

There is a body of anomalies in the analysis of both white-collar and organized crime. The most obvious anomalies in the study of organized crime 'concern the ethnic stipulations of conventional theory and emerge in attempts to apply a Sicilian-based paradigm to blacks, Hispanics, Orientals, and other groups' (Smith, 1982: 23). These stipulations have long constituted a deadlock for the analysis of conventional criminal groups. Anomalies concerning the study of white-collar and corporate crime, where ethnic specifications are absent, are mainly associated with the occupational role of the perpetrators. In Chapter 1 I discussed the difficulties encountered by criminologists in drawing clear definitional distinctions between corporate criminals and professional thieves. We have also seen the controversial interpretations and elaborations occasioned by Sutherland's statement that 'white-collar crime *is* organized crime'.

It has been argued that a fruitful response to these anomalies lies in a unified approach to organized crime, white-collar and corporate crime, a response which is not based on the status of the offender, but on the motives and methods of the offence (Calavita and Pontell, 1993). In the previous chapter cases of white-collar and corporate crime have been analysed through categories which belong to the fields of organizational theory and the theory of the enterprise. The same categories will be used in this chapter to describe examples of conventional organized crime in Europe.

Trust: A Red Herring

In describing organizational behaviour, Thompson (1967) identifies two distinct strategies. The first he terms a closed-system strategy, one which implies the search for certainty in a changing environment. The second is defined as an open-system strategy, and implies the incorporation of uncertainty within the organization. In the latter perspective, the organization recognizes its interdependence with the environment in which it operates. This is riddled with the risks and challenges posed by the market-place. The dynamics of the market require that the related risks are dealt with through specific organizational responses. This argument brings us back to the analysis of Knight (1921), who suggests that the immorality of profits is somehow absolved through the risks incurred by entrepreneurs and the responsibility they take in initiating and co-ordinating a productive process. The German term *Unternehmer* and the English *undertaker* also referred to individuals engaging their capital and energies in an extremely uncertain environment (Gallino, 1975).

Conventional organized crime faces an environment in which risk and uncertainty are compounded by the illegal nature of their undertakings. However, the variables risk and uncertainty play here a more complex role. The goods and services provided by organized criminal groups may contribute to the reduction of the uncertainty and risks experienced by those who demand them. For example, when organized criminal groups give continuity to the provision of illegal drugs, they resolve the problems related with the uncertain and irregular availability of these goods in the illegal market. Conventional organized crime, therefore, would seem to take risks in order to partly indemnify the risks incurred by its customers. An example of this dynamic is provided by protection rackets, where the role of organized crime apparently consists of guaranteeing the safety and smoothness of the environment in which businesses operate. It has been argued that in these cases the commodity sold is 'trust', a commodity which may be lacking in certain areas or periods (Gambetta, 1992). At first sight, the case presented below might be understood in these terms. It concerns the eastern area of Europe, where the tumultuous changes of the last few years and the establishment of a free-market economy are taking place in an environment unaccustomed to private economic initiative and the related trust.

Case 14

There are two rival organized groups operating in Warsaw. The former is called the 'Wolomin Group', and is named after the area where its leader grew up. The latter is known as the 'Pruszkow Mafia' from the affluent west of the city. Its leading figure calls himself 'Pershing', presumably in honour of the missile whose power he tries to emulate (Borger, 1994). The two groups are engaged in a constant territorial battle over protection money imposed on businesses. This battle includes kidnapping members of the rival gang and holding them for ransom. In Poland, protection rackets developed in the early 1990s, and according to official agencies it was almost non-existent before 1 January 1990, when 'capitalism was declared' (Marek, 1993). In the new climate of uncertainty, protection rackets supposedly filled the vacuum caused by the disappearance of state-controlled markets. Difficulties in adopting the rules of competition within a free-market economy forced businesses into seeking alternative ways of establishing a safe environment in which to operate. What is interesting about this case is the entrepreneurial character of this activity and its far-sightedness. The protection racket in Poland is not an end in itself, nor does it constitute a distinct stage in the development of organized crime. It has been argued that extortion activities are either independent of other criminal businesses or constitute a phase of accumulation eventually leading to new undertakings (Peterson, 1991). In Poland the protection racket business is linked from the outset to a variety of other illegal businesses. Protection money, for example, is frequently invested in illegal distilleries and in the expanding market of forged documents. The case of Poland, therefore, contradicts the assumption that organized crime goes through distinct phases where predatory, parasitic and finally entrepreneurial crimes respectively prevail (Peterson, 1991). Polish organized groups involved in extortion were proven to have associates operating in the USA, where a number of their members faced criminal proceedings for counterfeiting currency, passports, drivers' licences, immigration papers, social security cards, and birth certificates (Myers, 1991).

* * *

Extortion rackets are in operation in many European countries. For example, many leisure businesses are hit by this activity in the south of France, as well as in the larger Dutch and German cities (Calvi, 1994; van der Heijden, 1993). In England, where these rackets also operate, it is particularly difficult to quantify the phenomenon. This is due, among other things, to the virtual impossibility of distinguishing between cases of fraudulent insurance arson, when businesses are burned down by their proprietors, and racket arson, with businesses being burned down when their owners fail to keep up payments (The *Guardian*, 22 June 1991). In Italy, an estimated 15 per cent of businesses at the national level pay protection money. In some southern regions of the country the percentage is around 50 per cent (Censis, 1992).

However, protection rackets cannot simply be seen as providing 'trust' in situations where this 'commodity' is scarce. As we have seen in the previous case, protection money is invested in a number of other activities which are not parasitic in nature. Moreover, in some contexts extortion is aimed to partly or totally control the businesses which it victimizes. For example, businesses which fail to keep up payments may be offered to establish partnerships with extortionists. They may also be bought up completely if the financial situation of the victim is desperate. In these cases, the price of the 'merger' or the complete 'takeover' constitutes the last stage of the extortion process itself (Mancuso, 1990). In other cases, insolvent entrepreneurs who are exhausted both emotionally and materially by the extortion racket may be exempted from payment if they agree to 'invest' in ventures whose nature they officially pretend to ignore. These investments are frequently directed into the drugs economy (Ruggiero, 1995). Criminal entrepreneurs, in such cases, act like Sombart's speculators to which I referred earlier. They both exert fear and offer hope. They carry others along and involve them in their 'dreams' (Sombart, 1915). In these cases risk is shared with other actors and, contrary to the suggestions of Knight (1921), the marginalized condition of criminal entrepreneurs and the uncertainty of their status are partly neutralized by the alliance they establish with more officially powerful actors.

The Work Discipline of Theft

It should be reiterated that conventional organized crime does not confine its activities to a parasitical collection of 'taxes' in exchange for protection and trust. The undertakings of most organized criminal groups in Europe fall in the realm of the productive or the commercial sectors, characterized as they are by either the production or the circulation of illicit goods. In this sense, the offer of protection or trust by conventional organized crime is part of what Perrow (1961) describes as the official goals of such criminality, the operative goal being instead the expansion into new productive or commercial businesses. The example that follows is one such business. The reason for highlighting this case will be clearer when an attempt is made to identify some common characteristics shared by organized criminal groups. In choosing this case I bore in mind Smith's notion that the description of organized crime should avoid the application of a Sicilian-based paradigm to all variants of this type of offending.

Case 15

Estimates from the 1992 British Crime Survey suggest that the vast majority of the 15 million offences committed in England and Wales for that year were property crimes. Burglary and theft of or from vehicles were the most common offences. The proportion of stolen goods recovered was said to be declining, which would suggest an increased willingness on the part of the general public to purchase stolen second-hand goods. The number of stolen cars recovered also declined, 'indicating that theft of cars for other purposes (stripping, resale, export, etc.) is increasing more steeply than those used for "joyriding"' (Mayhew et al., 1993: xi). The business of stolen goods also includes items stolen from warehouses, factories and retailers. This business, therefore, includes brand new goods that can be sold along with legitimate goods in shops and markets. Purchasers of stolen items range from friends or neighbours of the thief to strangers in pubs (Foster, 1990; Sutton, 1993). More experienced thieves sell at auctions, markets, car boot sales, or through classified advertisements.

> The number of magazines solely concerned with classified advertisements has mushroomed in recent years and car boot sales now seem an immensely popular weekend activity. To what extent these second-hand outlets have provided a new market and so increased theft levels is unknown. (Sutton, 1993: 6–7).

However, an increasing proportion of stolen goods are sold to professional fences, particularly by those thieves who need urgently and constantly to convert goods into cash. Many burglars who intend to make a career out of their thefts may find it necessary to keep permanent contacts with a retailer. The same applies for shoplifters, many of whom in London work to order (Oxford, 1994). Professional fences usually encourage thefts of specific goods, or even particular brands, namely those goods and brands which meet purchasers' demand (Klockars, 1974). In London, professional fencing is not carried out as a sole activity, as fencers may sideline it with licit retail activities.

Car thieves and 'joyriders' may also be attracted into more structured activities. They may contact or be contacted by well-organized groups. They may be instructed by a receiver to strip the cars and provide the parts or to hand over the entire vehicle (Nee, 1993). In an interview carried out by Graef (1993: 54), a young man described how his reputation as a brave joyrider was noticed by prospective 'employers' who ended up offering him a more stable occupation:

> I do it for the money, of course, and for the buzz. They wrote about the chase in the paper. ... So people heard about it and came round asking me if I'd get cars for them. So I started ringing motors – changing the motor numbers – I mean delivering the cars to people who ring them or sell them abroad.

* * *

Among the inherent developments of professional fencing is the organization of theft from large businesses and other large-scale operations. Organized groups may provide information and finances for more complex thefts to be carried out (Walsh, 1977). This is the case with the import/export of stolen cars, a business which involves thieves, but also shipping and container transport companies. Cars stolen in France, for example, are often recovered in the ports of Rotterdam or Antwerp (Stoppelenburg, 1990). Although more expensive, container transport is increasing because it offers the advantage of security and secrecy. Stolen cars are shipped in containers officially loaded with other goods. 'In [one] instance, a number of stolen Mercedes cars were shipped to Sierra Leone in containers that, according to the documentation, contained school equipment being sent out by a well-known and respected charity organization' (Stoppelenburg, 1990: 29).

In Germany a trend has been identified in which car owners 'agree' to their car being stolen. They sell their vehicle to illegal exporters and once this reaches the country of destination, they report the car stolen. The owners, in these cases, are 'able to replace the "stolen" vehicle with a better, up-market model due to receiving both money from the sale of the car and an insurance payout' (Stoppelenburg, 1990: 28).

As we saw in Chapter 3, a number of rationalizations can be mobilized which render entrepreneurs 'venial sinners'. Among these is the description of entrepreneurs as altruistic perpetrators, as they mobilize other people's initiative and participation. Knight (1935), for example, points to the promotion of labour and the production and circulation of goods, all of which go beyond the individual benefits of entrepreneurs. In the case discussed above, the groups and individuals who co-ordinate and promote the acquisition and circulation of stolen goods seem to fit Knight's description, their 'altruism' being even more pronounced, one could argue, due to the condition of illegality in which they operate.

Merchants and Thieves

The following case concerns criminal entrepreneurs adopting innovative strategies and discovering the potential of new markets. In Schumpeter's terms, business is innovative when economic factors are arranged in a new combination, for example, new markets are identified and a new organizational set-up is consistently arranged.

Case 16

A transport company whose office was located in the port of Marseilles was prosecuted for cigarette contraband. This company bought directly from manufacturers and claimed that the cigarettes were destined for African and Latin-American countries. In this way it benefited from Customs rules and concessions given to businesses exporting outside the European Union. In reality, American-manufactured cigarettes were destined for European markets, where untaxed goods are sold (Calvi, 1994). The goods were sent by container to Philip Morris warehouses based in Belgium or Switzerland. From here, instead of being shipped to the official destination outside Europe, they were collected by transport firms operating in Belgium or Switzerland and diverted to Marseilles. Here, containers were unloaded and the cigarettes re-loaded on lorries destined for a number of European countries. According to a turncoat of the organization, business was proceeding so well that soon the establishment of another branch of the company would have been necessary. Saint-Raphaël was the designated town for the new branch. A number of customs officers working on the borders between France and the confining countries were also prosecuted in this case (Calvi, 1994). The interesting aspect of the case lies in the international nature of the organization involved. Among the distributors who bought in Marseilles were entrepreneurs operating in Spain, Italy, Germany, and Poland. A judge interviewed in Berlin, for example, said that cigarette middle-range distributors operating in the city were supplied by transport firms trading with France.

> These distributors resell to smaller groups or directly to street sellers. Among the smaller groups are those resident in the former East Germany who commute for business reasons. Commuters also include street sellers, who come to what was formerly known as West Berlin in the morning, and go back to the East in the evening. Selling cigarettes is also one of the only occupational options available to some illegal immigrants or refugees. I have investigated a case where Polish illegal immigrants acted as agents of criminal groups operating in Poland. These immigrants sold contraband cigarettes in Germany, and at the same time were the contacts of groups of importers based in Poland.

* * *

This case suggests that changes in the pattern of cigarette contraband in Europe may have recently occurred. During the 1960s French organizations enjoyed a virtual monopoly in the distribution. This monopoly ended when Italian groups, who previously controlled only retail distribution in their own towns, were in a position to commit themselves to large-scale investments and establish their presence in all spheres of organization and distribution. The entire cycle of 'trade' could now be mastered, from purchase of commodities abroad through wholesale distribution to street sale (Pizzorno and Arlacchi, 1985). Attempts were even made to set up local units producing 'American' cigarettes, whereby for example in Naples smokers would specify whether they wanted an 'Original American Contraband' or simply a 'Neapolitan Contraband' brand (Ruggiero, 1993b; Casillo, 1990). The case highlighted above seems to suggest that the Italian monopoly in contraband cigarettes is also declining, as new forms of multinational partnerships are being established. In the case described, the presence of criminal entrepreneurs from a number of European countries indicates the expansion of markets into the former Soviet bloc. In the new situation partnerships may have become necessary, as the previous smuggling networks proved insufficient. For example, before the opening of the new Eastern European markets, Italian distributors would buy cigarettes in Switzerland and limit risky movements to the crossing of the border between that country and Italy. With the potential offered by the new markets, the role of agents based in other staging countries became central. This led to partnerships with locally established groups in places outside Italy, including subsidiaries operating in the new markets themselves.

The high degree of innovation involved in this case is apparent in the way in which a monopolistic position was broken down, while a condition of oligopoly was established: an ideal implementation of Schumpeterian 'discontinuity' in the arrangement of economic combinations. In analysing this case the restlessness of Hermes also comes to mind. As McClelland (1961) argues, Hermes is an astute merchant but also a thief; he avoids repetition, he innovates, but is also a trickster. Anecdotal evidence shows that the new partnerships between criminal groups are tainted by mutual theft and overall dishonesty in transactions. Lorries destined for Poland, for example, are occasionally stolen or highjacked in Germany by suspiciously well-informed gangs.

Your Bag and Your Life

Money is among the goods provided by organized crime. For a number of circumstances which will be sketched in the following case, the illicit provision of this good is becoming pre-eminent in countries such as Italy. This contemporary form of usury retains all the ambiguity with which it was regarded before the banking system was established (Le Goff, 1987). As explained in the discussion of this case, the legal definition of this offence is blurred, though the very term usury still exists in the Italian criminal code. The vagueness of the legal definition puts perpetrators in a Purgatory where, as Le Goff argues, they will be able to save both their money and their (eternal) life.

Case 17

In Italy, an estimated 4 million businesses are the clients/victims of loan sharks (Sammarco, 1994). Although stigmatized by the Catholic Church and by Dante Alighieri, usury contributed to the early development of Italy in the aftermath of the unification of the country. The formation of a class of financiers was favoured, among other things, by the availability of parallel financial markets. Purchasers of Church land, which was put up for sale, made a constant recourse to these markets (Fiasco, 1994). The recent development of this unofficial market can be attributed to a number of circumstances. First, with the economic recession between the late 1980s and the early 1990s, many small and medium-range entrepreneurs were faced with the choice of either closing down or diversifying their activity. Because unpredicted lower profits made them heavily indebted to official financial institutions, entrepreneurs resorted to the illicit money market to either pay back their debts or start new activities. Second, the collapse of the Italian currency in international financial markets in 1992 forced banks to urgently claim back their credits from prime lenders. This was accompanied by unprecedented restrictions of the criteria governing new credit (Centorrino, 1994).

The typology of contemporary usurers can be broadly outlined as follows. There are professionals who earn more than officially claimed, and entrust their money to mediators or agencies involved in moneylending. Discretion guarantees that the actual financiers of these enterprises remain unknown. There are agencies linked to official banks, from which they receive credit and pass it over to their own customers. In this way, the official bank does not deal with lenders directly, and risks are directly incurred by such agencies. There are also banks which, after rejecting applications for credit, offer applicants alternative sources of credit, and put them in contact with agencies or individual moneylenders (Centorrino, 1994). Finally, there are organized criminal groups laundering their proceeds through usury. These groups may target businesses which appear to be experiencing financial difficulties, and through the offer of a loan and the predictable impossibility of repayment, aim at the acquisition of the business itself.

Loan sharks who offer services to businesses experiencing difficulties are often regarded as 'benefactors'. In such cases, clients and service providers establish a mute agreement which in a sense justifies the high interest rates. Lenders can claim they run high risks, both in terms of the money they commit and *vis-à-vis* law enforcement agencies. However, legislation in this field is easy to sidestep, because the crime described as 'usury' entails knowledge on the part of the lender of the financial difficulties experienced by his/her client, difficulties that the lender intentionally exploits. Lacking evidence of this knowledge, no proceedings can be initiated. Another difficulty for prosecutors lies in the fact that neither the criminal code nor any piece of administrative legislation establish the rate of interest beyond which banking can be defined as usury.

The case of illicit moneylending came to public attention in 1992, when the victims formed an association and established a 'rescue telephone line' for those persecuted by loan sharks. This was the result of a number of suicides allegedly committed by the victims of usury. The association demanded that the Italian state create an anti-usury fund for those so victimized. In Rome, between October 1992 and June 1993, 1300 cases of usury received a court hearing (Fiasco, 1994). As stressed above, insolvent businesses may be forced to sell their premises or goods to those who lent them money. When this involves conventional criminal groups usury is deemed to be part and parcel of the extortion industry, with contiguity and even overlap between criminal groups practising extortion and those practising usury (Colussi and Silvestri, 1994). Many businesses may resort to usury in order to pay protection money (Censis, 1992). The specific sector of the industry of usury controlled by conventional criminal groups is said to employ about 8000 individuals, including money collectors, mediators and squads specializing in 'warning' those in debt.

* * *

Although usually listed among the activities of conventional organized crime, loan-sharking is not given a central position in these activities. Moreover, the hypothesis that loan-sharks aim at gaining control of their customers' business is treated with scepticism (Rubinstein and Reuter, 1978). However, in the United States it has been noted that, with the end of Prohibition and the onset of the Great Depression, criminal groups 'found themselves in the enviable position of having a great deal of excess cash in a cash-starved economy, and this gave them an important source of continued income' (Abadinsky, 1990: 288). The case examined above confirms this analysis, although in a different context and time. It also echoes the experience of Joseph Valachi, who lent money to a legitimate businessman and eventually became his partner because the loan could not be repaid (Maas, 1968). Incidently, with Valachi's financial support and his ability to keep labour unions from organizing the factory, the business prospered (Abadinsky, 1990: 290).

Contemporary usury in Italy, as we have seen, does not only involve conventional organized crime, but also official actors. These may be the representatives of and be employed by members of organized crime, or may engage in loan-sharking independently. Conventional organized crime may be willing to deal with illegitimate lenders such as criminal entrepreneurs, and use 'clean' intermediaries to deal with legitimate entrepreneurs. Despite the unwritten code according to which usury is 'dishonourable', this activity is evolving into a corollary of other activities such as money laundering.

Like the 'rules' prohibiting centrally non-agreed killings and investments into illegal drugs referred to in the previous chapter, the rule prohibiting loan-sharking may be seen by conventional organized crime as part of a 'mock bureaucracy'. Therefore, in the daily conduct of business, the paraphernalia of this bureaucracy are ignored because inoperative (Gouldner, 1954).

Cui bono?

One of the criteria which permit the classification of organizational goals is identified by Blau and Scott (1963) as being: *cui bono?* – 'who benefits?' In the case highlighted below this question defies straightforward answers. As we have seen, some types of organization may benefit their members or participants, others their owners, others their clients, or the public at large. Earlier, I suggested that organizations engaged in deviant behaviour frequently attempt to portray the beneficiaries of their deviance as others than themselves. Let us see how successful this attempt is when it is made by organizations involved in a specific illicit production.

Case 18

In May 1990 thousands of Opium perfume bottles were seized in Spain. They were fakes produced, wittingly or otherwise, through the participation of a number of countries. 'A European co-production, this was assembled in Britain, using Spanish bottles, Dutch tops, Italian boxes and French perfume' (Thomas, 1990: 24). Fakes, mainly of perfumes, clothing, watches and leather goods, are produced and sold in a number of European countries. France's luxury goods industry is particularly hit: 7 out of 10 fakes are of French products, causing the textile industry alone to lose up to FF30 billion a year (Christie, 1994). Companies vulnerable to the 'competition' of fakes also include the record, motoring and medicine industries. Fake car components are widely available and difficult to detect by vendors, who may at times even be aware of the forged goods they are buying, but may nevertheless be prepared to purchase them because of lower prices. One in every three audio tapes sold worldwide is said to be an unauthorized copy. In 1990, the pharmaceutical firm Glaxo introduced a new hologram on its packets of the Zantac ulcer drug, which was virtually impossible to copy. Their action followed the seizure of 6000 counterfeit packets of the drug in Greece earlier the same year (Thomas, 1990). The medicine also found its way to the UK, the Netherlands and Switzerland. Many watches on sale in Italy read 'Made in Switzerland', but are made in Italy and contain lead to give them weight. Gucci T-shirts on sale in the streets of London are in fact bought in Turkey for 25p each (Thomas, 1990). The European market is 'flooded' by high-quality forgeries of Wedgwood ceramics whose quality is so good that even experts have been fooled (Alberge, 1994). Forging them is not difficult, as Wedgwood's potting techniques and the make-up of the materials are well known to potters, having been published. A judge in Paris said that many bars in the city serve illegally produced alcohol. He added: 'Liquor wholesalers stock both the real brands and the fake ones under the same label. They provide bars and discos with the variety the owners want. Illegally produced liquors include cognac and whisky'.

Once allegedly the preserve of illegal entrepreneurs based in the Far East, the production of counterfeit goods is said to have moved to European countries. A member of a British investigation unit said: 'It's got so bad you can go into *any* mill *anywhere* in Lancashire and you'll find someone counterfeiting' (Tredre, 1994). The police fear the industry is turning increasingly violent: 'When rival counterfeit gangs clashed in Manchester last year, a man was found attached to an advertising hoarding, nailed through his hands and feet' (Tredre, 1994).

Good-quality counterfeiting 'can sometimes be a long-term benefit in publicizing brand names, which in turn encourages legitimate purchasers of market leaders' (Levi, 1987: 44). The investigation of a judge I interviewed in Rome was concerned with a similar aspect of the counterfeiting business. But his hypothesis stretched well beyond the propaganda aspect. He said:

> Many purchasers are aware of the fact that they are buying forged goods, for example clothes. Nevertheless, they buy them because they are cheaper, and sometimes they are all right. This awareness equals that of official producers, who may think that the market of forged goods is too large to be ignored. In brief, some producers may come to an agreement with illicit producers and in a sense they may sell their label. In other cases, perhaps, they may decide to start an in-house production of their own counterfeit goods. In this way they can both sell their high-quality products and an inferior quality of the same products, in order to have access to both the official and the illegal market.

* * *

The development of the industry of counterfeit goods is caused by the monopolist position of producers, who ideally would enjoy exclusive rights in manufacturing and distributing certain goods (Mossetto, 1993). Producers may defend themselves by either prosecuting the counterfeiters or strictly labelling each good manufactured. In both cases the expenditure falls on consumers, while the monopolist position of producers is strengthened. This, in turn, may provide even more incentive to the counterfeit industry. In the countries of the European Union this illicit economy is estimated to employ around 100,000 individuals (Comité Colbert, 1992).

This case reveals how the criterion 'who benefits?' can be used by both licit and illicit organizations, both being in a position to claim that their deviant behaviour benefits those they victimize. As I argued in Chapter 3, licit organizations involved in criminal conduct can claim that their employees are indirect beneficiaries because jobs are retained thanks to the employers' deviance. Think, for example, of industries producing harmful commodities or disregarding safety regulations, or those paying lower wages than statutorily established, or even industries illegally exporting their products. Their violations of the law may be seen as benefiting employees, because in one way or another they keep them on the payroll. Similarly, as it has been suggested, large firms may benefit from the production of counterfeit goods by criminal organizations. Moreover, if the suspicion of the judge cited above eventually proves to be founded, we would face paradoxical examples of firms committing fraud against themselves. But in apparently victimizing themselves, they would in fact be trying to recapture the gains of those who victimize them. In other words, these firms would attempt to channel within their own profits the profits of crimes committed against them.

This case displays opposite dynamics to cases of corporate crime examined in the previous chapter. We have seen examples of firms operating in industrialized countries which transfer their productive apparatus, or sell their final products, in developing countries. Here, uncertainty and the lack of a deep-seated market culture almost justify their bending of the rules. As I have argued, in environments presenting risks, the stretching of moral values constitutes a sort of compensation for those who take those risks. Moreover, in these environments values themselves may differ and their violation may be deemed an acceptable price to pay in exchange for 'development'. By contrast, in the case of counterfeit goods immorality and illegality are not exported or transferred outside, but are incorporated within official and moral practices. The business of forged goods has moved from the Far East to European countries: developed countries could not allow the profits involved in this business to be retained outside their territories.

Competing in Crime

All this bears a striking resemblance to episodes occurring within the illicit drugs economy. In his 1993 presidential address to the American Academy of Criminal Justice Sciences, Robert Bohm (1993) focused almost entirely on the 'war on drugs' and its effects. The increase of drug use and related offences were said to be a by-product of this war. This ironic outcome is exemplified by the fact that 'despite the interdiction efforts of the US government over the last decade, the availability of powder cocaine has increased tenfold, its purity has quintupled, and its price has dropped' (Bohm, 1993: 531). It can be argued that the war on drugs was inspired by the desire to restore traditional international roles, with the developed countries claiming their historic role of producers rather than mere consumers. As a consequence, there is an increasing production of illicit drugs in the industrialized countries both for their own use and for others. The increased availability of drugs such as cocaine, and the unprecedented purity of this drug found in American inner cities, are due, among other things, to the development of nationally based industries producing drugs both for their domestic market and for foreign importers. With the dramatic increase in drug users in the developing countries, the traditional division of roles is restored: the poor provide raw materials and buy the finished product from the rich.

This example brings us to developments occurring in the former Soviet Union, where forms of organized crime are said to be thriving in the chaotic situation caused by the collapse of Communism. The establishment of a market economy in the former USSR, a process which is far from complete, produced a number of problems including unemployment, the increasing poverty of large sectors of the population, the collapse of the welfare system, and a sharp decline in living standards. Not surprisingly, the profound economic crisis was also reflected by the severe deterioration in the morbidity and mortality of the population (Ellman, 1994). The movement towards a market economy also caused an unprecedented wave of economic and organized crime. Almost 40 per cent of money circulating in Russia is thought to have been generated by illegal activity. Finally, the murder rate increased by 40 per cent between 1991 and 1993 (Blundy, 1994).

The activities of Russian organized groups range from the protection racket to trafficking in stolen cars, and the illegal import and export of all goods including arms, radioactive materials and drugs. These activities are creating vast new wealth for entrepreneurs, both legal and illegal, which is also visible in new businesses being established by Russians in European countries such as Germany. Other European countries have set up investigative units with the task of foiling attempts by Russian criminal groups to launder proceeds in their territories (Kelsey, 1994).

Organized crime was officially recognized by the Soviet government in the December 1989 speech of the then minister of internal affairs (Serio, 1991). However, if the recent exploits of organized crime in the former Soviet Union is the result of development related to the emerging free-market economy, forms of organized crime were also in operation from the outset of the Bolshevik Revolution. Comparisons with the Soviet era are not easy to make because, as is widely known, criminal justice practitioners, unable to eradicate crime, were forced to 'tamper with data on reported and cleared offences' (Nikiforov, 1994: 11). Kapuscinski (1994), who limits his historical analysis to the Communist era, identifies in the millions of young people and children who became homeless in the aftermath of the Revolution the ancestors of Russian organized crime. Many of these young people who could not be looked after by the state became professional thieves. A substantial section of them were recruited for surveillance purposes in concentration camps.

> The grandfathers of contemporary Mafia members in Russia are exactly these kids without a roof and often without a name. This is an important characteristic of post-Soviet society: it is the presence not so much of isolated delinquents, but an entire criminal category with a genealogy and a tradition which are completely different from the rest of society. (Kapuscinski, 1994: 170)

The devastation of the Second World War, the corruption of the Stalinist and Brezhnevian systems, and finally the collapse of Communism, all contributed to the structuring of these groups and their increasing influence. In this transitional society, where institutions of arbitration are still non-existent, the path of force is said to emerge. 'Weapons of all sorts have appeared on the black market, including armoured trucks and tanks, owing to the disintegration of the old superpower and the loosening of discipline in the army.... It is easier in this country to get a pistol and a grenade than a shirt or a cap' (Kapuscinski, 1994: 111).

Russian organized crime is not only involved in conventional criminal activities, its main characteristic being the ability to establish links with bureaucrats and licit entrepreneurs (Nikiforov, 1994; Róna-Tas, 1994). However, for the purpose of the argument developed in this chapter, the following case concerns a typically conventional criminal activity, namely the production and marketing of illegal drugs.

Case 19

It has been hypothesized that convertibility of the rouble could result in a large flow of Western hard drugs such as cocaine, heroin or crack into European Russia (Lee, 1992). Journalistic accounts claim that Western organized criminals have already started the 'promotional' distribution of these drugs at low prices (Vulliamy, 1992). This 'virgin' market is said to have enormous potential, as a multitude of young people are prepared to experiment with anything which comes from the West. However, according to reports from the Soviet Ministry of Internal Affairs, around 1.5 million individuals had already used drugs before the USSR itself collapsed. Throughout the 1980s, the average Soviet drug user was male, less than 30 years of age, employed, and fairly well educated (Lee, 1992). The most popular illicit drugs were hashish, marijuana, morphine, koknar (ground poppy straw), and opium. In Kazakhstan poppy straw extracts were as popular as hashish, and in the Soviet Union as a whole the drug culture was more opium-centred than in the West.

An important aspect of the drug economy was that

> home-brewed drugs such as koknar and khimka (a more refined version of koknar that is injected rather than ingested) seemingly account for a significant share of the Soviet drug market. In contrast, in the West, refined narcotics are widely available, so users have less incentive to manufacture their own drugs. (Lee, 1992: 182)

The collapse of the Soviet Union, therefore, found a drug market already receptive and relatively well developed. What changed after the opening of the borders was the pattern of use and the correspondent production and distribution. The Kazakhstan/Tajikistan area already had a tradition of drug crop production. Here, as well as in Kyrgyzstan, suggestions were made to legalize the cultivation of drugs. 'But bowing to international pressure and the threat of curtailment of foreign assistance, these countries subsequently outlawed drug production' (Shelley, 1994: 18). As a consequence, Moscow-based criminal groups intensified commercial contacts with the drug-producing areas, and soon the manufacturing of drugs became similar to that prevailing in Western countries. The appearance of synthetic drugs was increasingly recorded, and illegal laboratories producing amphetamines, morphine and heroin were discovered. It was also suggested that expanded contacts with the West would result in new opportunities for transferring drug-manufacturing technology to the former Soviet Union. In this way, rather than Western criminal groups feeding the East with drugs, Russian-based criminal groups seem now able to provide the West with their own drug products (Lee, 1992).

The increased demand for drugs and higher prices have caused the subsequent increase in users committing crime to support the financial costs of their habit, because 'the average Russian worker's monthly wage might not be sufficient to cover the cost of a single gram of opium' (Lee, 1992: 191). In the meantime, large manufacturing and distributing organizations emerged which displayed signs of internal specialization. Infrastructures were developed including transportation facilities, weapons, and communication equipment. A demarcation of roles similar to that displayed by Western variants of organized crime appeared between leaders, middlemen, couriers, manufacturers, distributors, informants, treasurers, security guards, money launderers (Urvantsev, 1990). Most importantly, a rigid division of labour was established whereby the badly paid work of production was left in the less economically developed areas. These areas, mainly inhabited by ethnic minorities and with high rates of unemployment, are associated in the official rhetoric with the core of the drug problem. On the other hand, the refining and distributing operations became the preserve of Russian groups, who also launder the proceeds. These groups are therefore dependent on the labour of the less-developed regions of the former Soviet territory.

* * *

The process just described shows similarities with developments in other drug-producing countries. Here, groups involved in the growth and sale of unrefined drugs slowly appreciated the enormous exchange value of the crops they were handling. They also understood that, by growing and refining drugs in their own territory, part of the added value produced would remain with them. As a consequence, the large availability of refined drugs in the producing countries caused the spread of these drugs among the younger generation, who slowly shifted from the use of natural traditional drugs such as opium or coca leaves to heroin and cocaine (Ruggiero, 1992a). In Russia, the younger generation seems to adopt a pattern of use and a drug culture which were long established in North America and Western Europe. In the former USSR traditional recreational use and home-based production are declining, while a hierarchical structure in the production and distribution of drugs is emerging. This structure is similar in many European countries, and it is to its broad description that the next section is devoted.

There are some characteristics which can be regarded as the hallmark of organized crime. These are particularly vivid in the drugs economy, which is why this specific economy deserves to be dealt with more extensively than others. Therefore, the following analysis may help to provide a definition of organized crime, which will be formulated in the concluding pages of this chapter.

The De-skilling of Criminal Work

In Europe the explosion of the drug phenomenon over the last two decades significantly altered the profile of criminal business (Ruggiero and South, 1995). New characteristics emerged within the criminal economies, which developed varying forms and degrees of organization. In Britain, for example, many commentators indicate the early 1980s as a turning-point for drug distribution. Supply, which was locally centred and poorly structured, became increasingly organized and regularized (Stimson, 1987). The explosion of the heroin phenomenon is said to have favoured this shift, which is commonly also described in relation to the variety of the substances available on the market and the respective producing countries. Chinese, Iranian and Pakistani illicit drugs successively predominated in the markets of British cities, a circumstance which leads many observers to investigate the trafficking routes and the criminal enterprises connected to these producing countries. This may have favoured the construction of an 'alien conspiracy' theory with regard to the drug business in Britain.

However, it is to be noted that import operations and distribution are not likely to be undertaken by the same groups. It is true that a large majority of apprehended importers and couriers are foreign nationals (Green, 1991). But these, often improvised, importers are in no position to master the distribution network in their host country. Therefore, they are forced to sell consignments to established local figures with whom they end up establishing business on a permanent basis. These local figures act as wholesalers and, after buying from importers, pass on quantities of drugs to a number of locally based middle-range distributors.

Some wholesalers are reported to have been previously engaged in armed robberies (Dorn et al., 1992). Presumably, they never managed to invest the proceeds of their raids in legitimate business, and their shift towards drugs was encouraged by the increasing use of firearms on the part of the police (Taylor, 1984). Drugs were welcomed as a long-overdue chance to put guns away. Journalistic accounts also suggest that, after an initial resistance to drug dealing, some professional criminals 'soon realized that here was a new way of making money that required no getaway car and ran less risk of informers. It had the added advantage that there was no victim running to the police' (Campbell, 1990: 5).

Middle-range distributors are in contact with specific communities where street dealers operate. Research suggests that at this level of drug distribution individuals and groups are found who are already involved in a variety of activities in the so-called irregular economy. This economy provides those who inhabit it with a 'facilitating subculture', but also with precise skills, structures and roles. 'The irregular economy provides multiple conduits for the distribution and exchange of drugs, and for a variety of other goods and services, prostitution, the disposal of stolen goods, and so on' (Auld et al., 1986: 172). It also provides a position within its structure which is modelled upon a more or less strict division of labour. It is my contention that the conversion of part of this irregular economy to the drug business made its internal division of labour increasingly rigid. Research, including my own, proves that those who benefit from this conversion are mainly individuals who already held an entrepreneurial or managerial position in the irregular economy, whereas those whose role was confined to the provision of 'pure criminal labour' experience, with the shift to drugs, an exacerbation of their economic dependence.

Many users experiment with drugs while inhabiting the irregular economy, where drugs add to other illicit goods already circulating. Those who develop habitual use, and in particular those who resort to property crime as a result of this, become increasingly dependent on that economy which provides them with both the doses and the market where their stolen goods are circulated. Often, they are forced to give up their 'wage', as transactions take on a non-monetary nature. The exchange therefore may not entail the trinomial 'good–money–drug', but simply the binomial 'good–drug'.

The illegal activities conducted by this type of user imply an immutable pattern of tasks within a career which is virtually stagnant. Users who have been followed up in their career show how their frenetic activities do not translate into upward mobility. A revolving-door situation prevents them from improving their skills. This also applies to users who were not 'working' in the irregular economy prior to their drug-using career: their lack of apprenticeship keeps them at the bottom of the drug hierarchy (Ruggiero, 1992a; 1993c; 1995).

In the drug economy, therefore, we witness the creation of an inexperienced 'army' of users and small dealers who service the market. This, on the other hand, shows a drive towards more structured and professional operations at the top of the distribution hierarchy. This specific division of labour, and the pattern of activities which are part of the drugs economy in England, describe a variant of organized crime which is found elsewhere in Europe. Let us examine, for example, the case of Italy.

The involvement of Italian organized crime in the drug economy dates back to the 1950s. One of the first large seizures occurred in 1952, when 6kg of heroin were found in the area between Palermo and Trapani (Santino and La Fiura, 1993). Among those arrested were distributors residing both in Sicily and the USA. Other traffickers and wholesale distributors operated in the north of Italy, where some industrialists managed to divert quantities of heroin from the legal to the illegal market. According to the Anti-Mafia Commission set up by the Italian parliament, for a period Lucky Luciano obtained drugs from these 'licit' dealers of pharmaceuticals (Commissione Antimafia, 1976; Pantaleone, 1976). When a laboratory for the processing of heroin was discovered near Milan, it was clear that Italian criminal groups also purchased the substance in the producing countries and, after refining it in Italy, exported it to the USA. This pattern of activity was destined to remain unaltered until a proper heroin market developed in Italy around the early 1970s.

It was during the course of the 1970s and the 1980s that the participation of organized crime in the drug economy assumed new characteristics. Judge Falcone's investigation proved that decisions regarding involvement in illegal drugs were never taken centrally, but were the result of personal initiative (Falcone, 1991). In other words, the drug business gave the old Mafia families the opportunity to claim independence from so-called consortia, commissions or *domes* (the organ where members of the different traditional Mafia families allegedly plan and co-ordinate their exploits). All the Mafia supergrasses confirmed that finances invested in drugs came neither from the common assets of the organization nor from the collective proceeds accumulated by members of a specific family. The money invested was part of individually owned finance (D'Avanzo, 1993). Members who entered the drug business, therefore, had the opportunity to build partnerships with other investors who were not part of their family or, for that matter, members of the Mafia (Arlacchi, 1992; Gambetta, 1992). The informant Antonino Calderone tells of the way in which some men of honour could sometimes become independent from their very family if their attempt to build up a remunerative drug business was successful.

In some cases the members of traditional organized crime in Italy performed the role of mediators, as they invested somebody else's money in the drug economy. In other cases, both imported drugs and drugs refined in Italian laboratories were sold to wholesale distributors who did not belong to traditional groups or families. In other words, due to the structure which distinguishes drug distribution, 'men of honour' were forced to deal with 'ordinary men'. Among middle-range distributors individuals emerged who had acquired skills and funds in previous criminal activities on the one hand, and entrepreneurs who were devoid of those skills but only owned funds on the other. In turn, small-scale distribution was also taken on by individuals who had never been associated with organized crime (Ruggiero, 1992a; 1995). None of the prevailing groups, including the Mafia, managed to establish a monopoly in the distribution of illegal drugs. Rather, they shared an oligopoly with regard to both the national territory and the specific local market which they supplied.

As for the user–distributors, official statistics show that very few are able to develop a real career in the economy of drugs, as they are intermittently arrested either after committing the same type of offence or while possessing the same quantity of drug (Istat, 1992). In other words, their career is 'blocked', for they prove incapable of ascending the distribution hierarchy and acquiring the professionalism needed to do so.

The drug business in Italy both remodelled traditional organized crime and shaped new organized groups which occupy, along with the former, the leading positions in it. The drug business fostered a process whereby the creation of a number of 'expendable labourers' servicing the market ran parallel with a drive towards more structured and professionalized operations. These developments are not oppositional. On the contrary, it is the employment of one which allows for the promotion of the other.

Similarly, in the early 1980s the drug economy in France was confined to the centres of major cities. In Paris, for example, dealing mainly occurred on the streets and was almost entirely limited to identifiable drug scenes: Belleville, Barbès, Les Halles, Chalon. In this context, the drug economy remained relatively poor and unstructured. Those who worked in this economy were involved in relationships of a mutualistic nature.

Police intervention dispersed this economy, which soon became more structured and took on a more rigid division of labour. In the suburbs, where most drug dealing was dispersed, the economy of drugs now offers jobs such as running, delivering, looking out, and so on. Dangerous and badly paid, these jobs are taken by the younger and more vulnerable users (Coppel, 1994; Conseil National des Villes, 1994).

A Fordist-type Criminal Labour

We can now try to identify some common traits in the cases dealt with so far. The criminal activities described in all the above cases constitute examples of organized crime. The business of stolen goods, extortion rackets, loan-sharking, tobacco smuggling, the manufacture and distribution of counterfeit goods, and the drugs trade could not be carried out without an entrepreneurial structure. However, the characteristics of these criminal businesses do not necessarily correspond to those commonly attributed to traditional organized crime such as the Mafia. The 'Sicilian' anomaly in the study of organized crime, to which I referred at the beginning of this chapter, can be superseded if among the organized criminal businesses which I have described some common elements are identified. I believe that one such element is the capacity of organized crime to *mobilize criminal labour*. In other words, we have organized crime when activities are structured in the guise of a 'collective' endeavour implying the recruitment of *criminal workers* and the payment to them of a wage. This definition leads us to reconsider an important aspect which has been often overlooked in the literature on the matter.

There are recurrent features in the definition of organized crime, among which is the notion that its members are endowed with criminal skills acquired by means of long-term apprenticeship. The well-known polemic between Donald Cressey and Joseph Albini obscures the fact that the above-mentioned notion belongs to both authors and many others after them. As we have seen, Cressey's description of organized crime is based on a so-called bureaucratic model, whereby different groups or families are said to co-ordinate and direct, within a commission formed by representatives of all groups, all activities carried out on the national territory (Cressey, 1969). Albini suggests instead that organized crime is not to be viewed as a nationwide conspiracy, but should be described as a series of local, relatively independent entities which are loosely structured and only informally co-ordinated (Albini, 1971). Now, these interpretations describe networks and relationships which, if differently structured, nevertheless involve similar actors, namely professional criminals or 'men of honour'. These actors are given a central location in many definitions of organized crime, thus conveying the idea that activities are only performed by criminals who are extremely skilled, have undertaken an exclusive career, and are often related either by familial or ethnic bonds. Other definitions, which do not only focus on professionalism, can help develop a more fruitful perspective.

According to Haller (1992), families constituting organized crime are not to be regarded as centrally controlled business enterprises. Rather, members independently conduct their activity. 'A family, then, is a group which is separate from a member's economic ventures and to which members belong roughly in the same way that legal businessmen might join a Rotary Club' (ibid.: 2). The author also argues that many members are not involved in permanent structures nor engaged in long-term partnerships. They may undertake one-off operations, make temporary alliances with legal or illegal entrepreneurs, and often recruit part-timers.

Employees of criminal organizations pose a serious threat to their employers. 'The entrepreneur aims then to structure his relationship with employees so as to reduce the amount of information available to them concerning his own participation and to ensure that they have minimal incentive to inform against him' (Reuter, 1983: 115). This threat can be reduced if employees are recruited among family members and close associates who guarantee a degree of loyalty. However, this is not possible for all illegal businesses, especially those with large and complex distribution structures. The criminal economies described above, for instance, do not lend themselves to centralized control by entrepreneurs, whose capacity to monitor the suitability and skills of employees is very limited. The precariousness of 'jobs', and the high turnover in criminal economies, are an indication of this.

The illegal businesses I have discussed show that organized crime needs a degree of 'disorganization'. In other words, it needs skilled, semi-skilled, improvised, opportunistic, and disorganized criminals simultaneously. In some economies individuals without a previous criminal career may constitute the majority of employees, but paradoxically their 'non-professional' and disorganized illegal acts end up benefiting their professional and organized employers. Surely, the notion that organized crime is a monolithic structure formed exclusively by professional affiliates loses pertinence when its involvement in the economies described above is observed. Here, organized groups are forced to renounce the traditional regulatory function commonly attributed to them. Petty, disorganized and opportunistic offences can no longer be controlled or regulated, as they become an important component of organized crime itself.

The variants of organized crime described above seem to differ less qualitatively than quantitatively. They are all characterized by the capacity to provide goods and services while creating jobs. In the contexts examined it is possible to sell one's 'criminal labour' in exchange for a wage. Organized crime, therefore, displays features of an industrial type, as it recruits both skilled and unskilled labour, like any other industry. It is the presence of these diverse figures holding varying degrees of professionalism and skills which should be regarded as a significant hallmark of organized crime.

The development of this type of criminality is accompanied, on the one hand, by the partial decline of independent groups and their subjection to more organized structures, and on the other, by the recruitment of a mass of 'delinquent workers' devoid of criminal expertise. Many are now pure employees with no decision-making role. In this respect, the analysis of organized crime can no longer focus exclusively on the variable 'professionalism'. The type of criminal organization prevailing in criminal economies displays a dual process whereby professionalism is fostered by non-professional activities and vice versa. The examples I have provided show how theft contributes to the increasing professionalism of fences, cigarette street selling to the expansion of smuggling companies, and so on.

This process entails the disappearance of what could be termed 'crime in association'. This form of illegal activity implies that tasks are collectively planned, the proceeds shared and further activities collectively attempted. Organized crime, in turn, entails a vertical structure, a low degree of co-operation among its members, or rather an abstract, 'Fordist' kind of co-operation among them. Planning and execution are here strictly separated (Fondazione Colasanto, 1990; Sales, 1992; Marino, 1993; Ruggiero, 1995; Ruggiero and South, 1995).

Economic definitions of organized crime, to which I have referred in a previous chapter, regard both criminals and law enforcers as rational actors choosing the ideal maximization of their returns (Becker, 1968; Stigler, 1970; Andreano and Siegfried, 1980). This breakthrough in criminological analysis has not been fully exploited. For, if it is true that the economic principles operating in the upperworld also apply to the activities of the underworld, some irritatingly conformist traits present in the former should also be found in the latter. I have tried to identify one such trait in the Fordist-type work offered by organized crime and the consequent exploitation of the *criminal labour force*. This labour force is unable to master, and lacks knowledge of, the entire economy in which it participates. Unlike 'criminal artisans', those employed by organized crime only master the limited segment of the labour process which they occupy.

Along with the cases already discussed, other activities carried out by organized groups show these characteristics. Take, for example, the organization of prostitution. Research conducted in France indicates that groups engaged in a contemporary form of slave trafficking are in operation. They help women from the former Communist countries to illegally enter France, where they provide them with 'safe' residence in brothels (Tomasevski, 1994). These assembly-line sex-labourers are in no position to control the economy in which they participate, let alone the profits they generate. Similar features are found in the organization of illegal gambling, which is rife in many European cities (Censis, 1992). Other examples are provided by alcohol-smuggling companies operating in Britain (McSmith, 1994). One such company recruited unemployed South Yorkshire miners to make daily trips to Calais, bringing back lorry-loads of untaxed beer and spirits. 'The miners hired accommodation in Dover and vans to ferry the drink to cash-and-carry warehouses in London' (The *Guardian*, 8 December 1994).

Even kidnapping, at least in a number of cases which occurred in Italy, seems set to adopt a 'Fordist-type' organization. Kidnapping is often commissioned by groups endowed with finances who resort to specialized contractors. These have enough information regarding potential targets, their location, whereabouts and assets. The contractors may carry out the operations directly or employ a number of teams to perform the different tasks: the physical abduction of the person, his or her transferral and detention, the negotiation with his or her family, and finally his or her release. Often the members of the teams are offered the job by mediators, and therefore they ignore the identity of their employer, of the victim and of the initial financier (Ruggiero, 1992b; Camon, 1994). They are employees who have never seen their employer.

In some European countries young people and adolescents are also employees of organized crime, whose rigid division of labour mirrors the worst aspects of the official economy (Occhiogrosso, 1993). Examples of women employed by organized groups are also frequent (Madeo, 1994; Siebert, 1994). English gangs specializing in stealing or forging cheque books also use women whom they pay with what could be termed a criminal piece rate system (Campbell, 1993; The *Guardian*, 13 December 1994). In countries with large ethnic minorities, disadvantages based on race, which are usually found within the official labour market, are in a sense reproduced within the criminal labour market. The most remunerative positions within criminal economies are frequently occupied by indigenous groups, whereas the most poorly paid and dangerous tasks are entrusted to minorities. For example, the number of Maghrebians, West Indians and Albanians serving a sentence for drug charges in Italy, France, Britain and Switzerland respectively is not the reflection of their higher involvement in the drug economies of these countries: rather, it is an indication of their occupying the most hazardous positions in those economies (Coppel, 1994; Luce, 1994; Ruggiero, 1993c; Ruggiero and South, 1995).

Applying organization theory to the analysis of organized crime has allowed for the elaboration of a number of themes. These are mainly related to the hostile and relatively dynamic environments in which organized crime operates. The uncertain and changing nature of law enforcement on the one hand, and the equally changing nature of demand for illicit goods and services on the other, are said to determine some important features of organized crime. For example: 'complex technology is avoided; organizations are small in size; there is little organizational complexity; and formalization exists only in a non-traditional, unwritten manner based on mutual understandings and a relatively discrete and concise set of operating procedures' (Southerland and Potter, 1993: 263). This analysis may be useful to challenge interpretations of criminal enterprises as centrally controlled conspiracies monopolizing illicit markets. It is true that organized crime is constituted by a series of partnerships set up around specific criminal projects, and that a very large, tightly controlled and organized criminal conspiracy could not function in operational reality (Southerland and Potter, 1993: 263–4). However, if we really believe that criminal enterprises come into existence and flourish because there is a strong public demand for the goods and services they offer, it is difficult to neglect the role played by 'labour' in these enterprises. One characteristic of this 'labour' is insecurity, which resonates with a similar insecurity informing organized crime with its customers. If we adopt the definitions suggested by Burns (1963), criminal enterprises could be described as *organismic* firms, because they have to constantly adapt to conditions of change and respond to new and unfamiliar problems arising incessantly.

Further consideration should be given to 'job insecurity' in organized crime and the type of Fordism operating in illegal economies. When Ford applied the first assembly line to his car factory, substantial incentives were given to the workforce in terms of salary and work stability. This was possible because the new production techniques were mainly used in the monopoly sector, where demand seemed to be assured for ever. Instead, in the illegal economy the Fordist type of work is accompanied by irregular demand and highly unstable markets: in other words, it serves the competitive sector (Ruggiero, 1995). In this sector, working conditions are poor, unemployment and underemployment high, and workers do not earn enough to save for periods of unemployment, sickness, or retirement.

In the analysis of Thompson (1982), the military analogy for the description of organizations is strongly rejected. Similarly, organized crime should not be viewed as a number of 'sub-units or elements [which] are commanded with respect to a coherent and unambiguous aim' (Thompson, 1982: 235). Organized crime is composed of 'nodes' where individuals pursue their partial objectives, which are unlikely to be rationally co-ordinated under one meta-objective. However, the role of organized crime, as that of management, is to try to reconcile all conflicting interests and aims in order to benefit the organization as a whole. As we have seen, organized crime tries to subsume rather than hamper disorganized crime.

If the analogy with the 'firm' is more than a hollow metaphor, relationships within organized crime should be viewed as those characterizing other licit enterprises, where the 'principal and agent' model often prevails. This model implies that the principal commands the agent to take actions on his/her behalf, and that the agent is motivated by a monetary reward (Strong and Waterson, 1987). In criminal enterprises 'principals' may be less visible than in official ones, they may sometimes only be mediators between principals and agents, who therefore end up never physically meeting. They may confine their influence to a sub-unit of the organization rather than controlling the organization as a whole. However, the relationships between principals and agents within each sub-unit is of a non-co-operative nature, because the two hold asymmetric resources and are driven by self-interest rather than common interest. In highlighting the capacity of organized crime to mobilize labour, I have attempted to describe how incentives are in place through which the agent's interests are harnessed to serve the purposes of the 'principal'. I have mentioned, for example, how organized crime engaged in the drug economy is unable, and indeed unwilling, to control petty crime, because offences committed by drug users make the drug economy flourish. This 'authority' view of criminal enterprises is also common in official economics, where concepts of power describe roles and conflicts in contractual organizations (Fitzroy and Mueller, 1984).

The forms of organized crime which I have described in this chapter derive their authority from their role as job providers. Employees build 'bonds of rejection' with this authority, as they would with official employers. These bonds permit dependence on those whom one fears and against whom one would like to rebel. 'The trouble is that these bonds also permit the authorities to use us: they can exercise control of a very basic sort over those who seem on the surface to be rebelling' (Sennett, 1993: 28).

The characteristics I have identified belong to most variants of organized crime, particularly when its involvement in conventional criminal activity is examined. It should be reiterated that these characteristics describe qualitative rather than quantitative aspects. Other variants of organized crime emerge when the degree of its involvement in the official economy is analysed. The following chapter presents cases in which organized crime 'has made it' into the licit economy. Here, organized crime meets corporate crime. This leap, as we shall see, did not occur in all European countries. In some contexts organized crime still 'stagnates' in conventional criminal activities, while the 'higher immoralities' (Mills, 1956) of business crime are jealously maintained as the preserve of legitimate actors.

6 Offers that Can't Be Refused

In the previous chapter I tried to identify some common characteristics shared by organizations involved in conventional criminal activities. I suggested that one such characteristic is their industrial-type division of labour, whereby acts are performed in exchange for an income. In other types of crime such as professional, craft or artisan crime, tasks are performed by an association of equals, in which bees are also architects. In organized crime, however, planning and execution are strictly separated. I have discussed cases in which organizations mobilize a specific 'criminal labour' in the production and/or distribution of illegal goods and services.

The examples provided earlier revolve around one variant of organized crime, and only refer to illicit enterprises which mainly confine their activities to conventional crime and the underworld. Other variants of organized crime can be identified when the degree of involvement of illicit enterprises in the upperworld is examined. Some criminal groups owe their power to their active presence in the official economy and in the political arena. This is the case, among others, of organized crime in Russia and Italy (Vaksberg, 1991; Rawlinson, 1993; Shelley, 1994; Varese, 1994; Commissione Antimafia, 1993; Lupo, 1993; Carter, 1994; Forgione and Mondani, 1994; Martens and Roosa, 1994). If in general the analysis of corporate and organized crime, as I have argued throughout this book, should proceed jointly, the cases examined in this final chapter indicate that the necessity of a joint analysis is based on a tautology, which is that licit and illicit entrepreneurs commit crime jointly. This chapter describes a number of such joint undertakings, and presents us with a typology which is not easy to specify in a clear-cut fashion. The encounters taking place between licit and illicit businesses may take the form of a mutual entrepreneurial promotion, but may also consist of the provision of specific services by the former to the latter and vice versa. Finally, these encounters may give rise to partnerships, where the identification of the provider and the recipient of such services is problematic. In some cases, moreover, the service which organized crime provides to official entrepreneurs may also be provided by other actors, including legitimate ones. We shall see an example of this when the illicit arms trade is discussed. Equally, the services offered by the official economy to organized crime are simultaneously addressed to other customers, including legitimate ones. In this respect, we shall discuss the laundering opportunities offered by banks to a variety of actors. In brief, the cases examined below seem to confirm the difficulty faced by attempts to draw neat boundaries between legal, illegal, semi-legal, Mafia and corrupt economies, a difficulty whose analysis is the main concern of this book. In the previous chapter ample space has been devoted to the drugs economy for its exemplar characteristics within conventional criminal economies. Similarly in this chapter, while some activities will be dealt with summarily, others will be given more space due to their outstanding importance for the analysis of both organized and corporate crime. These illegal activities are arms trafficking and money laundering.

The War of Art

The theft of art works is perhaps one of the most traditional services provided by criminal groups to official economic actors. Customers buying this service vary from art traders to private individuals, and include firms engaged in art auctions. There is finally a parallel art market, with galleries and minor museums resorting to this service. Works of art may be stolen with a view to demanding ransom money (McIvor, 1993; *The Independent*, 4 March 1994). In these cases, as for the Titian painting stolen in England and Edvard Munch's *The Scream* stolen in Oslo, the works are too famous to be exhibited in galleries and too expensive to be purchased by private individuals (*The Observer*, 8 January 1995). However, in 1994 relatively well-known stolen paintings were found in Parisian galleries where enchanted customers were poised to issue hefty cheques. The gallery directors involved had sold abroad other works including paintings by Chagall (*La Repubblica*, 29 November 1994). Ancient treasures from Turkey, including the Garlanded Sarcophagus, were found in US museums (*The Independent*, 27 April 1994). Russian and East European cultural treasures are being smuggled into the West (D. Brown, 1993). Antiques stolen in the Middle East and Turkey are offered to London auction houses (*The Observer*, 1 August 1993). The black market of art works is fed by both independent thieves and organized groups, with the latter usually acting as mediators between those hired for the actual commission of thefts and those who commission them. Particularly hit are France, Germany, Italy and Britain, where a commercial war has long been engaged for supremacy in the international black market of art (*La Repubblica*, 12 December 1991; *The European*, 6–12 May 1994).

The Art of War

While in the cases examined above a residual role is played by independent gangs, the service on which I focus in this section is so structured that in its provision little space seems to be left to such gangs.

Case 20

In 1993 a chemical warfare facility was 'discovered' in a location eight to nine miles from the outskirts of Madrid. Although covering an area the size of a small town, journalists described the facility as being extremely difficult to find (Hooper, 1993). The Spanish authorities stressed that this was only a defence facility, an army base where research and testing were conducted. These included the testing of protective clothing, detection equipment and decontaminants. However, it was admitted that the base also produced tear gas for riot control and napalm for industrial use. Finally, it was acknowledged that chemical warfare agents were produced in the facility, although the quantities produced were only suitable for research use. Judicial investigation focused on the quantities of agents produced and aimed to establish whether the facility should be considered a research centre or a factory. The public prosecutor had to establish whether the plant kept production below one tonne per day, a limit imposed by the Chemical Weapons Convention signed by the Spanish government.

The investigation followed an enquiry led by the United Nations into the use of chemical weapons in the Iran–Iraq conflict. Spanish-manufactured weapons were found among other weapons and chemicals which, under international regulations, should not have been there. A judge in Madrid said:

> The first embarrassing conclusion of the investigation was that the chemical arms found in Iraq by the United Nations were produced in that army base, a base which was officially listed as a factory. This was inconsistent with the claim by high-rank military staff that it was a research centre. How did those arms come into Iraq's possession? Illegal arms trade is usually carried out through the joint efforts of a number of actors including manufacturers, state officials, and mediators. In this case we were faced with an anomaly, because the factory was state owned, so the manufacturers and state officials overlapped. If these officials also acted as mediators with the importing country, then the actors all belonged to the same category. However, the investigation, which is still under way, is trying to ascertain whether organized criminal groups were also involved in the capacity of smugglers. This would make the case similar to others occurring in Europe, where organized crime provides the illegal conduits

for the smuggling of arms and acts as a *trait-d'union* between manufacturers, politicians and importers.

* * *

The features identified by this Spanish judge were also highlighted by investigators based in other European countries. First, there are arms manufacturers and financial institutions supporting them. These have work relationships with army officials and security services, whose role includes the monitoring of the quality and quantity of arms produced. The monitoring exercise is officially intended to ensure that producers meet international requirements and guidelines (Goldblat, 1994). In countries such as France and Italy, where the arms industry is largely state owned, managers of this industry may be former army officers. Therefore, the army and the arms industry experience a permanent exchange of high-rank personnel between them (Arlacchi, 1988; *Courrier International*, 10 March 1994). Second, there are mediators or wholesale traders, who are closely linked with producers and also act as financial guarantors for transactions between producing and importing countries. Third, there are politicians who take decisions regarding the transfer of arms abroad. They are in charge of supervising the route followed by weapons and ensure that embargoes imposed on certain countries are respected.

The arms business, therefore, may become illegal in a number of respects. The illegality may reside in the quality and quantity of arms produced, which are subject to international restrictions and regulations. Frequently, inspectors in charge of monitoring these aspects of the arms industry are part of an international élite which is closely associated with manufacturers, and may therefore be exposed to corruption (Palermo, 1988). The illegality may also reside in the false claim regarding the country for which the arms are destined. Finally, illegal practices may be adopted by financial institutions through which payments for illegal sales are processed. These institutions conceal the identity of purchasers and sellers along with the sums involved. In cases investigated in Italy during the 1980s, organized crime provided illegal arms traders with transport services and ensured that contacts were maintained with international mediators, some of whom were operating in the importing countries. A manufacturer based in Milan officially exported arms to Jordan and Qatar, with goods being loaded in the port of Livorno. Judge Carlo Palermo found that no ports in Jordan or Qatar ever received these cargoes, and that Italian manufacturers illegally sold to countries such as Lebanon, Libya and Iran.

In the confession given to investigators by a corrupt army general, the two most common ways of sidestepping national and international regulations were described. The first consists of concealing the 'end user' of the goods exported, and implies the forging of documents in a way that mentions no country under embargo. The second consists of falsifying the 'final use' of the goods exported, thus concealing the warfare nature of the goods (Palermo, 1988).

Investigations conducted in Italy found that countries which do not suffer an embargo may also find it convenient to import arms illegally for the benefit in terms of bribes that the illegal trade brings to the politicians and mediators involved. 'For the purchasing countries, the interest in bribes almost outweighs their interest in arms' (Palermo, 1988: 108). The same seems to apply to the exporting countries, where the interest in bribes among politicians and mediators may also outweigh their interest in arms sales.

In some circumstances conventional organized crime may provide a service to arms manufacturers and mediators. In the case mentioned above, for example, this service, which consisted of the provision of shipping facilities, was performed by import–export companies registered in Milan and owned by Turkish, Syrian and Bulgarian entrepreneurs. These entrepreneurs not only specialized in arms, but had developed skills and knowledge in the illegal trafficking of all sorts of goods. They also relied on branches operating in Liechtenstein, where the financial aspects of the trade were dealt with through the local 'liberal' banking system.

As mentioned above, the major actors involved in illegal arms trafficking are manufacturers, politicians or army officials, and mediators. The involvement of organized crime in this traffic reflects the extent to which organized crime itself establishes links, or even overlaps, with one of those actors. In Italy, despite having achieved such links and overlaps, the Mafia has only marginally or indirectly been involved in the arms trade. One case pursued by investigators regarded a financier, who was also a mediator and a diplomat, charged with money laundering through a financial institution he had set up in the Seychelles. He was not selective in the provision of his services, as he laundered money for the Mafia, for arms manufacturers, mediators, tax evaders, and corrupt politicians. A mediator himself, he had required the smuggling services offered by the Mafia in a number of illegal arms deals (Beccaria, 1992).

The cases just mentioned are not as frequent as one might assume. The illicit arms business seems too lucrative a trade to be left in the hands of conventional criminals. Moreover, costs and risks associated with illegal trafficking encourage manufacturers to devise other trading strategies. In recent years a shift became apparent from the 'black' to the grey market of arms. While the former still sees the participation of conventional organized crime, the latter seems to function without the contribution of such an uncomfortable ally. Let us examine examples of both.

Conventional criminal groups seem to occupy the sector of the black market in which light armaments and second-hand weapons are mainly found. For example, a British group of traffickers was arrested in New York for attempting the illegal importation of 15,000 AK47 assault rifles into the USA. The documents seized indicated that the group acquired rifles in Poland and sold them to a number of countries including Croatia (Norton-Taylor, 1991). Polish organized crime also provides manufacturers and army officials with smuggling services. In 1993, a cargo officially carrying ceramic pots and tiles was raided in a British harbour. The find included Polish-manufactured 'assault rifles, pistols, explosives, tens of thousands of ammunition, bayonets, knives and grenades' (Bowcott and Campbell, 1993). In Italy, 15 people were charged with illegally exporting arms to a number of African countries. The weapons were manufactured in the north of the country, while the smuggling service was provided by organized crime based in the south (*La Repubblica*, 8 January 1992). German-manufactured weapons were intercepted by Swiss customs authorities in 1992. The truck-load of arms had been sold to mediators, and by these to members of the Neapolitan Camorra who were poised to re-sell them in the former Yugoslavia (Commissione Antimafia, 1994). Czech-produced arms were seized in 1993 while en route to Bosnia. The development of a 'black' market of arms in Czechoslovakia should be located within the economic context of the country, which throughout the 1980s was among the top arms manufacturers. President Havel's efforts to halt arms exports caused a dramatic decline in foreign currency earnings, and 'crippled the Slovak economy, which during the Cold War had been largely dependent on the arms industry' (Beard, 1993). Finally, it was also proved that Russian organized crime smuggled Czech weapons into the former Yugoslavia (Moder, 1994).

It is on the 'war market' of the former Yugoslavia, where international embargoes have caused the expansion of the 'black' market in arms, that the services offered by organized crime are highly valued. Austrian, German, French, Italian, Israeli, Hungarian, Romanian and Czech weapons find their way on to this war market through the participation of conventional criminal groups from both West and East Europe (Longo and Moder, 1994; Observatoire Géopolitique des Drogues, 1994; Narcomafie, 1994a).

The redefinition of the boundaries between a hidden and a grey market of weapons, with conventional organized crime mainly involved in the former market, should be analysed against the background of recent developments in Europe. The collapse of the Communist block is alleged to have triggered an unprecedented array of conversion policies across Europe. But paradoxically, since the end of the Cold War, progress on disarmament, linked to an irreversible programme of demilitarizing the economy, mainly occurred in the former Soviet Union, whose objective was to prove to the West that it had abandoned its previous 'bellicose' intentions. At the same time, in many Western countries the restructuring of the arms industries was left to market forces, 'with the inevitable consequence that many companies have consolidated around defence work and defence exports' (Project on Demilitarisation, 1994: 3). The failure of Western countries to curtail their arms production is both the result and the motive of the competitive edge they enjoy in the market (Campaign Against Arms Trade, 1994). Even before the collapse of the Soviet Union, the British Institute for Defence Studies reported that 'no longer are Soviet ... manufactured weapons the main commodity of the illicit arms dealer, as more and more of his clients insist on modern Western-manufactured equipment' (Malcher, 1989: 337). During the late 1980s dealers were inundated with requests for both American and European weapons, and would-be purchasers were willing to pay up to 11 times the manufacturer's price. All dealers offered an end-user certificate for an additional 2 per cent of the total price of the arms (Mazarr, 1993). Countries no longer willing to accept Soviet influence had already started to obtain weapons from Western manufacturers (Cupitt, 1993). The increase in demand caused a restructuring of the arms trade and the expansion of a grey market which is still under way.

According to Karp (1994: 178), grey transactions in arms are neither entirely legal nor entirely illegal. A 'necessary evil', the grey market represents 'policy in flux, as exporting and importing governments experiment with new diplomatic links'. The 'black' market is of use to countries that face international restrictions and embargoes, but it is not suited to trading large quantities of major weapons, let alone manufacturing technologies. The grey market is therefore said to be an arena of diplomatic innovation, and in many cases its secretive nature is alleged to arise from confusion within governments, 'as with Britain's controversial exports of dual-use machine tools from Matrix-Churchill in 1988–89, a deal apparently sanctioned by one part of the British government' (Karp: 1994: 187). But what role does 'legal confusion' play in the definition of an illegal market as a grey market?

Some commentators on the 'arms to Iraq affair' involving British manufacturers and sections of the government have highlighted the increasing interpenetration between cabinet ministers and the arms industry in Britain (Cowley, 1992; Friedman, 1993; Sweeney, 1993; Pilger, 1994; Foot and Laxton, 1994). When the biggest gun ever manufactured in Britain was seized by customs officials, the manufacturers 'had informed the Department of Trade and Industry that they were manufacturing pipes which might need export licences, and ... had been told they could go ahead as they pleased. No inspection had been ordered' (Foot and Laxton, 1994: 3).

British companies exporting arms to Iraq used false 'end user' certificates, claiming that the goods were destined for Jordan (*The Economist*, 18

December 1993; Phythian and Little, 1993). While their guilt was evident, the complicity of government departments was to be proved. The case collapsed when ministers signed certificates designed to withhold information from the defence (Norton-Taylor, 1995). With these certificates ministers had in fact invoked 'public interest' immunities to suppress the publication of government papers. 'The classified documents appear to show that a policy change in 1988, relaxing the policy on sales of defence-related equipment to Iraq, was still in force within weeks of Baghdad's invasion of Kuwait in August 1990' (Dawnay, 1992). British ministers have a duty to claim public interest immunity in respect of specific documents the production of which would be contrary to the public interest (National Peace Council, 1994). 'There is now overwhelming evidence that British and other intelligence services – with their governments behind them – did not merely monitor arms deals with Iraq but promoted them' (Cowley, 1992: 270).

This case shows how the development of the grey market in arms increasingly reduces the role played by conventional organized crime in the arms trade. In the grey market the function previously performed by organized crime is taken on by official actors. Chris Cowley, an engineer involved in 'Project Babylon', the construction of the 'supergun' destined for Iraq, described this function as 'encouragement', a term which incorporates the notions of promoting, guaranteeing and facilitating illegal arms transfers.

> At last, here was clear evidence from the inside of political encouragement for exporters of war supplies to Baghdad. The strenuous attempt, through the issuing of public interest immunity certificates by four ministers, to prevent this coming out simply shows how much the politicians wanted to keep this encouragement secret. (Cowley, 1992: 270).

In a similar case, which occurred in the late 1980s, German companies were accused of helping to build an 'Auschwitz in the desert', namely a poison gas factory in Libya (Boyes, 1994). Two executives were prosecuted and received a custodial sentence. In Belgium, whose capital is said to be to arms what Bordeaux is to wine (Bigler, 1989), two government officials were brought to court for soliciting a bribe over the purchase of Italian Agusta military helicopters (Marthoz, 1994). The murder of political leader André Cools was linked to his knowledge of the hidden aspects of the arms contract (Clarke, 1994). As we have seen above, the British company directors of the 'arms to Iraq' affair were acquitted, while no politicians were prosecuted. In Belgium and Germany, however, politicians were prosecuted and sentenced. This would suggest that in dealing with business crime, Britain adopts a system of 'compliance' as compared with punishment, a system based on the primary role of regulatory agencies and internal inspectorates rather than the agencies of the criminal justice system. Bearing in mind the notorious punitiveness of the British against other types of offenders, this 'reflects the extent to which the British system of criminal justice is willing to trust some groups more than others' (Nelken, 1994b: 223).

However, the difference between official responses to the illegal trafficking in arms also depends on the degree to which individual countries rely on the armament sector to redress their trade balance. In Britain and France, arms sales are vital to the economy, as proved by the virtual monopoly held by the two countries with regard to transfer agreements with developing countries (*Arms Trade News*, 1994). Relentless demand from these countries is singled out as the dominant factor in determining both the centrality of arms production in Britain and France and the 'tolerance' they show towards grey transactions. However, the plea of Saudi Arabian officials to 'stop coming here pushing arms down our throats' (Plommer, 1994) puts demand in perspective, and seems to allude to other aspects of today's arms trade. This is simultaneously an instrument of economic development for the manufacturing countries and an instrument of foreign policy for their governments. In Chapter 4 we saw examples of arms contracts linked to the granting of financial aid, within what could be termed coercive diplomacy. The most recent of these examples concerns Indonesia which, compared with some poorer countries, and despite its appalling human rights record, has scored suspiciously high in the aid stakes. The British interest in selling arms to the country in exchange for financial aid might explain this apparent anomaly (Durham, 1994).

In interviews with members of Campaign Against Arms Trade and Project on Demilitarisation, the concept of the grey market was expanded and clarified in the following terms. There is an increasing integration of civil and military technology, with 'spin-offs' from one to the other. Overlaps are frequent between the two technologies, with the best of the civil sector being used in the manufacture of arms and vice versa. This makes the illicit arms trade easier, as does the internationalization of arms production. Brazil, for example, is among the leading arms exporters because it is also a prime customer of Britain in the import of technology and military consultancy. In other words, the leading arms producers of the developed countries need not move their plants to developing countries, but only transfer their technology and know-how. This practice triggers a 'saturation process' whereby the developing countries are put in the position of producing their own weapons and exporting them (Pacheco and Büll, 1994).

To conclude this section, it is worth summarizing the role played by organized crime in the illegal arms trade. Some authors have suggested a typology of traders which include 'big-time dealers', 'munitions manipulators', and 'gun-runners' (Thayer, 1969; Sampson, 1977; Martin and Romano, 1992). The first are private dealers who rely on the support of government officials. The second step is when big-time dealers fear the negative consequences and the legal risks of specific deals. The versatility of this second category of dealers allows them to circumvent embargoes and deliver weapons along with other goods, be they licit or illicit. They have direct contact with arms manufacturers or mediators and utilize the same illegal smuggling channels and facilities through which they move other goods from one country to another. Gun-runners, which form the third category, are only in contact with larger dealers and mediators, and are confined to the less-remunerative sectors of the illegal arms trade, namely the light weapon trade. We have seen examples in which organized crime provides the legal economy of armaments with smuggling services. In some countries this service covers all varieties of weapons, and organized crime may therefore be hired by or act as big-time dealer, munitions manipulator and gun-runner alike. In other countries, the role of organized crime may be limited to that of gun-runner. In other words, in some contexts upward mobility for organized crime is easier than in others. This seems due less to the different effectiveness of law enforcement agencies in specific countries than to the willingness of the respective national élites engaged in the arms trade to 'share' their business with outsiders.

When analysts invoke 'legal confusion' to account for the growth of the grey market in arms (Karp, 1994), they neglect how grey transactions permit the monopolization of profits by the arms élites. In some European countries arms manufacturers do not need organized crime to conduct their business, because the prevailing climate in which they operate is conducive to the export, legal or otherwise, of their goods. The following case shows the treatment given to those opposing this climate, namely those who act illegally in order to import rather than export arms.

Case 21

Gordon Foxley, a Ministry of Defence official who received a £1.3 million backhander from non-British arms manufacturers, was sentenced to four year's imprisonment in 1994 (Macerіean, 1993; Norton-Taylor, 1994). By placing arms orders abroad, Foxley was accused by British manufacturers and unions to have cost thousands of jobs. Foxley's defence lawyer provided a summary of the case in the following terms: 'The case was one of placing orders on behalf of the British government for arms and ammunition with foreign countries. These were commissioned by the defendant, who was also accused of banking monies by using a fairly complicated network.' Foxley's son was gaoled for six months for destroying incriminating Swiss bank statements during the police investigation into his father's affairs. Journalistic accounts of the case stressed the 'high life' and luxury enjoyed by Foxley as opposed to the misery suffered by arms industry workers. This, along with the prevailing way in which the arms industry in general is viewed in Britain, may have affected the court decision. In the opinion of the defence lawyer:

> Foxley was convicted in a way which was quite unusual. The Crown Court heard no witnesses, but only used written documentation, such as international letters exchanged between the defendant and arms producers abroad. This business documentation was regarded as sufficient evidence. It was found that money came from foreign manufacturers and was eventually deposited in Switzerland. However, the British government did want to buy the goods that Foxley was providing. The question was whether or not British manufacturers could have supplied the same goods at lower prices. The underlying rationale of the prosecution was that there had been economic loss for the British economy, although this was never officially mentioned. The fact that the documentation was not cross-examined by means of hearing witnesses was not an orthodox way of proceeding. In other words, the International Justice Co-operation Act was not respected. This requires that evidence is also provided by witnesses residing abroad and are in one way or another involved in the case. The Act also provides that documents should not be used for purposes other than those specified in the Court's request. The British authorities failed to specify why they required the information from abroad. Finally, sentencers did not take the personality or the age of the defendant into any account. This case relates in a paradoxical way to the 'arms to Iraq' case. In Foxley's case the interests of the British arms manufacturers were under threat. In the arms to Iraq case, the British arms manufacturers were the defendants.

Poisons

The dynamics of the illicit arms trade are similar to those operating for the trafficking of radioactive material. Here, the smuggling route is simply reversed, as it frequently runs from the developing to the developed countries. Again, a number of actors are involved in this business, with organized crime providing a service to 'clean' entrepreneurs and traders (*La Repubblica*, 15 August 1994). However, smugglers may also include amateurs and small groups who are devoid of the power and structure of traditional organizations. In a case which occurred in 1994, for example, six Bulgarians were arrested while smuggling 19 containers of radioactive material. The police were 'amazed at the ignorance of the suspected thieves, [and] found no evidence of any trafficking network' (*The Independent*, 15 September 1994).

In another example, a German businessman was arrested with six grams of plutonium. Finally, three members of a Spanish criminal organization were found in possession of 300 grams of radioactive material on their arrival at Munich from Moscow (Radford, 1994). Investigators believe that, although the market in radioactive material is open to all sorts of businesspeople, criminal enterprises have a competitive edge because they are able to establish partnerships with organized criminals in the countries were this material is stolen. Criminal enterprises are also said to be more persuasive in corrupting officials. However, in the confession of an Italian smuggler, the role of traditional organized crime was put into perspective, while diplomats, secret service agents and government officials were described as the major protagonists of the trade (Barbacetto, 1994).

The disposal of hazardous industrial waste offers a clearer example of a service provided by organized crime to the official economy.

Case 22

Cases of illegal industrial waste disposal have been investigated by the Dutch Ministry of Justice. A researcher in this ministry, who is also a well-known writer on the subject, described the dynamics of this illegal service as follows. Processing industrial waste without a licence and sidestepping environmental regulations is cheaper and faster.

> One can also 'degrade' the waste products as being less toxic [burnt at a lower temperature for a lower price], or describe it in the books as 'raw material'; e.g., toxic oil residues described as heating oil. For the illegal broker it is also important to have available [illegal] dumping sites or corrupt officials to turn a Nelsonian eye. Another important asset is the availability of transport firms, usually subsidiary companies, which, if necessary, can take the blame for illegal transport and dumping. (van Duyne, 1993: 123–4).

Dutch illegal enterprises operating in this sector are said to offer service packages which comprise the provision of false invoices, chemical reports, transport facilities, and permits to dump waste.

> Floris Blanchefloor, a bankrupt entrepreneur, appeared to be the background figure behind a number of 'environmental technical' front companies. His enterprise was a small one: Floris Blanchefloor was the leader, assisted by his girlfriend Greenheart. Karl Clinker was an important associate because he had a firm, Eco Cycle Ltd, which was used as a front for various transactions.

A chemist was also involved who provided false chemical certificates from a non-existent specialized laboratory.

> Important was the availability of a Belgian firm, Whiteroad Ltd, which transported most of the wastage to the Belgian dumping site Graywell. Blanchefloor used the firm Eco Cycle to collect large quantities of waste from at least 12 disposers, and had it transported by Whiteroad to the Belgian dumping site Graywell. However, before passing the border the transport made a little detour to the firm Terre de Mère, where the wastage was covered with a thin layer of earth. In his administration the dump site manager recorded the load as 'loose earth from market gardening'. However, not all the wastage was transported to Graywell: reports mentioned that some loads … simply disappeared somewhere in Belgium. (van Duyne, 1993: 124)

Other informants based in Holland suggested that some legally registered dumping companies do also operate illegally. They either establish partnerships with illegal firms or run their own in-house parallel illegal business. The choice between the two services is the result of how much the customer is prepared to spend. An investigator argued: 'It is otiose to question whether customers are aware of the illegal nature of the cheaper option: its very cheapness speaks for itself.'

* * *

A similar case became known in the Netherlands as the 'Uniser affair', and involved the illegal processing of chemical substances for customers such as 'Shell, Chevron and Gulf Oil. … Local and national authorities had either known that Uniser was incapable of legally processing the quantities of waste it contracted, or had at least been culpably negligent in their lack of concern and supervision' (Brants, 1994: 115).

The illegal disposal of hazardous waste has been thoroughly studied in the USA, where in some cases the involvement of organized crime reaches all aspects of the business, from the control of which companies are officially licensed to dispose of waste to those which earn contracts with public or private organizations and to the payment of bribes to dump site owners or the possession of such sites (Block and Scarpitti, 1985; Szasz, 1986; Pennsylvania Crime Commission, 1993; Salzano, 1994). Paradoxically, the development of this illegal service runs parallel with an increase in environmental awareness, the latter forcing governments to raise costs for industrial dumping, which indirectly encourages industrialists to opt for cheaper solutions.

Cases similar to the one described above occurred in Germany, from where criminal groups transported hazardous waste into French territory (Moore, 1994). And in England, where the head of a legal waste-disposal firm based in North Yorkshire was sentenced for running a parallel illegal dumping business (The *Guardian*, 8 February 1995). In Italy, traditional organized crime based in the south has often offered waste-disposal services to entrepreneurs operating in the north. Among the firms serviced in 1990 was ACNA, which produces dioxane and operates in Lombardy. In describing this activity of organized crime in Naples, the Commissione Antimafia (1994: 6) commented: 'The seawater of large parts of the Naples province is polluted mainly because of illegal waste dumping, authorized dumping constituting only 10 per cent of the total waste actually disposed of in the bay of Naples.'

As the USA is negotiating with representatives of the Marshall Islands in the Pacific Ocean and the Mescalero Apaches to open waste dumps in their respective territory and reservation, European criminal organizations are also trying to find disposal sites in the developing countries or recently converted partners (Bryce, 1994; The *Guardian*, 16 August 1994). A bogus Italian company shipped tons of hazardous waste to Nigeria under the label 'industrial supplies' (Vir, 1988; Moore, 1994). As for newly converted partners: 'Parallel with offers of economic aid, the West is using Russia as a dumping ground for toxic waste' (Vidal, 1993).

While in a number of European countries stricter regulations are being discussed (Cranor, 1993), waste-disposal companies are already moving to other continents where their services can be sold more easily – see, for example, the attempt by British-based Attwoods, partly led by Denis Thatcher, to open a landfill in a rural community in Pennsylvania. 'Attwoods had entered the lucrative American garbage market by acquiring an American company, Industrial Waste Services Inc., which, it became clear, had been implicated in racketeering activities' (Block, 1993: 91).

Trafficking in Humans and Human Parts

An illegal trade in human beings has developed in all European countries (Enzensberger, 1992). Many of these human beings are in search of employment, which in many cases will be illegal. Illegal migration and illegal employment presuppose illegally operating entrepreneurs. Organized crime provides a service to such entrepreneurs, as they smuggle human beings on request. 'In the textile industry, the unskilled sector and, above all, the building trade, practices dominate which are reminiscent of the slave markets of the past' (Enzensberger, 1992: 32). However, entrepreneurs are not charged for this smuggling service, as it is usually those smuggled who pay. Refugees from Iran, Iraq, Pakistan and Afghanistan often land on the island of Gotland in Sweden, and the trip costs them more than US$1000. They board boats from Estonia or Latvia, where traffickers act as sorting agents (*The European*, 22–28 December 1994).

A Chinese group operating in Turin offered more than smuggling services. The investigation started after a Chinese, who turned out to be an illegal immigrant, was found shot dead. One of his colleagues helped in the investigation, which unravelled an organization engaged in both the trafficking and the 'employment' of immigrants. These were 'housed' under quasi-military surveillance, and worked under similar coercion in order to pay the sum due for their transportation to Europe. The murdered immigrant had failed to keep up with payments (Mascarino, 1994).

In a Kent fruit farm 81 immigrants were arrested: they had paid money to get to England, where they were illegally employed and paid £15 a day (Sharrock, 1993). The case I wish to highlight occurred in October 1994.

Case 23

There is a narrow strait separating Albania from the coast of the Italian region of Puglia. Here the coastguard patrol is particularly severe, as dozens of small boats are alleged to illegally carry Albanians into the Italian territory. A boat with two Albanians was caught, but it was going the wrong way. They had just dropped a score of people on the coast and were returning to Albania, where customers for the next trip were waiting. No fewer that 5000 individuals per month are estimated to cross the sea in similar small boats. This is the new strategy adopted by those who dream of a new beginning in Italy, after the previous biblical exodus failed.

> Albanians filled with television images of Maseratis and shapely models wearing Valentino and Gucci clothes continue to see Italy as a *dolce vita* country. Only now they rely on organized crime rather than the goodwill of the Italian government to help them fulfil their dream. (Endean, 1994)

A consortium of criminal groups operating in Puglia and their associate counterparts based in Albania are under investigation for similar cases of trafficking in humans.

In Puglia, organized crime is composed of three major criminal groups respectively known as the *Sacra Corona Unita*, the *Famiglia Salentina Libera* and *La Rosa*. Allegations that these organizations are extensions of the Sicilian Mafia or the Neapolitan Camorra in the territory of Puglia proved to be untrue. Instead, as evidence gathered by investigative judges has shown, organized crime in this region is a response by local professional gangs to the 'colonizing' attempts made by the more powerful organizations operating in the neighbouring regions of Campania, Calabria and Sicily. Organized crime in Puglia replicates some aspects of traditional criminal organizations, including secrecy and the sect rituals such as blood oaths and initiation rites (Maritati, 1992; 1993). Returning to our specific case, senior customs officers indicated that trafficking in humans is a very lucrative business in the region, especially when the groups organizing it establish joint ventures with 'clean' entrepreneurs. These commit themselves to hiring those who are delivered to them in the small businesses they run, which are usually part of the parallel unofficial economy. In other words, 'packages' are offered to Albanians who wish to reside in Italy, with men being given insecure, seasonal, unregistered work in the countryside or in the crime industry, and women being destined for striptease clubs or brothels.

* * *

Trafficking in humans is not only carried out by conventional organized crime, but also by other enterprises involved in sexual exploitation of young males and females (Council of Europe, 1993). There are also agencies specializing in the recruitment of women from developing countries seeking work. No matter their skills and experience, these women almost invariably become servants. They are frequently duped, 'being promised the work of their choice only to find on arrival that the employer gives them no choice – or rather the non-choice of returning home immediately at their own expense' (Anderson, 1993: 109). Although legally registered, these recruitment agencies apply what amounts to a debt bondage to those seeking a job in a developed country. The illegality of their business also lies in the level of the recruitment fee, which is far higher than the one officially stated. The British Anti-Slavery Society claimed that:

> Many of the women fall into debt by borrowing at exorbitant interest rates to pay recruitment fees, or by taking an advance payment from the recruiter. Before they can even begin to send money to their families – the prime purpose of working overseas – they have to redeem these debts. (Anderson, 1993: 110)

In Britain, the slave condition of these domestic workers is also apparent in the rule indicating that, on their entry into the country, the name of the employer must be stamped on their passports. A leaflet issued by the British Home Office reads: 'The stamp placed in your passport by the Immigration Officer will record the name of your employer. You cannot work for anyone else' (quoted in Anderson, 1993: 113). Similar agencies, operating in Germany, trade in Asian women destined for marriage. 'An exotic wife costs between 5000 and 10,000 German marks' (*La Stampa*, 27 October 1994).

Groups operating in Russia and Romania trade in children and offer their services to parents wishing to adopt them (Conradi, 1994; Boggan, 1994). Such a trade network was also discovered in Greece, where the infants sold were mainly of Gypsy origin (Marinellos, Dervinioti and Zarakovitou, 1993). It is often the case that children smuggled into developed countries end up in care after being rejected by those who bought them. A British mother who rejected a two-year-old complained: 'She never, ever, called me mummy.' Another lamented that the baby she had bought had turned into a difficult toddler: 'She never says thank you for anything' (Lightfoot, 1994).

According to the World Health Organization and to some officials of the Crime Prevention and Criminal Justice Branch of the United Nations, a black market in body parts has developed. The involvement of organized crime in this trade was proved on a number of occasions, for example when a group of 'organ brokers' were arrested and tried in Turkey in 1991. They received large sums for securing organs from poor farmers, which were then sold to wealthy patients in England (Ward, 1991). San Salvador, Guatemala and Brazil are also said to be attractive markets for European brokers (López, 1994; Grignetti, 1994). Germany is said to be overwhelmed by offers of human organs. 'Patients' Associations and Transplant Units are inundated with letters and faxes from the developing countries offering kidneys for a couple of thousand marks' (Narcomafie, 1994b: 38). In Russia, children's homes are visited by dubious adopters who are prepared to take children with any ailment, from a harelip to Down's syndrome and severe mental disturbance. 'Their only stipulation is that they have no heart trouble. What reasonable conclusion can you draw from that?' (O'Shaughnessy, 1994).

You can Bank on It

The examples highlighted above show how organized criminal groups perform an ancillary role with respect to sectors of the official economy. They provide a variety of services to, and act as a supplementary infrastructure for, the legal economy. In a sense, they constitute a parallel clandestine 'tertiary' sector which helps step up the circulation of commodities. However, as I have suggested above, this clandestine tertiary sector is often set up by licit entrepreneurs themselves, who thus retain the revenues which would otherwise be earned by outsiders. The illegal or grey arms trade is a case in point, with the bulk of the business being conducted by either government officials or respectable mediators.

In the last section of this chapter I shall examine cases in which the roles are reversed, that is, cases of service provision performed by official actors for the benefit of organized crime. Money laundering is one such service, one that seems embedded in the intrinsic necessity to encourage finances, including those originated by crime, to find a proper valorization.

Case 24

Switzerland is second only to the Arab Emirates as regards the average income per person. 'The raw material of the Arab Emirates is oil, that of the Helvetian Emirates is money, other people's money' (Ziegler, 1990: 14). The Swiss National Bank holds the third-largest gold reserves in the world.

> This minuscule country, which only covers 0.15 per cent of the inhabited surface of the planet, and whose population amounts to 0.03 per cent of the population of the globe, plays a considerable role in the world: it is the second financial market, the first market for gold, and the first market for the insurance business. (Ziegler, 1990: 14)

The money flow to Switzerland is constituted by 'clean' money derived from licit profits, 'grey' money deposited by white-collar fraudsters such as tax evaders and corrupt politicians from most European countries as well as from the developing countries, and 'dirty' money originated by criminal activities. The case of the Magharian brothers is but one example of how dirty money is easily laundered in Swiss banks. The two brothers travelled almost fortnightly to Switzerland and made an informal deal with the managers of Crédit Suisse, the second-largest bank in the country. Part of their money was converted into gold, while part was transferred to Turkish banks in accounts owned by the brothers. They were prime customers and were therefore able to strike favourable bargains. For example, the transfer of money and the purchase of gold was undertaken against the guarantee offered by collaterals based in Turkey who were associates of the customers. Initially the two brothers did not think it necessary to establish a front business in Switzerland, and only eventually were they so advised by the bank (Zuberbühler, 1989). The Magharians established a joint venture with a prominent Swiss businessman, Dr Hans Kopp, who specialized in the trade of precious stones. When the investigation into the two brothers started, and as evidence arose that they were laundering profits derived from the illegal drug trade, Hans Kopp severed his relationship with the two. He was alleged to have received a telephone call from the Swiss minister of justice tipping him off to the investigation. 'The problem was that the Swiss minister of justice happened to have been his wife, Elizabeth' (Robinson, 1994: 135).

* * *

The necessity of money laundering is one of very long standing in relation to most financially motivated crimes (Gilmore, 1993). One of the purposes of criminal activity is not so much the one-off making of large profit as the reinvestment of profits on a larger scale, be it in further criminal activity or legal activity (McClean, 1992). Furthermore, professional criminals rely on financial institutions to hide and launder their proceeds. This is the case with robber gangs, whose structure corresponds less to the definition of 'organized crime' provided in the previous chapter than it does to 'crime in association' or artisan crime. For example, the robbery that was to become known in London simply as 'Brink's-Mat' was thoroughly planned so that the money taken would be immediately laundered by a team of respectable businessmen (Campbell, 1994). So was the robbery of the Knightsbridge Safe Deposit Box Centre, in which one of the accomplices was both a manager of the Centre and the person charged with laundering the sum taken (Morton, 1992; Viccei, 1992). However, money-laundering services are alleged to have become more relevant than ever in the past, due in particular to the high earnings produced by the illegal drugs business. This business, which is transnational in nature, avails itself of money-laundering operations which are equally transnational. These operations may easily take place thanks to confidentiality, which is central to the banker/customer relationship (Jack Report, 1989; Jack, 1993). Pressures by governments to make this relationship more transparent are met with suspicion and reluctance by bankers, who see the disclosure of information regarding customers as a 'formidable burden' (Jack, 1993). However, there is a tendency to accept the breach of the confidentiality obligation on the generalized ground of public interest. The illegal drugs business is deemed to fall within the most sensitive terrain of public interest.

Arguably, the case examined above could not have occurred after July 1992, when the Swiss authorities introduced new banking regulations. Under the new rules *anonymous accounts* are no longer available, and customers or their legal representatives must be fully identified. Clients are also required to provide documentary evidence of the origin of the sums deposited through the display of invoices or business contracts (Robinson, 1994). However, a judge interviewed in Zurich argued that not only can these documents easily be forged, but they can even be genuinely produced when clients belong to large criminal organizations. These can provide authentic evidence of their earnings in licit businesses which they conduct alongside criminal activities. Even under the new regulations, the Swiss authorities are reluctant to take action against suspect customers, as action can only be initiated when foreign governments provide precise substantiation, and meet extremely strict formal guidelines, regarding the illegal undertakings of customers.

Establishing one's 'fiscal residence' in Switzerland is one way of outflanking the new regulations, and can be done by means of front persons or businesses. This practice brings enormous advantages to wealthy individuals, including the possibility of negotiating the amount of tax payable to the Swiss authorities without proof of the sums of money earned. My respondent said that this practice attracts mediators involved in the illicit funding of political parties across Europe. The Kollbrunner case, for example, proves how a front person, or even a personal secretary of a political party leader, can bargain with the Swiss authorities over the amount of tax payable irrespective of the amount of money flowing into his/her account. Kollbrunner was the manager of a company based in Switzerland, whose real activity consisted of recycling the bribes taken by members of the Italian Socialist Party (Cipriani, 1993). At times, the bargain may even entail an inverse proportionality between earnings and tax, which is one of the ways in which the Swiss authorities attract money into their territory.

Breach of confidentiality in the name of public interest has become a very selective process. For example, it has been stressed that the requirement on banks to act upon suspicion may be taken too far (Jack, 1993). This is a euphemism to pinpoint how the new banking regulations seem designed to favour the more powerful criminal organizations, and may end up applying only to customers who are unable to conceal their criminal curricula. Barriers are being erected to limit access into the money-laundering market, which will therefore more strictly select its actors. As Levi (1991b) argued, with the decline of bank secrecy sophisticated offenders can either generate business fronts or just divert they money towards less-regulated areas.

Before giving a brief account of these less-regulated areas, it should be noted that the stricter regulations introduced in Europe are embedded in the assumption that the bulk of the money laundered in European banks is drug-related, and on the willingness of governments to impede its circulation along with all other proceeds of organized crime. 'Actually, amongst the various operations determining the international pool of dirty money, drug trafficking should certainly not be considered as the most prominent one' (Arlacchi, 1994b: 90). The most relevant portions of hot money derive from tax evasion, flight capital and the proceeds of irregular or hidden economies, which are distinguished from the overtly criminal economies. Flight capital includes money made available by developed to developing countries in the form of financial aid, which is not spent or invested locally, but returns to the developing countries as illegally exported capital. This money is 'often deposited with the very bank that gave the credits in the first place' (Arlacchi, 1994b: 98).

The new banking regulations introduced in Europe sound like an invitation to organized criminal groups to establish high-rank alliances and partnerships, or to find alternative money-laundering opportunities. One such alternative consists in the more powerful organized groups opening up their own banks or other laundering enterprises such as casinos (Cipriani, 1989; *Il Corriere della Sera*, 8 July 1991). Failing this, offshore financial markets are available where furtive money can avoid regulatory attention and taxes.

The term 'offshore' is a relative one, and implies the existence of an 'onshore'. A firm's offshore is taken to mean all activities not undertaken by the firm in its home country, but by its branches based abroad (Roberts, 1994). As banks engage in competitive deregulation, an increasing invisibility characterizes transactions performed by their foreign branches to the point that the distinction between onshore and offshore becomes blurred. 'The closing of BCCI in July 1991 and the consequent unravelling of the bank's "web" of involvements dramatically demonstrated the interlinking of onshore and offshore finance' (Roberts, 1994: 93). This interlinking underlies a process whereby customers are offered a number of services within what is termed 'global custody'. A multitude of operations are initiated under global custody including security transfer, mergers and acquisitions, risk reduction and tax minimization. 'The ability to use the uneven global topography of taxation to gain advantage is now an imperative' (Roberts, 1994: 96). Among the most notorious offshore banks are those operating in the Cayman Islands, whose authorities show a firm determination to remain a British colony. Here, 'the pomp and pageantry of the colonial government ... are used to sell the Islands as changeless (and hence stable) to both tourists and financiers' (ibid.: 108).

Financial services provided to organized crime have been the focus of international investigation in the wake of spectacular bankruptcies (Arel, 1992; Herring, 1993; Passas, 1993; Punch, 1993). I have described how the new banking regulations introduced in most European countries may fail to stop the provision of such services. Instead, among the likely developments of such new regulations, there could be an increase in the cost of laundering operations in terms of corruption and risk. The climate of suspicion may also provide an environment conducive to frauds in which organized or white-collar criminals are victimized. In 1992, two cases occurred involving respectively a Hungarian and a Canadian businessman who wanted to launder hot money in Switzerland and, after secretive bargaining, had their money stolen by fraudsters posing as bank managers (Robinson, 1994). But perhaps the most sensational of such cases was the 'Sindona affair' in Italy, where the 'banker of the Mafia' disappeared with the proceeds of crime which were entrusted to him. This seemed the ideal conclusion of an economic cycle: organized crime accumulated profits illegally, and when trying to make these profits legal was victimized by those who normally make their profits legally (Cipriani, 1989; Lodato, 1992).

Mutual Entrepreneurial Promotion

Investment opportunities are among the other services provided to organized crime by the licit economy and the official political apparatus. This formulation need not convey the idea of a rigid separation of roles between service providers on the one hand and service recipients on the other. Partnerships are often established in which it is difficult to ascertain who is promoting whom. The following examples may clarify this point.

In 1994 the Court of Auditors of the European Community gave a detailed account of waste and fraud occurring within the Community. Among the countries singled out, ironically, was Denmark, which had previously rejected the Maastricht Treaty for the perceived disadvantages that the Treaty and the European Union in general was said to bring to the country (Court of Auditors, 1994). In the case of Denmark, 'for 57 out of 95 cases selected from the export refund population, EFD [the Control Danish Paying Agency] could not produce supporting lists for reconciliation purposes. Out of the total sample of 131 cases, 39 could not be reconciled because of differences in the supporting lists. A full reconciliation was only possible for 26 cases' (Court of Auditors, 1994: 54).

The EU's agricultural expenditure in the form of subsidies represents an attractive source of finance for both legitimate enterprises and organized crime across Europe. Between 1971 and 1988, all countries of the Union reported cases of irregularities, with the highest number of cases occurring in Germany and Britain. As for the amounts of money involved, Italy scored twice as high as Germany and ten times higher than Britain (Passas and Nelken, 1993). In Italy, in other words, fewer cases of fraud reaped much higher revenues, a circumstance which illustrates the higher degree of 'professionalism' of fraudsters in that country. Frauds are said to be created by the complexity of subsidy schemes (Leigh and Smith, 1991), and it is perhaps due to this complexity that the ideal EU frauds are the result of partnerships involving both organized crime and official actors. The former find it necessary to learn administrative and commercial techniques that the latter appear willing to teach. Moreover, both legal and illegal actors need some contacts with officials in their national territory and possibly in the EU bureaucracy. For example, a £50 million fraud investigated in Britain revealed how important it was for the company involved to maintain a good working relationship with the 'policy community' which lobbies for agricultural interests at European level (Collins, 1990). In this case top-quality beef, whose exportation attracts European subsidies, was replaced with cheap cuts (Ministry of Agriculture, 1992). A similar case which occurred in Italy, with a company replacing what officially was the export of fillet meat with chicken feet, revealed a web of corruption involving customs officials who turned a blind eye to the actual nature of the goods exported (*La Stampa*, 7 December 1994).

When conventional organized crime engages in this type of fraud, it has to follow similar modalities already established by their 'licit' counterparts. Pietro Scavuzzo, a supergrass of Cosa Nostra, revealed that it was not enough for members of the organization to become entrepreneurs: they needed to establish partnerships with colleagues who could teach them the techniques to maximize profits. Those involved in the farming business also 'needed to have some contact with officials of the Ministry of Foreign Commerce and of the EU' (*Il Corriere della Sera*, 21 October 1993).

The importance of establishing partnerships with licit entrepreneurs does not only characterize organized crime. Professional criminals may also find such partnerships crucial. For example, one of my interviewees, a London-based barrister, drew my attention to a number of frauds committed by joint ventures of 'clean' financial advisers and 'wheeler-dealers' with a criminal record. One of these ventures, which brought some £3m in illegal revenues, consisted of the sale of goods which the offenders were only supposed to store on behalf of customers. The two main characters involved were a business adviser who had been educated in both England and France and a second-hand car dealer with a previous criminal record. It is impossible to establish which of the two had transmitted to the other the techniques and the 'sub-cultural rationalization' which facilitated the commission of the offence.

The following case saw the involvement of conventional organized crime which, while displaying the characteristics identified in the previous chapter in relation to conventional criminal activities, also constitutes an ideal example of 'making it' on to the official economic scene.

Case 25

During the night of 23/24 November 1980 the south Italian regions of Campania and Basilicata were hit by an earthquake which killed 2735 and injured 8850. The most important section of a report issued by the Antimafia Commission investigating organized crime in Naples, the main city in Campania, was devoted to an analysis of this 'natural' event (Commissione Antimafia, 1994). This event provided the backcloth against which the Camorra underwent the most spectacular development in its history. The investment opportunities taken by the Camorra in the aftermath of the earthquake enabled this criminal enterprise to gain an unprecedented position in the local economy and eventually to launch ventures internationally. The equivalent of some £20 billion financial aid was allocated by public and private, and national and international bodies to the regions hit by the earthquake. The reconstruction and refurbishment of both privately and publicly owned buildings, and the restoration of services and urban infrastructures, were entrusted to the local mayors and municipal administrators. Due to the emergency situation, mainly stemming from the large number of people who were left homeless, limited discretionary power was given to the municipalities. Mayors and administrators turned discretion into arbitrariness, and funds were allocated on the basis of personal and political clientelism. Advisers, consultants and subcontractors were systematically chosen from among faithful cliques who could guarantee, through the mobilization of votes, the re-election of those mayors and administrators (Marro, 1990).

> The Camorra acted as guarantors of the electoral success of dishonest administrators, and contributed to the maintenance of the political stability necessary for the reconstruction to take place. In cases where mayors and administrators did not bow to the logic of collusion, the Camorra made recourse to violence. For example, Marcello Torre, mayor of Pagani [a small town near Naples] was murdered on 11 December 1980, because he had refused to contract a Camorra-owned company for the removal of the debris provoked by the earthquake. This execution occurred days after the earthquake, and constituted a 'signal' addressed to public administrators, who were thus 'warned' over the consequences of their lack of co-operation. (Commissione Antimafia, 1994: 108)

The earthquake was said to have caused a 'last opportunity syndrome' among both public administrators and organized crime. Both saw it as a unique chance to make it for good. This chance was perfectly timely for the Camorra, which was seeking ways to re-invest the proceeds of its criminal activity, including drugs trafficking. Organized crime in Naples did not limit its role to the cornering of contracts for its own firms, but also established an informal 'allocation panel' endowed with decision-making power over the 'licit' firms to be given this or that contract. Some of these firms were willing to pay a pre-established percentage of their earnings to the Camorra. Some never completed the works, while some only existed on paper. Companies based in northern Italy were also encouraged to make a tender for public works, and a building co-operative of Bologna won an important contract after agreeing to pay 5 per cent of the potential earnings to the Camorra, and another 5 per cent to politicians. Numerous other examples of north-based companies involved in price-fixing, collusion and bribery with local administrators, or sharing works with firms owned by organized crime, prompted one commentator to declare: 'A beautiful North–South alliance' (Papuzzi, 1991: 39).

* * *

To complete the examination of this case it should be added that many buildings which were damaged by the earthquake had been built during the course of the 1960s by companies associated with organized crime, and the poor quality of the material utilized was deemed among the causes of their collapse. Incidentally, these dynamics, whereby those causing social damage eventually try to take advantage from redressing it, also became apparent when members of the Camorra planned the establishment of drug rehabilitation centres for drug abusers, and when a firm associated with the Sicilian Mafia won a contract for the building of a high-security court in which members of the Mafia were due to be tried (Falcone, 1991).

This specific field of entrepreneurial promotion, revolving around the building business, is also offered to organized crime operating in other European countries. Qualitatively similar, for example, was the case investigated in southern France concerning the assassination of Yann Piatt, a local administrator. The assassination took place against the background of the complex web of alliances involving politicians, developers and organized crime in that area (Gaetner, 1992; *Il Corriere della Sera*, 2 March 1994; Groussard and Leauthier, 1994; Lennon, 1994; *Infomatin*, 2 March 1994). These alliances proceeded undisturbed throughout the 1960s and 1970s, prompting writers such as Graham Greene (1982: 7) to write:

> Let me issue a warning to anyone who is tempted to settle for a peaceful life on what is called the Côte d'Azur. Avoid the region of Nice, which is the preserve of some of the most criminal organizations in the south of France: they deal in drugs; they have attempted with the connivance of high authorities to take over the casinos, they are involved in the building industry which helps to launder their illicit gains.

These warnings were proven founded when in 1990 Jacques Médecin, mayor of Nice, escaped to Latin America after being investigated over his relationship with organized crime. Between 1966 and 1990 he had offered investment opportunities in the building industry to criminal enterprises operating in the south of France. These enterprises: 'Renovated and refurbished entire city neighbourhoods, built a congress house and a sumptuous theatre' (Gaetner, 1992: 235).

A judge interviewed in France analysed this case in the context of the peculiar relationship between local and central authorities in the country. He argued that many French cities are run in a 'feudal' fashion, with local administrations resembling mini-states endowed with absolute powers. He explained:

> Cities such as Nice, Marseilles, Bordeaux and Cannes are to be regarded as mini-states, where the representatives of the national state are omnipotent in

every sphere of the local political, cultural and economic life. Marseilles, for example, used to belong to Gaston Defferre, and more recently it seems to belong to Monsieur Tapie. These individuals act as feudatories invested by the central power to supervise over all aspects of the social life of their local subjects. For example, the name Médecin in Nice is everywhere, and can be found in or behind all the relevant private enterprises playing a role in the local economy, but also in most cultural associations and public initiatives. Even the Madonna which is submerged under the sea in the old port bears a huge plate with the name of Madame Médecin, the mayor's wife. It is this feudal aspect of public life that makes it difficult to unravel the actual origin of finances and the nature of the alliances between those who own them, be they legitimate or illegitimate actors.

Conclusion

Many philosophers of the seventeenth and eighteenth centuries were concerned to elaborate a 'theory of property' with a view to establishing the legitimacy of the new industrial system and the market economy. They sought to devise a concept of social justice which would make restrictions upon property-holders unjustifiable. John Locke's conception of property, for example, was informed by his own view of the relation between man and his Maker (Reeve, 1991). Property entitlement was therefore inscribed in a theological context. Locke argued that human beings are under an injunction to improve the gift of our wise and generous Maker, therefore resources and wealth belong to those who appropriate them and convert them into wealth.

Raffaele Cutolo, a leader of organized crime in Naples, defended himself in court by expressing his own 'theory of property', though this was devoid of theological overtones. He accused his accusers of persecuting him and his associates while condoning criminal businessmen. After all, he stated, the Camorra commits offences which are routinely committed by many 'clean' entrepreneurs. He concluded: 'People are just jealous because we can make gold out of fleas.'

John Locke and Raffaele Cutolo epitomize two analogous ways in which resources can be appropriated and converted into wealth. Their 'theories' allude to the fact that corporate and organized crime can be observed from a similar perspective. In this book, notions derived from the history of merchants and entrepreneurs, and the theory of organizations and the firm, have provided a vantage point for observing the two types of offending. The cases examined and the dynamics tentatively described seem to suggest that economic order embodies criminal disorder *ab initio*.

This is not new. Max Weber explained how the 'original crime' of the economy was the aim of religious innovation. The Protestant Reformation, for example, removed the anachronistic rejection of usury, a rejection which hampered industrial development. Usury was not the only 'lie' embedded in the economy, the fundamental sin being inherent in the gap between price and value, price and profit. Daniel Defoe personified the 'lie' of commerce in the 'man that stands behind the counter'. This man, he said, will be a perfect hypocrite, if he will be a complete tradesman (Defoe, 1727). In a number of his writings, the author struggled unsuccessfully (or pretended) to prove that 'business ethics' is not an oxymoron (Faller, 1993).

In the previous pages a number of illicit economies have been described in which conventional organized crime is involved. In these activities some common traits have been identified, among which is a distinctive internal division of labour. The definition of organized crime has been linked to this particular division of criminal labour, which is based on the growing separation between planning and execution. While all the variants of organized crime in Europe seem to share this characteristic, some appear to be pariah forms of criminal enterprise, in the sense that the criminal options open to them are limited. On the one hand, these enterprises are in need of the goods and services, including protection, that more powerful criminal enterprises can deliver. On the other hand, they are incapable of accessing the official economy to a significant degree. More powerful variants of organized crime, which expand their activities into the licit arena of business, both maintain the characteristics described above and adopt those typifying corporate actors. They are offered the opportunity to engage in value-adding partnerships with legitimate entrepreneurs, in a mutual economic promotion and through the exchange of services. Their 'going legal', in other words, adds to their criminal opportunities.

A number of final considerations can be drawn from the material presented in this book. Sutherland's theorization seems to imply that deviant techniques and rationalizations are learned within specific homogeneous enclaves or professional groups. In a number of cases examined above, on the contrary, learning processes appear to cross the boundaries of social groups, as criminal know-how is transmitted to a variety of actors. In other words, techniques are exchanged and skills enhanced within an economic arena inhabited by legal, semi-legal and illegal businesses.

The cases of corporate deviance presented in Chapter 4 reflect a selection operating both in the criminal justice system and in the overall economy. The perception of some corporate acts as deviant depends on a number of forces, including the pressure exerted by powerless groups against specific corporate activities. The use of the criminal justice arena on the part of pressure groups, for example, is instrumental in identifying some corporate behaviours as harmful or criminal. However, as stressed in Chapter 1, pressure exerted by powerful groups against one another may also have a role in determining which corporate activities and behaviours are more penalized than others. One should be aware, therefore, that some of the cases of corporate deviance presented in this book reflect the selective processes generated by both these forces. On the other hand, one should also consider that other practices and behaviours remain untouched by processes of stigmatization and penalization. Hence the book analyses practices which, as Conklin (1977) suggested, are harmful, perhaps semi-legal, but 'not criminal'.

The dynamics analysed in this book seem to confirm the inappropriateness of those moralistic overtones which often accompany the explanation of crimes of the powerful. Contrary to analysts adopting such overtones, these types of crime constitute neither exceptional behaviours nor social pathologies. They do not result from the weakening of the bonds linking individuals to society, but from the strengthening of such bonds. As opposed to orthodox analysis, which as we have seen in Chapter 1 even Chaucer would endorse, crimes of the powerful seem not to be caused by 'greed', but by wealth and power. This power includes the possibility of imposing criminal definitions on competitors rather than on oneself.

What distinguishes the pariah forms of organized crime from the more prosperous ones is their respective degree of involvement in the official as well as the illegal economy. Criminal groups who do not 'make it' into the legal economy are denied those 'multiple social affiliations' which would improve their life chances (Blau, 1994). These affiliations would simultaneously expand the scope of their criminality. In this respect it is legitimate to ask: is excess of socialization, rather than lack of it, one of the causes of crime?

This question brings us back to Sutherland's suggestion that both poverty and wealth may cause criminal behaviour. The analysis of conventional organized crime provided in Chapter 4 indicates that activities conducted by criminal enterprises rely heavily on the recruitment and exploitation of labour. 'Crime as work' is a notion which defies the search for 'strong' causes of offending, especially when these putative causes are associated *tout court* with poverty and unemployment, in turn due, as Gordon (1980) suggests, to 'capitalism'. Criminal labourers *do* work, they *are* employed. Only occupational alternatives which actually compete with their illegal jobs, in terms of status and income, may entice them to early retirement from crime.

In turn, the notion 'work as crime', a notion explored throughout Chapter 4, not only defies the search for a strong cause of crime, but makes it almost unnecessary. Hence the scepticism vis-a-vis aetiological issues throughout this book. Crime seems one of the options offered to all individuals, who are faced with a structure of opportunities arising from both the legal and the illegal arenas. In sum, each official position occupied in society seems to entail possibilities to alter or escape such position through the adoption of a set of illegal practices. These are specific to the social position occupied. The availability, scope and remuneration of illegal options change according to status and income. Where both are low, illegal options are limited, extremely risky and, overall, bring poor benefits. Looking at the cases examined in this book, one could argue that more opportunities available in the official arena translate into more opportunities being created in the illegitimate one. Factors which serve the purpose of conducting legitimate business may also serve to promote unlawful behaviour (Vaugham, 1983). Moreover, access to material resources runs parallel with access to justifications of criminal behaviour, as wealth and status increase the need to deny criminal intent (Conklin, 1977). This will make violation of law more likely. In this sense, the second part of Sutherland's formula applies, namely that wealth, rather than poverty, causes crime.

References

Abadinsky, H. (1990), *Organized Crime*, Chicago: Nelson-Hall.
Aglietta, M. (1979), *A Theory of Capitalist Regulation*, London: New Left Books.
Albanese, J.S. (1982), 'What Lockheed and La Cosa Nostra Have in Common', *Crime and Delinquency*, 28: 211–32.
Alberge, D. (1994), 'Ceramics World Hit by Wedgwood Fraud', *The Independent*, 8 June.
Albini, J. (1971), *The American Mafia: Genesis of a Legend*, New York: Appleton-Century-Crofts.
Amnesty International (1994), *Concerns in Europe: France*, London: Amnesty International.
Anderson, B. (1993), *Britain's Secret Slaves*, London: Anti-Slavery International.
Andreano, R. and Siegfried, J. (eds) (1980), *The Economics of Crime*, New York: John Wiley.
Arel (Agenzia Ricerche e Legislazione) (1992), *Criminalità e finanza*, Bologna: Il Mulino.
Arlacchi, P. (1983), *La mafia imprenditrice*, Bologna: Il Mulino.
Arlacchi, P. (1988), 'Introduzione', in Palermo, C., *Armi e Droga*, Roma: Editori Riuniti.
Arlacchi, P. (1992), *Gli uomini del disonore*, Milano: Mondadori.
Arlacchi, P. (1994a), *Addio Cosa Nostra. La vita di Tommaso Buscetta*, Milano: Rizzoli.
Arlacchi, P. (1994b), 'Corruption, Organized Crime and Money Laundering World-Wide', in Punch, M., Kolthoff, E., van der Vijver, K. and van Vliet, B. (eds), *Coping with Corruption in a Borderless World*, Deventer/Boston: Kluwer.
Arms Trade News, August–September 1994 ('Arms Transfer Agreements with the Third World').
Ashe, M. and Counsell, L. (1993), *Insider Trading*, London: Tolley.
Atkinson, D. (1994), 'Shady UK Financial Advisers Make Irish Republic their Base', The *Guardian*, 14 August.

Auld, J., Dorn, N. and South, N. (1986), 'Irregular Work, Irregular Pleasure. Heroin in the 1980s', in Matthews, R. and Young, J. (eds), *Confronting Crime*, London: Sage.

Bagnasco, A. (ed.) (1990), *La città dopo Ford*, Torino: Bollati Boringhieri.

Bantman, B. (1994), 'Un scandal toujours plus fort' *Libération*, 21 September.

Barbacetto, G. (1994), 'Noi, venditori dell'Apocalisse', *L'Europeo*, 25 July.

Baumhart, R. (1961), 'How Ethical Are Businessmen?', *Harvard Business Review*, 39: 6–19.

Beard, M. (1993), 'The Explosive Way to Pay for Czech Security', *The European*, 19–25 November.

Beccaria, G. (1992), 'Palmeti, coralli e mafia', *Il Corriere della Sera*, 11 June.

Becchi, A. and Rey, G. (1994), *L'economia criminale*, Roma/Bari: Laterza.

Becker, G. (1968), 'Crime and Punishment: An Economic Approach', *Journal of Political Economy*, 76 (2) : 169–217.

Bergman, D. (1991), *Deaths at Work. Accidents or Corporate Crime*, London: Inquest/London Hazards Centre/Workers' Educational Association.

Bigler, R.M. (1989), 'Overview of the International Sale of Arms and its Global Politics', in Unsinger, P.C. and More, H.W. (eds), *The International Legal and Illegal Trafficking of Arms*, Springfield, Ill.: Charles C. Thomas.

Blackhurst, C. (1994), 'Files on Pergau Project Withheld', *The Independent*, 3 February.

Blau, P.M. (1994), *Structural Contexts of Opportunities*, Chicago: University of Chicago Press.

Blau, P.M. and Scott, W.R. (1963), *Formal Organizations. A Comparative Approach*, London: Routledge & Kegan Paul.

Block, A. (1980), *East Side–West Side. Organizing Crime in New York 1930–1950*, Cardiff: University of Cardiff Press.

Block, A. (1991), *Perspectives on Organizing Crime. Essays in Opposition*, Dordrecht: Kluwer.

Block, A. (1993), 'Defending the Mountain Top. A Campaign Against Environmental Crime', in Pearce, F. and Woodiwiss, M. (eds), *Global Crime Connections. Dynamics and Control*, London: Macmillan.

Block, A. and Chambliss, W. (1981), *Organizing Crime*, Amsterdam: Elsevier.

Block, A. and Scarpitti, F.R. (1985), *Poisoning for Profit: The Mafia and Toxic Waste in America*, New York: William Morrow.

Blundy, A. (1994), 'Moscow Puts Out a Contract', The *Guardian*, 27 May.

Boggan, S. (1994), 'British Woman Fixes Babies-For-Cash Deals', *The Independent*, 15 July.

Bohm, R. (1993), 'On the State of Criminal Justice: 1993 Presidential

Address to the Academy of Criminal Justice Sciences', *Justice Quarterly*, 10(4): 529–40.

Borger, G. (1994), 'Most Businesses in Warsaw Pay Protection Money', The *Guardian*, 3 November.

Bosworth-Davies, R. (1993), 'An Analysis of Compliance Officer Attitudes Towards Insider Dealing', *Crime, Law and Social Change*, 20: 339–57.

Bottomore, T. (1981), 'The Decline of Capitalism, Sociologically Considered', in Heertje, A. (ed.), *Schumpeter's Vision. Capitalism, Socialism and Democracy After 40 Years*, Eastbourne/New York: Praeger.

Bowcott, O. and Campbell, D. (1993), 'Arms Find Raises Fears for Ulster Stability', The *Guardian*, 25 November.

Bowen, D. (1994), 'Insider Dealing', *The Independent*, 10 July.

Box, S. (1983), *Power, Crime and Mystification*, London: Tavistock.

Boyes, R. (1994), 'German MPs Press Bonn to Explain Role in Libya Gas Project', *The Times*, 5 March.

Braithwaite, J. (1984), *Corporate Crime in the Pharmaceutical Industry*, London: Routledge & Kegan Paul.

Braithwaite, J. (1985), 'White-Collar Crime', *Annual Review of Sociology*, 11: 1–25.

Braithwaite, J. (1993), 'Transnational Regulation of the Pharmaceutical Industry', *Annals of the American Academy of Political and Social Science*, 525: 12–30.

Brants, C. (1994), 'The System's Rigged – Or Is It?', *Crime, Law and Social Change*, 21(2): 103–25.

Brown, D. (1993), 'Looted Icons Surface in Jerusalem Mall', The *Guardian*, 20 November.

Brown, P. (1993), 'Britain Backs Trade Gag on Logging Fears', The *Guardian*, 29 March.

Bryce, R. (1994), 'Adding Insult To Injury', The *Guardian*, 12 August.

Buchanan, J. (1980), 'A Defence of Organized Crime?', in Andreano, R. and Siegfried, J. (eds), op. cit.

Burns, T. (1963), 'Industry in a New Age', *New Society*, 31 January: 17–20.

Calavita, K. and Pontell, H. (1993), 'Savings and Loans Fraud as Organized Crime: Toward a Conceptual Typology of Corporate Illegality', *Criminology*, 31(4): 519–48.

Calder, J. (1992), 'Al Capone and the International Revenue Service: State-Sanctioned Criminology of Organized Crime?', *Crime, Law and Social Change*, 17(1): 1–23.

Calvi, F. (1994), *L'Europa dei padrini: La mafia all'assalto dell'Europa*, Milano: Mondadori.

Camon, F. (1994), 'Massima insicurezza', *La Stampa*, 15 June.

Campaign Against Arms Trade (1994), *Campaigning for Conversion at the BAe AGM*, Bulletin, 125, February.
Campbell, B. (1993), *Goliath. Britain's Dangerous Places*, London: Methuen.
Campbell, D. (1990), *That Was Business. This Is Personal*, London: Secker & Warburg.
Campbell, D. (1994), *The Underworld*, London: BBC Books.
Carter, D.L. (1994), 'International Organized Crime: Emerging Trends in Entrepreneurial Crime', *Journal of Contemporary Criminal Justice*, 10 (4): 239–66.
Casillo, S. (1990), 'Il trionfo delle aziende fantasma', *Micromega*, 4: 143–60.
Cassels, J. (1993), *The Uncertain Promise of Law: Lessons from Bhopal*, Toronto: University of Toronto Press.
Cassese, A. (1994), *Umano-disumano. Commissariati e prigioni nell'Europa di oggi*, Roma/Bari: Laterza.
Cantanzaro, R. (1988), *Il delitto come impresa. Storia sociale della mafia*, Padova: Liviana Editrice.
Catanzaro, R. (1994), 'Violent Social Regulation: Organized Crime in the Italian South', *Social and Legal Studies*, 3(2): 267–70.
Censis (Centro Studi Investimenti Sociali) (1992), *Contro e dentro. Criminalità, istituzioni, società*, Milano: Franco Angeli.
Centorrino, M. (1990), *L'economia 'cattiva' del Mezzogiorno*, Napoli: Liguori.
Centorrino, M. (1994), 'Un fallimento del mito-mercato', *Narcomafie*, II(9): 8–9.
Centorrino, M. and Signorino, G. (1993), 'Criminalità e modelli di economia locale', in Zamagni, S. (ed.), *Mercati illegali e mafie. L'economia del crimine organizzato*, Bologna: Il Mulino.
Ceretti, A. (1992), *L'orizzonte artificiale. Problemi epistemologici della criminologia*, Padova: Cedam.
Chambliss, W. (1978), *On the Take. From Petty Crooks to Presidents*, Bloomington: Indiana University Press.
Chandler, A. (1977), *The Visible Hand*, Cambridge, Mass: Harvard University Press.
Chomsky, N. (1992), *Deterring Democracy*, London: Vintage.
Christie, A. (1994), 'Fake Goods Go Up in Smoke as French Take Tough Line', The *Guardian*, 22 June.
Cipriani, A. (1989), *Mafia. Il riciclaggio del denaro sporco*, Roma: Napoleone.
Cipriani, G. (1993), *I mandanti. Il patto strategico tra massoneria, mafia e potere politico*, Roma: Editori Riuniti.
Clarke, H. (1994), 'Cools Murder Linked to Knowledge of Agusta Deal', *The European*, 28 January–3 February.

Clarke, M. (1990), *Business Crime: Its Nature and Control*, Cambridge: Polity.
Clegg, S. and Dunkerley, D. (1990), *Organization, Class and Control*, London: Routledge.
Clinard, M.B. (1979), *Illegal Corporate Behaviour*, Washington, DC: US Department of Justice.
Clinard, M.B. (1983), *Corporate Ethics and Crime. The Role of Middle Management*, Beverly Hills: Sage.
Clinard, M.B. and Yeager, P.C. (1980), *Corporate Crime*, New York: Macmillan.
Cloward, R. and Ohlin, L. (1960), *Delinquency and Opportunity*, New York: The Free Press.
Coco, N. and Serra, C. (1983), *Devianza, conflitto, criminalità*, Roma: Bulzoni.
Cohen, A. (1955), *Delinquent Boys: The Culture of the Gang*, New York: The Free Press.
Cohen, A. (1977), 'The Concept of Criminal Organization', *British Journal of Criminology*, 17 (2): 97–111.
Cohen, A. (1990), 'Foreword and Overview', in Huff, R. (ed.), *Gangs in America*, London: Sage.
Coleman, J.S. (1982), *The Asymmetric Society*, Syracuse: Syracuse University Press.
Coleman, J.W. (1987), 'Toward an Integrated Theory of White-Collar Crime', *American Journal of Sociology*, 93: 406–39.
Collins, N. (1990), 'The European Community's Farm Lobby', *Corruption and Reform*, 5: 235–57.
Colussi, G. and Sivestri, F. (1994), 'Iugeri al sole o coltello alla gola', *Narcomafie*, II(8): 4.
Comité Colbert (1992), *La contrefaçon en Italie*, Paris: Comité Colbert.
Commissione Antimafia (1976), *Relazione sul traffico mafioso di tabacchi e stupefacenti nonché sul rapporto tra mafia e gangsterismo americano*, Roma: Poligrafico dello Stato.
Commissione Antimafia (1993), *Mafia e politica*, Roma/Bari: Laterza.
Commissione Antimafia (1994), *Rapporto sulla Camorra*, Roma: l'Unità.
Committee of Public Accounts (1994), *The Proper Conduct of Public Business*, London: HMSO.
Conklin, J.E. (1977), *Illegal But Not Criminal: Business Crime in America*, Englewood Cliffs, NJ: Prentice-Hall.
Conradi, P. (1994), 'Russian Adoption Curbs Alarm Western Couples', *The European*, 22–8 December.
Conseil National des Villes (1994), *L'économie souterraine de la drogue*, Paris: Conseil National des Villes/Maison des Sciences de l'Homme.

Coppel, A. (1994), 'Il sistema di socialità delle droghe', *Narcomafie*, 2(2): 21–2.

Council of Europe (1993), *Sexual Exploitation, Pornography and Prostitution of, and Trafficking in, Children and Young Adults*, Strasbourg: Council of Europe.

Counsell, G. (1993), 'Glaxo Sacks Five over Banned Sales Techniques', *The Independent*, 15 November.

Courrier International, 10 March 1994 ('Dossier: Marchands de Mort').

Court of Auditors (1994), *Annual Report Concerning Financial Year 1993*, Official Journal of the European Communities: Information and Notices, vol. 37, 24 November.

Cowe, R. (1994), 'Tobacco Road to Uzbekistan', The *Guardian*, 17 May.

Cowley, C. (1992), *Guns, Lies and Spies*, London: Hamish Hamilton.

Crainer, S. (1993), *Zeebrugge: Learning from Disaster. Lessons in Corporate Responsibility*, London: Herald Charitable Trust.

Cranor, C. (1993), *Regulating Toxic Substances: A Philosophy of Science and the Law*, Oxford: Oxford University Press.

Cressey, D. (1953), *Other People's Money*, Glencoe, Ill.: Free Press.

Cressey, D. (1969), *Theft of the Nation: The Structure and Operations of Organized Crime*, New York: Harper & Row.

Cressey, D. (1989), 'The Poverty of Theory in Corporate Crime Research', in Laufer, W.S. and Adler, F. (eds), *Advances in Criminological Theory. Volume One*, New Brunswick: Transaction.

Croall, H. (1992), *White-Collar Crime*, Milton Keynes: Open University Press.

Cupitt, R.T. (1993), 'The Political Economy of Arms Exports in Post-Communist Societies: The Cases of Poland and the CSFR', *Communist and Post-Communist Studies*, 27: 87–103.

Dalla Chiesa, N. (1983), 'Mafia e potere oggi', *Democrazia e Diritto*, XXIII (4): 31–40.

Dalton, M. (1959), *Men Who Manage*, London: Wiley.

D'Avanzo, G. (1993), 'Faccia a faccia Riina-Buscetta', *La Repubblica*, 17 November.

Dawnay, I. (1992), 'Judicial Inquiry Ordered into Iraqi Defence Contracts', *The Financial Times*, 11 November.

Defoe, D. (1727), *The Complete English Tradesman*.

Donegan, L. (1993), 'MP Who Quits Over BT Shares Offence Gets State-Funded Job', The *Guardian* 9 August.

Dorn, N., South, N. and Murji, K. (1992), *Traffickers. Drug Markets and Law Enforcement*, London: Routledge.

Douglas, J.D. and Johnson, J.M. (eds) (1977), *Official Deviance*, Chicago: Lippincott.

Downes, D. and Rock, P. (1988), *Understanding Deviance. A Guide to the Sociology of Crime and Rule Breaking*, Oxford: Clarendon Press.

Durham, M. (1994), 'Making a Killing with British Aid', *The Observer*, 13 November.

Durham, M. and Nelson, D. (1994), 'The Tangled Web of Arms and British Aid', *The Observer*, 6 February.

Durkheim, E. (1960), *The Rules of Sociological Method*, London: Macmillan.

Edelhertz, H. and Overcast, T. (1982), *White-Collar Crime: An Agenda for Research*, Lexington: Lexington Books.

Edelhertz, H. and Overcast, T. (1993), *The Business of Organized Crime*, Loomis, Calif.: Palmer Enterprises.

Ellman, M. (1994), 'The Increase in Death and Disease under "Katastroika"', *Cambridge Journal of Economics*, 18(4): 329–55.

Endean, C. (1994), 'Albanians Risk All To Run Blockade of Bari', *The European*, 21–7 October.

Enzensberger, H.M. (1992), 'The Great Migration', *Granta*, 42: 17–51.

Erhel, C. (1994), 'Sang: Fabius, Dufoix, Herve bientôt mis en examen', *Libération*, 21 September.

Ermann, M.D. and Lundman, R.J. (eds) (1978), *Corporate and Governmental Deviance*, New York: Oxford University Press.

Ermann, M.D. and Lundman, R.J. (1982), *Corporate Deviance*, New York: Holt, Rinehart and Winston.

Etzioni, A. (1964), *Modern Organizations*, Englewood Cliffs, NJ: Prentice-Hall.

Falcone, G. (1991), *Cose di Cosa Nostra*, Milano: Rizzoli.

Falcone, G. (1992), 'Struttura e dinamica delle organizzazioni criminali in Italia', *Sicurezza e Territorio*, 3: 13–20.

Faller, L.B. (1993), *Crime and Defoe*, Cambridge: Cambridge University Press.

Ferracuti, F. (ed.) (1988), *Forme di organizzazioni criminali e terrorismo*, Milano: Giuffré.

Fiasco, M. (1994), 'Oggi il leccofermo si chiama franchising', *Narcomafie*, II(7): 10.

Fijnaut, C. (1990), 'Organized Crime: A Comparison Between the United States of America and Western Europe', *British Journal of Criminology*, 30(3): 321–40.

Fitzroy, F. and Mueller, D.C. (1984), 'Co-operation and Conflict in Contractual Organisations', *Quarterly Review of Economics and Business*, 24: 24–50.

Fondazione Colasanto (1990), *Sintesi delle principali attività svolte*, Napoli: Fondazione Colasanto/Osservatorio sulla Camorra.

Foot, P. and Laxton, T. (1994), 'Thatcher, Major, Saddam and the Merchants of Death', *A Private Eye Arms to Iraq Special*, November.
Forgione, F. and Mondani, P. (1994), *Oltre la cupola*, Milano: Rizzoli.
Foster, J. (1990), *Villains. Crime and Community in the Inner City*, London: Routledge.
Fox, A. (1966), *Industrial Sociology and Industrial Relations*, London: HMSO.
Friedman, A. (1993), *Spider's Web. Bush, Saddam, Thatcher and the Decade of Deceit*, London: Faber & Faber.
Friends of the Earth (1992), *Mahogany Is Murder*, London: Friends of the Earth.
Friends of the Earth (1993), *Timber: The UK Timber Industry's 'Think Wood' and 'Forest Forever' Campaigns*, London: Friends of the Earth.
Gaetner, G. (1992), *L'argent facile. Dictionnaire de la corruption en France*, Paris: Stock.
Gallino, L. (1975), *Dizionario di sociologia*, Torino: UTET.
Gallino, L. (1985), *Il lavoro e il suo doppio*, Bologna: Il Mulino.
Gambetta, D. (1992), *La mafia siciliana. Un'industria della protezione privata*, Torino: Einaudi.
Garofoli, G. (1983), 'Areas of Specialised Production and Small Firms in Europe', *Economia Marche*, 11(1): 53–84.
Geis, G. (1968), *White-Collar Criminal. The Offender in Business and the Professions*, New York: Atherton Press.
Geis, G. (1992), 'The Heavy Electrical Equipment Antitrust Cases of 1961' in Ermann, M.D. and Lundman, R.J. (eds), *Corporate and Governmental Deviance*, 4th edition, New York: Oxford University Press.
Geis, G. and Jesilow, P. (eds) (1993), *White-Collar Crime*, Special Issue of *The Annals of the American Academy of Political and Social Science*, 525, January.
Giacopuzzi, G. (1994), 'Corruzione in Spagna', *Narcomafie*, II(8): 29–31.
Gilmore, W.C. (1993), 'Money Laundering: The International Aspect', in The David Hume Institute, *Money Laundering*, Edinburgh: Edinburgh University Press.
Godson, R. and Olson, W.J. (1995), 'International Organized Crime', *Society*, 32(2): 18–29.
Goldblat, I. (1994), *Arms Control. A Guide to Negotiations and Agreements*, Oslo: International Peace Research Institute.
Gordon, D.M. (1980), 'Capitalism, Class, and Crime in America', in Andreano, R. and Siegfried, J. (eds), op. cit.
Gottfredson, M. and Hirschi, T. (1990), *A General Theory of Crime*, Stanford, Calif.: Stanford University Press.

Gouldner, A.W. (1954), *Patterns of Industrial Bureaucracy*, New York: The Free Press.

Gow, D. (1994), 'Mystery of the Lost Tycoon and Missing Billions', *The Observer*, 17 April.

Gow, D. and Tomforde, A. (1993), 'Bad Blood on their Hands', The *Guardian*, 6 November.

Grabosky, P. and Sutton, A. (eds) (1989), *Stains on a White Collar*, Sydney: Federation Press.

Graef, R. (1993), *Living Dangerously. Young Offenders in Their Own Words*, London: HarperCollins.

Green, G.S. (1990), *Occupational Crime*, Chicago: Nelson-Hall.

Green, G.S. (1993), 'White-Collar Crime and the Study of Embezzlement', in Geis, G. and Jesilow, P. (eds), op. cit.

Green, P. (1991), *Drug Couriers*, London: Howard League for Penal Reform.

Greene, G. (1982), *J'accuse. The Dark Side of Nice*, London: Bodley Head.

Greilsamer, L. (1992), *Le proces du sang contaminé*, Paris: Le Monde Editions.

Greilsamer, L. (1993), 'Au proces des initiés de l'affaire Pechiney–Triangle', *Le Monde*, 27–8 June.

Grignetti, F. (1994), 'Bambini venduti per i trapianti', *La Stampa*, 22 September.

Groussard, D. and Leauthier, A. (1994), 'Affaire Yann Piat: Entendus, les politiques sont laisses libres', *Libération*, 3 March.

Hagan, F. and Benekos, P. (1992), 'What Charles Keating and "Murph the Surf" Have in Common. A Symbiosis of Professional and Occupational and Corporate Crime', *Criminal Organizations*, 7(1): 7–20.

Hagen, E. (1962), *On the Theory of Social Change*, Homewood, Ill.: Irwin-Dorsey.

Hagen, E. (1980), *The Economics of Development*, Homewood, Ill.: Irwin-Dorsey.

Hall, M. (1992), 'The $225,000,000 Habit', *The Observer Magazine* 8 November.

Haller, M. (1992), 'Bureaucracy and the Mafia: An Alternative View', *Journal of Contemporary Criminal Justice*, 8(1): 1–10.

HCDA (Hackney Community Defence Association) (1991), *A Crime Is a Crime Is a Crime*, London: HCDA.

HCDA (Hackney Community Defence Association) (1992), *Fighting the Lawmen*, London: HCDA.

Herring, R.J. (1993), 'BCCI: Lessons for International Bank Supervision', *Contemporary Policy Issues*, XI (2): 76–86.

Hobbs, (1995), *'Bad' Economies*, Oxford: Oxford University Press.

Hoffmann, G.H. (1990), *Tales of Hoffmann: The Experience of an International Business Investigator*, Amsterdam: Hoffmann Investigations Ltd.

Hooker, L. (1994), 'Austrians Find Rich Pickings In Hungarian Land Market', The *Guardian*, 27 May.

Hooper, J. (1993), 'Spain Finally Admits to Chemical Warfare Plant', *The Observer*, 14 November.

Hopkins, A. (1980), 'Crimes Against Capitalism: An Australian Case', *Contemporary Crises*, 4: 421–32.

Ianni, F. (1972), *A Family Business. Kinship and Social Control in Organized Crime*, New York: Russell Sage Foundation.

Il Corriere della Sera, 8 July 1991 ('Viaggio nei segreti della Costa Azzurra, lavanderia di denaro sporco').

Il Corriere della Sera, 21 October 1993 ('Comprammo un vicequestore').

Il Corriere della Sera, 2 March 1994 ('Midi, politici assassini').

Infomatin, 2 March 1994 ('Enquete sur l'assassinat de Yann Piat').

Istat (Istituto Nazionale di Statistica) (1992), *Statistiche Giudiziarie*, Roma: Poligrafico dello Stato.

Jack, R.B. (1993), 'Introduction', in The David Hume Institute, *Money Laundering*, Edinburgh: Edinburgh University Press.

Jack Report (1989), *Banking Services: Law and Practice*, London: HMSO.

Johnson, E. (1962), 'Organized Crime: Challenge to the American Legal System', *Criminal Law, Criminology and Police Science*, 53 (4): 1–29.

Kapuscinski, R. (1994), *Imperium*, Milano: Feltrinelli.

Karp, A. (1994), 'The Rise of Black and Grey Markets', *The Annals of the American Academy of Political and Social Science*, Special issue: 'The Arms Trade', 535: 175–89.

Keat, R. and Abercrombie, N. (1991), *Enterprise Culture*, London/New York: Routledge.

Kefauver Committee (1951), *Report on Organized Crime*, New York: Didier.

Kelsey, T. (1994), 'A Land of Old Roubles', *The Independent*, 12 July.

Kerenyi, C. (1958), *The Gods of the Greeks*, Harmondsworth: Penguin.

Kerr, C., Dunlop, J.T., Harbison, F.H. and Myers, C.A. (1964), *Industrialisation and Industrial Man*, New York: Oxford University Press.

Klockars, C. (1974), *The Professional Fence*, New York: Free Press.

Knight, F.H. (1921), *Risk, Uncertainty and Profit*, New York: Houghton Mifflin.

Knight, F.H. (1935), *The Ethics of Competition and Other Essays*, London: Allen & Unwin.

Kochan, N. and Whittington, B. (1991), *Bankrupt. The BCCI Fraud*, London: Victor Gollancz.

Kontrolpean, K. (1995), 'Spain: The GAL', *Statewatch*, 5(1): 16–17.

Kramer, R.C. (1982), 'Corporate Crime: An Organizational Perspective', in

Wickman, P. and Dailey, T. (eds), *White-Collar and Economic Crime; Multidisciplinary and Cross-National Perspectives*, Lexington: Lexington Books.

Lacey, R. (1991), *Little Man: Meyer Lansky and the Gangster Life*, New York: Century Books.

Laitinen, A. (1993), 'Present Trends of Domestic and International Corporate Crime in Finland', paper presented at the 11th International Congress of Criminology, Budapest, 22–7 August.

Landesco, J. (1969), *Organized Crime in Chicago*, Chicago, Ill.: University of Chicago Press.

La Repubblica, 12 December 1991 ('Ecco l'Italia dell'arte rapita e venduta').

La Repubblica, 8 January 1992 ('Armi e mercenari: a giudizio un principe').

La Repubblica, 23 December 1993 ('Riina sepolto vivo all'Asinara').

La Repubblica, 15 August 1994 ('Il traffico del plutonio va bloccato a Mosca').

La Repubblica, 29 November 1994 ('Così la governante rubò 50 Chagall').

La Stampa, 6 May 1990 ('Rapivano bambini per non fallire' by P. N.).

La Stampa, 26 July 1993 ('Germania Est, privatizzatori pentiti' by M. V.).

La Stampa, 27 October 1994 ('Nel mondo 100 milioni di schiavi').

La Stampa, 7 December 1994 ('Esportiamo filetto: erano zampe di gallina').

Lee, R. (1992), 'Dynamics of the Soviet Illicit Drug Market', *Crime, Law and Social Change*, 17(3): 177–233.

Lefevre, G. (1902), *Le traité 'De Usura' de Robert de Courcon*, Lille: Université de Lille.

Le Goff, J. (1977), *Tempo della chiesa e tempo del mercante*, Torino: Einaudi.

Le Goff, J. (1987), *La borsa e la vita. Dall'usuraio al banchiere*, Roma/Bari: Laterza.

Leigh, L.H. and Smith, A.T.H. (1991), 'Some Observations on European Fraud Laws and their Reform with Reference to the EEC', *Corruption and Reform*, 6: 267–84.

Le Monde, 11 August 1993 ('L'affaire d'espionage industriel au profit de Volkswagen').

Lennon, P. (1994), 'La Côte de Crime', The *Guardian*, 4 March.

Levi, M. (1981), *The Phantom Capitalists*, London: Heinemann.

Levi, M. (1987), *Regulating Fraud. White-Collar Crime and the Criminal Process*, London: Tavistock.

Levi, M. (1991a), 'Sentencing White-Collar Crime in the Dark? Reflections on the Guinness Four', *The Howard Journal of Criminal Justice*, 30(4): 257–79.

Levi, M. (1991b), 'Regulating Money Laudering', *British Journal of Criminology*, 31(2): 109–25.

Lightfoot, L. (1994), 'Couples Abandon Romania Orphans', *Sunday Times*, 6 November.
Lilly, J.R., Cullen, F.T. and Ball, R.A. (1989), *Criminological Theory. Context and Consequences*, Newbury Park: Sage.
Lipiez, A. (1987), *Mirages and Miracles: The Crisis of Global Fordism*, London: Verso.
Lodato, S. (1992), *Potenti. Sicilia, anni Novanta*, Milano: Garzanti.
Lombardo, R. (1991), 'Organized Crime: A Control Theory', *Criminal Organizations*, 6(2): 8–13.
Lombroso, C. (1971 [1876]), *L'uomo delinquente*, Roma: Napoleone.
Longo, F. and Moder, M. (1994), 'Dal confino al confino: carriera di un poliziotto scomodo', *Narcomafie*, II(9): 6–7.
López, L. (1994), 'Dangerous Rumours', *Time*, 18 April.
Luce, E. (1994), 'Swiss War on Balkan Drug Groups Hits Immigrants', The *Guardian*, 3 December.
Lupo, S. (1993), *Storia della mafia*, Roma: Donzelli.
Maas, P. (1968), *The Valachi Papers*, New York: Putnam's.
Maceriean, N. (1993), 'Bosses Win Bribes War', *The Observer*, 7 November.
Madeo, L. (1994), *Donne di mafia*, Milano: Mondadori.
Maisi, M. (1993), *Far politica in Sicilia*, Milano: Feltrinelli.
Malcher, A. (1989), 'Sophisticated Weapons and Their Availability', *The Police Journal*, LXII(4): 337–9.
Mancuso, P. (1990), 'La conquista dell'impresa', *La Città Nuova*, V(2): 18–22.
Mannheim, H. (1975), *Trattato di criminologia comparata*, Torino: Einaudi.
Mansfield, M. (1994), *Presumed Guilty. The British Legal System Exposed*, London: Mandarin.
March, J.G. (1990), 'The Technology of Foolishness', in Pugh, D.S. (ed.), op. cit.
Marek, A. (1993), 'Measures to Control Organised Crime: The Situation in Poland', paper presented at the 11th Congress of Criminology, Budapest, August 22–7.
Marinellos, G., Dervinioti, H. and Zarakovitou, A. (1993), 'Cashing in Children', The *Guardian*, 2 November.
Marino, G. (1993), *Bella e mala Napoli*, Roma/Bari: Laterza.
Maritati, A. (1992), 'Puglia. Dai tentativi di infiltrazione alla Sacra Corona Unita', *Asterischi*, I(2): 71–85.
Maritati, A. (1993), 'La criminalità organizzata in Puglia', in Occhiogrosso, F. (ed), *Ragazzi della mafia*, Milano: Franco Angeli.
Marro, E. (1990), 'Il terremoto, grande affare', *Il Corriere della Sera*, 22 November.

Mars, G. (1994), *Cheats at Work*, Aldershot: Dartmouth.

Martens, F.T. and Roosa, S.B. (1994), 'Exporting RICO to Eastern Europe: Prudent or Irresponsible', *Journal of Contemporary Criminal Justice*, 10 (4): 267–89.

Marthoz, J.P. (1994), 'Echoes of Italy in Belgian Scandals', *The European*, 28 January–3 February.

Martin, J.M. and Romano, A.T. (1992), *Multinational Crime*, Newbury Park: Sage.

Martinoli, G. (1985), 'Dimensioni economiche dell'illecito in Italia', in Centro Studi Investimenti Sociali (Censis) (ed.), *Dossier Illecito*, Roma: Censis.

Mascarino, E. (1994), 'Schiavi nella sartoria cinese', *La Stampa*, 22 September.

Mayer, J.P. (1956), *Max Weber and German Politics*, London: Faber & Faber.

Mayhew, P., Aye Maung, N. and Mirrless-Black, C. (1993), *The 1992 British Crime Survey*, London: HMSO.

Mazarr, M.J. (1993), 'A Farewell to Arms Control?', *International Security*, 17: 188–96.

McClean, J.D. (1992), *International Judicial Assistance*, Oxford: Clarendon Press.

McClelland, D.C. (1961), *The Achieving Society*, Princeton, NJ: Van Nostrand.

McIntosh, M. (1975), *The Organisation of Crime*, London: Macmillan.

McIvor, G. (1993), 'Cat Burglars Steal Museum's Picassos', The *Guardian*, 9 November.

McMullan, J.L. (1992), *Beyond the Limits of the Law. Corporate Crime and Law and Order*, Halifax: Fernwood.

McSmith, A. (1994), 'Business Booms for the Booze Smugglers', *The Observer*, 11 December.

Mead, G.H. (1934), *Mind, Self, and Society. From the Standpoint of a Social Behaviorist*, Chicago: University of Chicago Press.

Melville, H. (1984 [1857]), *L'uomo di fiducia*, Milano: Feltrinelli.

Merton, R. (1968), *Social Theory and Social Structure*, New York: The Free Press.

Mill, J.S. (1844), *Essays on Some Unsettled Questions of Political Economy.*

Mills, C.W. (1956), *The Power Elite*, Oxford: Oxford University Press.

Ministry of Agriculture (1992), *Appropriation Accounts. Volume Three*, London: HMSO.

Moder, M. (1994), 'L'Europa nel mercato dei cavalli di Frisia', *Narcomafie*, II(4): 11–13.

Mokhiber, R. (1988), *Corporate Crime and Violence. Big Business Power and the Abuse of Public Trust*, San Francisco: Sierra Club Books.

Moore, M. (1987), 'Organized Crime as Business Enterprise', in Edelhertz, H. (ed.), *Major Issues in Organized Crime Control*, Washington, DC: Government Printing Office.

Moore, R.H. (1994), 'The Activities and Personnel of Twenty-First Century Organized Crime', *Criminal Organizations*, 9(1): 3–11.

Morton, J. (1992), *Gangland. London's Underworld*, London: Warner.

Mossetto, G. (1993), 'L'economia della contraffazione', in Zamagni, S. (ed.), *Mercati illegali e mafie. L'economia del crimine organizzato*, Bologna: Il Mulino.

Mouzelis, N.P. (1967), *Organisation and Bureaucracy. An Analysis of Modern Theories*, London: Routledge & Kegan Paul.

Myers, L. (1991), 'Two Tied to Polish Mafia', *Chicago Tribune*, 6 June.

Narcomafie (1994a), 'Ex Jugoslavia: Guerra di Mercato', special issue, II(4).

Narcomafie (1994b), 'Quando il corpo diventa merce', II(1): 38.

National Peace Council (1994), 'More Questions Than Answers?', *NPC Newsletter*, 1 June.

Nee, C. (1993), 'Careers in Car Crime', *Research Bulletin* (Home Office Research and Statistics Department), 33: 1–4.

Nelken, D. (1994a), 'White-Collar Crime', in Maguire, M., Morgan, R. and Reiner, R. (eds), *The Oxford Handbook of Criminology*, Oxford: Clarendon.

Nelken, D. (1994b), (ed.), *The Futures of Criminology*, London: Sage.

Nikiforov, A.S. (1994), 'A Response to Joseph Serio's "The Soviet Union: Disorganization and Organized Crime"', *Criminal Organizations*, 8(3–4): 10–12.

Norrie, A. (1993), *Crime, Reason and History. A Critical Introduction to Criminal Law*, London: Weidenfeld and Nicolson.

Norton-Taylor, R. (1991), 'British Firm Raided in US Push Against Gun Running', The *Guardian*, 18 November.

Norton-Taylor, R. (1994), 'MoD Official Jailed for £1.3m Bribes', The *Guardian*, 27 May.

Norton-Taylor, R. (1995), *Truth Is a Difficult Concept: Inside the Scott Inquiry*, London: 4th Estate.

Nouchi, F. (1993), 'Les leçons du procès du sang contaminé. Un devoir de verité', *Le Monde*, 21 July.

Observatoire Géopolitique des Drogues (1994), 'L'ombra della grande Albania', *Narcomafie*, II(7): 42–43.

Occhiogrosso, F. (1993), *Ragazzi della mafia*, Milano: Franco Angeli.

O'Shaughnessy, H. (1994), 'Murder and Mutilation Supply Human Organ Trade', *The Observer*, 27 March.

Oxford, E. (1994), 'Child Shoplifters Work to Order', *The Independent*, 19 January.

Pacheco, C.B. and Büll, M.R. (1994), *Dossier America*, São Paulo: Nova Linha Editorial.
Padilla, F.M. (1992), *The Gang as an American Enterprise*, New Brunswick, NJ: Rutgers University Press.
Palermo, C. (1988), *Armi e Droga*, Roma: Editori Riuniti.
Palmer, J. and Bannister, N. (1994), 'British Steel Fined £24m over Cartel', The *Guardian*, 17 February.
Pantaleone, M. (1976), *Mafia e droga*, Torino: Einaudi.
Papuzzi, A. (1991), 'La repubblica del terremoto', *L'Indice*, 6: 39.
Parsons, T. (1982), *On Institutions and Social Evolution*, Chicago: The University of Chicago Press.
Passas, N. (1990), 'Anomie and Corporate Deviance', *Contemporary Crises*, 14: 157–78.
Passas, N. (1993), 'Structural Sources of International Crime: Policy Lessons from the BCCI Affair', *Crime, Law and Social Change*, 20: 293–309.
Passas, N. and Nelken, D. (1993), 'The Thin Line Between Legitimate and Criminal Enterprise: Subsidy Frauds in the European Community', *Crime, Law and Social Change*, 19: 223–43.
PCOC (President's Commission on Organized Crime) (1986), *The Impact: Organized Crime Today*, Washington, DC: Government Printing Office.
Pearce, F. (1976), *Crimes of the Powerful: Marxism, Crime and Deviance*, London: Pluto.
Pearce, F. and Tombs, S. (1990), 'Ideology, Hegemony, and Empiricism: Compliance Theories and Regulation', *British Journal of Criminology*, 30: 423–33.
Pearce, F. and Tombs, S. (1991), 'Policing Corporate "Skid Rows": A Reply to Keith Hawkins', *British Journal of Criminology*, 31: 415–26.
Pearce, F. and Tombs, S. (1993), 'US Capital Versus the Third World: Union Carbide and Bhopal', in Pearce, F. and Woodiwiss, M. (eds), *Global Crime Connections. Dynamics and Control*, London: Macmillan.
Pennsylvania Crime Commission (1993), *1992 Report*, Conshohocken, Pa.: Commonwealth of Pennsylvania.
Perrow, C. (1961), 'The Analysis of Goals in Complex Organizations', *American Sociological Review*, 26: 854–66.
Perrow, C. (1970), *Organizational Analysis. A Sociological View*, London: Tavistock.
Peterson, M. (1991), 'The Changes of a Decade', *Criminal Organizations*, 6 (3–4): 20–2.
Petronio, A. (1949), *Satyricon. Romanzo d'avventure e di costumi*, Milano: Bietti.
Phythian, M. and Little, W. (1993), 'Parliament and Arms Sales: Lessons of the Matrix Churchill Affair', *Parliamentary Affairs*, 46: 293–308.

Pilger, J. (1994), 'Death for Sale', The *Guardian Weekend*, 12 November.

Pizzorno, A. and Arlacchi, P. (1985), *Camorra, contrabbando e mercato della droga in Campania*, Roma: Commissione Parlamentare sul Fenomeno della Mafia.

Plommer, L. (1994), 'Weapon-Toting West Bleeds Saudis Dry', The *Guardian*, 17 December.

Polsky, N. (1967), *Hustlers, Beats and Others*, Harmondsworth: Pelican.

Project on Demilitarisation (1994), *Western Hypocrisy on Arms Conversion*, Leeds: POD/Leeds University.

Pugh, D.S. (ed.) (1990), *Organization Theory. Selected Readings*, Harmondsworth: Penguin.

Punch, M. (1993), 'Bandit Banks: Financial Services and Organized Crime', *Journal of Contemporary Criminal Justice*, 9(3): 175–96.

Putterman, L. (ed.) (1986), *The Economic Nature of the Firm*, Cambridge: Cambridge University Press.

Quinney, R. (1964), 'The Study of White-Collar Crime: Toward a Reorientation in Theory and Research', *Journal of Criminal Law, Criminology and Police Science*, 55: 208–14.

Quinney, R. (1970), *The Problem of Crime*, New York: Dodd, Mead.

Radford, R. (1994), 'The Heavy Metals That Are Too Hot to Handle', The *Guardian*, 17 August.

Radice, E. (1993), 'Tangenti in pillole. Quattro avvisi per le mazzette in farmacia', *La Repubblica*, 26 August.

Rawlinson, P. (1993), 'Pervasive Criminalnoma', *Arguments and Facts International*, March: 6–7.

Reed, M.I. (1993), *The Sociology of Organizations. Themes, Perspectives and Prospects*, Hemel Hempstead, Herts: Harvester-Wheatsheaf.

Reeve, A. (1991), 'The Theory of Property', in Held, D. (ed.), *Political Theory Today*, Cambridge: Polity Press.

Reuter, P. (1983), *Disorganized Crime. Illegal Markets and the Mafia*, Cambridge, Mass.: The MIT Press.

Reuter, P. (1984), *Racketeering in Legitimate Industries. A Study in the Economics of Intimidation*, Santa Monica, Calif.: The Rand Corporation.

Reynolds, M.O. (1980), 'The Economics of Criminal Activity', in Andreano, R. and Siegfried, J. (eds), op. cit.

Roberts, S. (1994), 'Fictitious Capital, Fictitious Spaces: The Geography of Offshore Financial Flows', in Corbridge, S., Martin, R. and Thrift, N. (eds), *Money, Power and Space*, Oxford: Blackwell.

Robinson, J. (1994), *The Laudrymen. Inside the World's Third Largest Business*, London: Simon & Schuster.

Roebuck, J. and Weeber, S.C. (1978), *Political Crime in the United States*, New York: Praeger.

Róna-Tas, A. (1994), 'The First Shall Be Last? Entrepreneurship and Communist Cadres in the Transition from Socialism', *American Journal of Sociology*, 100(1): 40–69.

Rubin, P.H. (1980), 'The Economics of Crime', in Andreano, R. and Siegfried, J. (eds), op. cit.

Rubinstein, J. and Reuter, P. (1978), *Bookmaking in New York*, New York: Policy Sciences Center.

Ruggiero, V. (1992a), *La Roba. Economie e culture dell'eroina*, Parma: Pratiche.

Ruggiero, V. (1992b), 'The Kidnapping Industry and the State in Italy', *Criminal Organizations*, 7(3): 21–2.

Ruggiero, V. (1993a), 'Organized Crime in Italy: Testing Alternative Definitions', *Social and Legal Studies*, 2: 131–48.

Ruggiero, V. (1993b), 'The Camorra: "Clean" Capital and Organised Crime', in Pearce, F. and Woodiwiss, M. (eds), *Global Crime Connections*, London: Macmillan.

Ruggiero, V. (1993c), 'Brixton, London: A Drug Culture Without a Drug Economy?', *The International Journal of Drug Policy*, 4(3): 83–90.

Ruggiero, V. (1994), 'Corruption in Italy: An Attempt to Identify the Victims', *The Howard Journal of Criminal Justice*, 33 (4): 319–37.

Ruggiero, V. (1995), 'Drug Economics. A Fordist Model of Criminal Capital', *Capital and Class*, 55: 131–50.

Ruggiero, V. and South, N. (1995), *Eurodrugs. Drug Use, Markets and Trafficking in Europe*, London: University College London Press.

Ruggiero, V. and Vass, A. (1992), 'Heroin Use and the Formal Economy', *British Journal of Criminology*, 32(3): 273–91.

Sales, I. (1992), 'La criminalità organizzata tra modernizzazione e poteri dello stato', *Asterischi*, 2: 11–20.

Salzano, J. (1994), 'It's Dirty Business: Organized Crime in Deep Sludge', *Criminal Organizations*, 8(3–4): 17–20.

Sammarco, V. (1994), 'Schiavisti in doppiopetto', *Narcomafie*, II(7): 9.

Sampson, A. (1977), *The Arms Bazaar*, London: Viking.

Samuelson, P. (1981), 'Schumpeter's Capitalism, Socialism and Democracy', in Heertje, A. (ed.), *Schumpeter's Vision. Capitalism, Socialism and Democracy After 40 Years*, Eastbourne/New York: Praeger.

Santino, U. and La Fiura, G. (1990), *L'impresa mafiosa*, Milano: Franco Angeli.

Santino, U. and La Fiura, G. (1993), *Dietro la droga*, Torino: Gruppo Abele.

Schelling, T.C. (1967), 'Economic Analysis of Organized Crime', in The President's Commission on Law Enforcement and the Administration of Justice, *Task Force Report: Organized Crime*, Washington, DC: Government Printing Office.

Schrager, L.S. and Short, J.F. (1977), 'Toward a Sociology of Organizational Crime', *Social Problems*, 25: 407–19.
Schumpeter, J. (1961a) *Capitalism, Socialism and Democracy*, London: Allen & Unwin.
Schumpeter, J. (1961b), *The Theory of Economic Development*, New York: Oxford University Press.
Scott, J. (1989), 'Ownership and Employer Control', in Gallie, D. (ed.), *Employment in Britain*, Oxford: Blackwell.
Semier, P. and Lynn, M. (1993), 'Italian Bribe Claims Rock Drug Firms', *The Sunday Times*, 3 October.
Sennett, R. (1993), *Authority*, London/Boston: Faber & Faber.
Serio, J. (1991), 'The Soviet Union: Disorganization and Organized Crime', *Criminal Organizations*, 6(2–3): 3–7.
Sgubbi, F. (1990), *Il reato come rischio sociale*, Bologna: Il Mulino.
Shapiro, S.P. (1984), *Wayward Capitalists. Target of the Securities and Exchange Commission*, New Haven: Yale University Press.
Shapiro, S.P. (1990), 'Collaring the Crime, Not the Criminal: Reconsidering the Concept of White-Collar Crime', *American Sociological Review*, 55: 346–65.
Sharrock, D. (1993), 'Police Arrest 81 Illegal Immigrants', The *Guardian*, 22 July.
Shaw, C. (1930), *The Jack-Roller: A Delinquent Boy's Own Story*, Chicago: University of Chicago Press.
Shaw, C. and Mckay, H. (1972), *Juvenile Delinquency and Urban Areas*, Chicago: University of Chicago Press.
Shelley, L.I. (1994), 'Post-Soviet Organized Crime', *Criminal Organizations*, 9(1): 14–22.
Short, M. (1991), *Crime Inc. The Story of Organized Crime*, London: Thames-Mandarin.
Siebert, R. (1994), *Le donne, la mafia*, Milano: Il Saggiatore.
Silverman, D. (1970), *The Theory of Organizations*, London: Heinemann.
Simon, D.R. and Eitzen, D.S. (1982), *Elite Deviance*, Boston: Allyn & Bacon.
Slapper, G. (1994), 'Crime without Punishment', The *Guardian*, 1 February.
Smith, D.C. (1980), 'Paragons, Pariahs, and Pirates: A Spectrum-Based Theory of Enterprise', *Crime and Delinquency*, 26: 358–86.
Smith, D.C. (1982), 'White-Collar Crime, Organized Crime, and the Business Establishment: Resolving a Crisis in Criminological Theory', in Wickman, P. and Dailey, T. (eds), *White-Collar and Economic Crime: Multidisciplinary and Cross-National Perspectives*, Lexington: Lexington Books.
Smith, D.C. (1991), 'Wickersham to Sutherland to Katzenbach: Evolving an

"Official" Definition of Organized Crime', *Crime, Law and Social Change*, 16 (2): 135–54.

Smith, D.C. and Alba, R.D. (1979), 'Organized Crime and American Life', *Society*, 16: 32–8.

Sombart, W. (1915), *The Quintessence of Capitalism. A Study of the History and Psychology of the Modern Business Man*, London: T. Fisher Unwin.

Southerland, M.D. and Potter, W.G. (1993), 'Applying Organization Theory to Organized Crime', *Journal of Contemporary Criminal Justice*, 9(3): 251–67.

Statewatch (1994), 'Europol: Defining Organized Crime', July–August, 4 (4): 12.

Stigler, G. (1970), 'The Optimum Enforcement of Law', *Journal of Political Economy*, 78 (3): 526–36.

Stimson, G. (1987), 'The War on Heroin: British Policy and the International Trade in Illicit Drugs', in Dorn, N. and South, N. (eds), *A Land Fit for Heroin?*, London: Macmillan.

Stoppelenburg, H. (1990), 'Import/Export of Stolen Motor Vehicles', *The Police Journal*, LXIII(1): 28–33.

Strong, N. and Waterson, M. (1987), 'Principals, Agents and Information', in Clarke, R. and McGuinness, T. (eds), *The Economics of the Firm*, Oxford: Blackwell.

Sutherland, E. (1939), *Principles of Criminology*, Chicago: Lippincott.

Sutherland, E. (1956), 'Crime of Corporations', in Cohen, A., Lindesmith, A. and Schuessler, K. (eds), *The Sutherland Papers*, Bloomington: Indiana University Press.

Sutherland, E. (1983), *White-Collar Crime: The Uncut Version*, New Haven: Yale University Press.

Sutherland, E. and Cressey, D. (1960), *Principles of Criminology*, 6th edition, Chicago: Lippincott.

Sutton, M. (1993), 'From Receiving to Thieving: The Market of Stolen Goods and the Incidence of Theft', *Research Bulletin* (Home Office Research and Statistics Department), 34: 3–8.

Sweeney, J. (1993), *Trading with the Enemy. Britain's Arming of Iraq*, London: Pan.

Sykes, G. and Matza, D. (1957), 'Techniques of Neutralization: A Theory of Delinquency, *American Sociological Review*, 22: 664–73.

Szasz, A. (1986), 'Corporations, Organized Crime, and the Disposal of Hazardous Waste: An Examination of the Making of a Criminogenic Regulatory Structure', *Criminology*, 24(1): 1–27.

Taylor, L. (1984), *In the Underworld*, London: Unwin.

Teece, D. (1982), 'Towards an Economic Theory of the Multi-Product Firm', *Journal of Economic Behaviour and Organization*, 3: 39–63.

Thayer, G. (1969), *The War Business: The International Trade in Armaments*, New York: Simon & Schuster.
The Economist, 18 December 1993 ('Trading in Hypocrisy').
The European 28 January–3 February 1994 ('Germany Frowns on Next-Door Tax Haven').
The European 29 April–5 May 1994 ('Deutsche Staff Face Schneider Inquiry' by C. P.).
The European, 6–12 May 1994 ('Old Master Reveals Trail of Art Thieves').
The European, 22–28 December 1994 ('Afghan Refugees Found on Baltic Island').
The Financial Times, 2 August 1993 ('NatWest Fined £10,000 Over BES Advertisement' by N. C.).
The *Guardian*, 22 June 1991 ('Recession Adds Fuel to Arson Racket').
The *Guardian*, 9 January 1993 ('Falling Marine Standards Add to Risk of Oil Disasters').
The *Guardian*, 3 September 1993 ('The Big Wheels of Scandals' by D. G.).
The *Guardian*, 20 May 1994 ('Schneider Leaves £200m Bank Bill' by D. G.).
The *Guardian*, 16 August 1994 ('Radioactive Isle Volunteered As Nuclear Dump').
The *Guardian*, 10 September 1994 ('Baby-food Firms Rapped').
The *Guardian*, 8 December 1994 ('Dole Pitmen Turn Smugglers').
The *Guardian*, 13 December 1994 ('Informer Got Big Reward from American Express After Setting Up Gang to Forge Travel Cheques').
The *Guardian*, 8 February 1995 ('Head of Waste Firm Imprisoned for Illegal Dumping').
The Independent, 4 March 1994 ('£700,000 Ransom Demanded for Stolen Painting').
The Independent, 27 April 1994 ('Turkish Jubilation Over Recovery of Ancient Sarcophagus').
The Independent, 15 September 1994 ('Bulgaria Arrests Nuclear Thieves').
The Observer, 1 August 1993 ('Iraqis Thwarted in Bid to Sell Kuwaiti Loot').
The Observer, 8 January 1995 ('£5m Titian Stolen a Week After Police Warning').
The Times, 15 January 1994 ('Why the Mafia Cannot Regulate the Mafia' by M. M.).
Thomas, T. (1990), 'A New Golden Gate for Great Pretenders', *The European,* 19–21 October.
Thompson, G. (1982), 'The Firm as "Dispersed" Social Agency', *Economy and Society*, 11(3): 233–50.
Thompson, J.D. (1967), *Organizations in Action*, New York: McGraw-Hill.

Thrasher, F. (1927), *The Gang: A Study of 1,313 Gangs in Chicago*, Chicago: University of Chicago Press.
Tickell, O. (1993), 'Britain's Mahogany Suppliers Guilty of Illegal Logging', The *Guardian*, 15 October.
Tomasevski, K. (1994), *Foreigners in Prison*, Helsinki: European Institute for Crime Prevention and Control.
Tredre, R. (1994), 'Fakers Set Up Their £300m Shop in Britain', *The Observer*, 12 June.
Urvantsev, V. (1990), 'Will We Curb the Drug Business?', *Pravda*, 23 November.
Vaksberg, A. (1991), *The Soviet Mafia*, New York: St Martin's Press.
van der Heijden, A.W.M. (1993), 'Measuring Organized Crime', paper presented at the 11th Congress of Criminology, Budapest, 22–7 August.
van Duyne, P.C. (1993), 'Organized Crime and Business Crime-Enterprises in the Netherlands', *Crime, Law and Social Change*, 19(2): 103–42.
Varese, F. (1994), 'Is Sicily the Future of Russia? Private Protection and the Russian Mafia', *Archives Européennes de Sociologie*, XXXV (2): 224–58.
Vaugham, D. (1983), *Controlling Unlawful Organizational Behaviour*, Chicago: University of Chicago Press.
Viccei, V. (1992), *Knightsbridge*, London: Blake.
Vidal, J. (1993), 'Drawing the Poison', The *Guardian*, 23 April.
Vidal, J. (1994), 'Pulling the Strings: European Aid', The *Guardian*, 11 February.
Vir, A.K. (1988), 'Africa Says No To Toxic Dumping Schemes', *Environmental Action*, 5: 26–8.
Vulliamy, E. (1992), 'Cocaine Builds a Bridge to the East', The *Guardian*, 14 March.
Walsh, M.E. (1977), *The Fence*, Westport, Conn.: Greenwood.
Ward, D. (1991), 'The Black Market In Body Parts', *Criminal Justice International*, 7(5): 1–6.
Weber, M. (1947), *The Theory of Social and Economic Organisation*, New York: The Free Press.
Weber, M. (1976), *The Protestant Ethic and the Spirit of Capitalism*, London: Allen & Unwin.
Weber, M. (1977), *Le sette e lo spirito del capitalismo*, Milano: Rizzoli.
Webster, P. (1994), 'French Minister Condoned Police Shooting of Youths', The *Guardian*, 13 October.
Wells, C. (1993), *Corporations and Criminal Responsibility*, Oxford: Clarendon Press.
Whyte, F.W. (1943), *Street Corner Society*, Chicago: University of Chicago Press.
Williams, G. (1983), *Textbook of Criminal Law*, London: Stevens.

Wolf, S. (1985), 'The Legal and Moral Responsibility of Organisations', in Pennock, J.R. and Chapman, J.M. (eds), *Criminal Justice*, New York: New York University Press.

World Development Movement (1994), *Inquiry into the Pergau Hydro-Electric Project, the Aid and Trade Provision and its Implications for Overseas Aid Expenditure*, London: World Development Movement.

Young, P. (1993), *Disasters. Focusing on Management Responsibility*, London: Herald Families Association.

Young, T.R. (1981), 'Corporate Crime: A Critique of the Clinard Report', *Contemporary Crises*, 5: 323–35.

Zeitz, D. (1981), *Women Who Embezzle and Defraud*, New York: Praeger.

Ziegler, J. (1990), *La Suisse lave plus blanc*, Paris: Seuil.

Zincani, V. (1989), *La criminalità organizzata. Strutture criminali e controllo sociale*, Bologna: Clueb.

Zuberbühler, D. (1989), *Rapport du directeur suppléant du Sécretariat de la Commission Fédérale des Banques*, Berne: Conseil Fédéral.

Index